Structures and Transformations

The Romance Verb

CHRISTOPHER J. POUNTAIN, MA, PhD
Assistant Lecturer in Romance Philology, University of Cambridge, and Fellow of Queens' College, Cambridge

CROOM HELM
London & Canberra
BARNES & NOBLE BOOKS
Totowa, New Jersey

Croom Helm Ltd, Provident House, Burrell Row,
Beckenham, Kent, BR3 1AT
Croom Helm Australia, PO Box 391, Manuka,
ACT 2603, Australia

British Library Cataloguing in Publication Data

Pountain, Christopher J.
Structures and transformations: the romance verb.
1. Romance languages––Verb
I. Title
445 PC145

ISBN 0-7099-2047-4

First published in the USA 1983 by
Barnes & Noble Books
81 Adams Drive
Totowa, New Jersey, 07512

Library of Congress Cataloging in Publication Data

Pountain, Christopher J.
Structures and transformations.

Bibliography: p.
1. Romance languages––Verb. I. Title.
PC145.P68 1983 440 83-12287
ISBN 0-389-20436-6

Printed and bound in Great Britain

CONTENTS

LIST OF TABLES

FOREWORD

This work is a considerably revised version of my Cambridge Ph.D. dissertation, "Aspects of verb-form usage in French and Spanish", which was approved in 1978. The prime aim of my research was not originally that of setting one approach to language description against another, but rather less ambitiously of describing a set of data; however, such a comparison eventually became inevitable, and so I feel justified in offering this book with its more wide-ranging title. I should make it clear that it is not an exhaustive treatment of all aspects of Romance verb-form usage, nor is it an attempt to work in the vanguard of descriptive linguistics. I see it much more as a stocktaking exercise, an approach to a well-known problem with well-known techniques, but an approach which nevertheless deserves to be tried. For there is a real danger that advances in descriptive linguistics are so rapid that their possible impact on the description of whole areas of data may go unrealised; and conversely, that the philologists, the data-hunters, may feel so bemused by these advances that they may hesitate to apply them. I hope that this book may at least encourage debate, and hence contact, between linguists and philologists who have not been sufficiently in the habit of scrutinising each other's achievements.

The subject-matter surely needs no defence. The Romance verb is a fascinating crossroads where morphology, syntax, semantics and pragmatics meet, whether one works on the synchronic or diachronic plane of investigation. It is a tantalising area to work in, and also a humbling one, for many of its complexities remain disarmingly opaque. I look forward to its further study, and hope that this book may at least provide a basis for that, if only by way of an exposure of its mistakes.

For

Marjorie, my mother,

and

to the memory

of

Eric, my father.

ACKNOWLEDGEMENTS

My thanks go primarily to three people, Martin Harris, Joe Cremona and Pieter Seuren, who as my teachers at Cambridge first led me to appreciate the strengths and weaknesses of 'structures and transformations'. I would like to thank Joe Cremona and Roy Harris, who, as Examiners of the thesis on which this book is based, made many detailed, and always constructive, criticisms, as well as giving me encouragement in seeking its publication. T.B.W. Reid, an earlier critic, deserves (lamentably posthumous) thanks for saving me from many unworthy errors in the reading of Old French. My friends and colleagues Andrew Crompton and Nigel Vincent have offered me valuable informal help and advice at various stages in the preparation of this work, although I fear they may not recognise it in the results. Other specialist colleagues and several native informants have given generously of their time to help me with points of detail, and I would like to mention in particular Christine Whitbourn, John Slattery, Luisa Anderson, Marta Pesarrodona, Teresa de Carlos, Marie-Claire Sharpe, Annie Arguile, Betty Tarantino and Anna Merchant. My biggest debt of gratitude goes to Martin Harris again as my patient research supervisor; his influence will be apparent throughout the work, and his encouragement has ensured its completion. My wife, Mary, helped me with the compilation of the Index and has been an unfailing support throughout the preparation of the final copy. Lastly, my thanks to Croom Helm, and in particular to Tim Hardwick, for undertaking the publication of this work.

ABBREVIATIONS

Language Names

CL	Classical Latin
VL	Vulgar Latin
O/MFr	Old/Modern French
O/MSp	Old/Modern Spanish
O/MIt	Old/Modern Italian
Ptg	Portuguese
Cat	Catalan
Rum	Rumanian

Syntactic Categories

S	Sentence
NP	Noun Phrase
N	Noun
VP	Verb Phrase
V	Verb
Adv	Adverbial
PrepP	Prepositional Phrase

Other Symbols and Conventions

*	Syntactically unacceptable
?, ??	Syntactically of doubtful acceptability
!	Semantically unacceptable
X > Y	Y derives historically from X
X < Y	X derives historically from Y
X ==> Y	Y derives from X by transformation
X <== Y	X derives from Y by transformation
X =imp= Y	X implies Y
X = Y	X and Y are semantically congruent

See also pp. 19, 21 and 155, and the Index, where all specialised terms and their abbreviations are listed.

Chapter One

A PROGRAMME FOR HISTORICAL ROMANCE SYNTAX

This study arose out of a desire to examine the verb-forms of Romance in a diachronic perspective, an aim which may seem well-worn at first sight. However, the following of this trail led through many interesting and uncharted areas. It begins with the claim that amongst the many factors which are crucial to an understanding of verb-form usage, syntax, hitherto somewhat neglected, has an important part to play. Two constructions in particular, conditional sentences and what I shall call '*when*-sentences' (i.e., sentences containing subordinate temporal clauses), shed light on the 'syntactic' functions of verb-forms: I first of all examine these structures from the point of view of synchronic description, and then trace the history of verb-form usage in these structures in French, Spanish and Italian, and, to a lesser extent, in other Romance languages.

The syntactic properties of verb-forms are indeed a no-man's land, largely ignored both by those structuralists who devoted their attentions to the morphological patternings of the 'verb-system', and by generative grammarians who are principally interested in the grosser features of sentence structure. Likewise, the constructions which I examine in this book have received only limited attention in the past. These things in themselves should constitute a sufficient apologia. However, I have a more broadly-based theme, too. It has become the fashion to oppose Chomskyan transformational-generative models of linguistic description to models which are classed as 'taxonomic structuralist'. Clearly, there are important reasons why such an opposition is desirable, and why generative models have greater power than taxonomic models. But we cannot afford to ignore the achievements of the taxonomists.

Either these achievements can be incorporated into a generative model of language, or - and I shall profess a fair degree of sympathy with this view - the taxonomic model itself may have offered insights into the workings of language which should be revalued. The relation between "structures and transformations" is hence the general theme of this study, and the purpose of this introductory Chapter is to set the stage for subsequent detailed discussion.

THE PRINCIPLES OF STRUCTURALISM

The direction for structuralist investigation of language on the synchronic plane was set by Saussure (1916). Although subsequent work has stressed many different aspects of language and made many refinements in methodology, it is still possible to give a general characterisation of structuralist principles.

The basic assumption is that the subject matter under investigation is not an amalgam of disparate elements but consists of elements which can be viewed as part of a 'system'; that is, these elements have value through the relations they contract with each other, and they participate in processes which characterise the 'system' as a whole and are particular to it. Piaget (1968:6-7) gives the following general definitions:

> En première approximation, une structure est un système de transformations, qui comporte des lois en tant que système (par opposition aux propriétés des éléments) et qui se conserve ou s'enrichit par le jeu même de ses transformations, sans que celles-ci aboutissent en dehors de ses frontières ou fassent appel à des éléments extérieures...
>
> En seconde approximation... celle ci [la structure] doit pouvoir donner lieu à une formalisation.

Whether structure is inherent or whether it is only to be imposed by the linguist is a nicety which need not detain us: the expectation is that it will be possible to establish units and classes of units in a description of language on the basis of the relations that these units contract with each other. The relations identified are of two kinds: (a) syntagmatic, that is to say, 'linear' relations between units which occur sequentially in a chain of utterance, and (b) paradigmatic, or relations between units which may replace and contrast with each other in a particular syntagmatic context. A distinctive feature of the structuralist approach is that, on the whole, greater prominence was given to paradigmatic relations than to syntagmatic. The notion of paradigmatic contrast, or 'opposition', is fundamental to the structuralist view of language: units are regarded as genuinely contrasting when they can appear, with distinctive value, in the same context; and when two or more units can be predictably associated each with characteristically different contexts, they can be regarded as variants of the same unit. An interesting notion which arises from the structuralist tradition is that of the 'system'. Saussure (1916:116) characterised language in the following terms:

> ... la langue est un système de pures valeurs que rien ne détermine en dehors de l'état momentané de ses termes.

It is possible to view this 'macro-system' as comprising a number of sub-systems, and we may provisionally say that where a closed (i.e., finite) set of units may be considered as belonging to the same paradigmatic class, they constitute a 'system'. It is convenient, for instance, to speak of 'personal pronoun systems', 'case systems' and - as in this study - 'verb systems' (or, more precisely, 'verb-inflection systems').

Typically, the structuralist programme is to identify and classify the phonemes and morphemes of a language. As far as syntagmatic relations are concerned, the combinatorial possibilities of phonemes and morphemes may be dealt with to a certain extent, but syntax usually receives scant attention. With the advent of the generativist approach to syntax, we have been educated to view syntax as primarily syntagmatic in nature, and as concerned with relations of order, agreement and dependency; syntax is hence very unlike phonology and morphology in that it is difficult to conceive of it as paradigmatic in nature at all. Thus, the more satisfying results obtained by a paradigmatically-orientated approach to language in phonology and morphology no doubt account for the neglect of syntax by the structuralists; Chomsky (1968:15, 17) also points to Saussure's implication that syntax was part of "parole" (loosely translatable as 'speech behaviour') rather than of "langue" (the common 'bank' of linguistic items on which speakers might draw and the acknowledged object of structuralist investigation), which perhaps also played a part in diverting attention from syntax. It is an interesting question, therefore, to see with what success structuralist principles might be applied to syntax[1].

GENERATIVE GRAMMAR

The historical roots of Chomskyan linguistics are in American synchronic linguistics of the 40's and 50's, a brand of structuralism which had confined its interests to observation and classification on the phonetic, phonological and morphological levels, and insisted on the strict separation of these levels severally from semantics. Chomsky initially broadened its sights in three ways: (a) he laid emphasis for the first time on the study of syntax, which indeed was to become the 'centre' of linguistic description; (b) he re-introduced a 'mentalist' methodology into linguistic investigation, the primary object of linguistic description being set as the "competence" (i.e., all that complex array which represents the native speaker's intuitive knowledge of his language) rather than the "performance" (i.e., what the native speaker actually says) of speakers, so that the judgment of the native speaker became the paramount criterion in the validation of linguistic descriptions; (c) he demonstrated the necessity for a higher degree of abstraction than ever before in linguistic descriptions. These three innovations changed radically the nature of linguistic investigation, since they bring into play a number of imponderables. First of all, syntax cannot be dealt with in a taxonomic manner as successfully as can phonology and morphology, since it is clearly impossible to list all the sentences of a language in the same way as it is (potentially) possible to list all the phonemes or morphemes of a language: sentence construction, in Humboldt's often quoted phrase, "makes infinite use of finite means" (Chomsky (1966:Chapter 1)). Secondly, setting up the native speaker's "competence" as the object of description means that the raw data of investigation is only indirectly observable (and indeed, there is a good deal of debate over what exactly is to be admitted as a proper part of that data[2]). Lastly, the licensing of abstraction in description opens the way for speculation as to the form such abstraction will take, or will be allowed to take. Linguistic descriptions must consequently be construed as hypotheses - the data potentially infinite, the source only indirectly investigable, the descriptive mechanism abstract. Investigation by the setting up and subsequent confirming or disconfirming of hypotheses gave linguistics for the first time an explicit share in established scientific method, with all the constraints that involves - for instance, the premium set on the testability or refutability of a hypothesis[3]. Great stress is laid on the criterion of "simplicity" in adjudicating between rival hypotheses: the more generalised a hypothesis is, the 'stronger' it is, and the ad hoc solution (i.e., one which describes or even explicates only one isolated linguistic phenomenon) is shunned. This last aspiration is responsible for the kind of research which either attempts to show that the adoption of a particular solution in fact assists in the description of several apparently unrelated phenomena or which postulates an abstract category or mechanism on the basis of several different motivating phenomena[4].

As the highest level of adequacy a linguistic theory can achieve, Chomsky (1957:Chapter 8) puts forward the notion of "explanation". This is a term which has caused a good deal of confusion, and not surprisingly, since the notion is an elusive one. In general terms, "explanation" goes beyond simple observation or classification of data: an "explanatory" solution will reveal something of the overall working of language - the causes of ambiguity or constructional homonymy, for example. In essence, this feature of Chomskyan theory embodies the requirement that descriptions must not content themselves with listings, random or classified, of data, but must seek to reveal how certain linguistic phenomena take effect. It is most important not to confuse this notion of "explanation" with logical necessity or historical causation.

Chomsky's famous observation that human language is distinguishable from animal communication because of the ability of human beings to produce and comprehend "original" sentences from an early age, and the better-publicised conclusion from this that the ability and disposition to learn language is innate in human beings, led to a concentration of interest on the properties of human language in general. Particular languages are considered as individual manifestations of human language, and it therefore became interesting to search for formal and substantive universals of linguistic description. An important new slant is thus given to comparative linguistics.

The apotheosis of the Chomskyan linguist's endeavour is the establishment of a 'model' of language of which individual human languages will be exponents. The search for such a 'model' has an added piquancy since it is possible that a demonstrably appropriate model of language will reveal a good deal about the psychological nature of human language in general. Accordingly, great store is set by hypotheses whose investigation challenges or illuminates our conception of the 'model'[5].

In this study, I make use of the Chomskyan distinction between a 'surface' or 'overt' level of structure and an 'abstract' or 'underlying' level, these levels being linked by 'transformations'. I have found it convenient too to refer to and use the device of the 'tree-diagram' for the representation of structures, and to speak accordingly of clauses (Ss) being 'higher' than or 'embedded' in other clauses. A clause in which another clause is embedded is referred to as the 'matrix clause'. I do not consider that the solutions offered in this study are firm evidence for any one generative model. In Chapter 4, for instance, it may equally easily be imagined either that conditional verb-form sequences are selected in accordance with primitive semantic units, or that semantic readings are assigned according to generated verb-form sequences. In Chapter 3, I make a case for the representation of time-referential categories in the grammar by the device of an abstract element of underlying structure; yet other categories of time-reference, and all overall aspectual values, will be seen as assignable by processes of semantic interpretation. In describing semantic relations among sentences, I distinguish between 'presuppositions' (by which I will mean the truth-conditions necessarily entailed by a sentence) and 'implications' (by which I will mean all that semantic information which follows from a sentence but which is not necessarily stated explicitly in it)[6].

THE STRUCTURALIST APPROACH TO LANGUAGE CHANGE

Perhaps the most significant contribution to diachronic linguistics within a structuralist framework has been made by Martinet, a convenient summary of whose stance is given in Martinet (1970:172-207). This kind of approach insists that a linguistic unit must be viewed (a) as discharging a function within the language as a whole and within particular sub-systems of the language, and (b) from the standpoint of relative frequency of occurrence and the consequent functional "load" and information value it carries. Change is hence conceived as the altering function and functional load of a unit within sub-systems of a language.

The particular interest of the structuralist view of language change is that it fields hypotheses concerning the causal explanation of change. The two principal suggestions put forward are, first, that change is brought about and constrained by a tension between the tendency of speakers to exercise an economy of effort and the need for a speech-community to preserve efficiency in communication, and, secondly, that a unit may be affected by "pressure" from the system or systems in which it participates. A classic example of these principles at work is found in the history of intervocalic plosive consonants in Sp, where the following general movement between CL and OSp can be hypothesised:

$$
\begin{array}{lclcl}
\underline{\text{CL}} & & \underline{\text{OSp}}\ (1) & & \underline{\text{OSp}}\ (2) \\
\text{-CC}_{[-\text{voice}]}\text{-} & > & \text{-C}_{[-\text{voice}]}\text{-} & > & \text{-C}_{[-\text{voice}]}\text{-} \\
\text{-C}_{[-\text{voice}]}\text{-} & > & \text{-C}_{[+\text{voice}]}\text{-} & \left.\begin{array}{c}\\ \\ \end{array}\right\} > & \text{-C}\begin{bmatrix}+\text{voice}\\+\text{continuant}\end{bmatrix}\text{-} \\
\text{-C}\begin{bmatrix}+\text{voice}\\-\text{continuant}\end{bmatrix} & > & \text{-C}\begin{bmatrix}+\text{voice}\\+\text{continuant}\end{bmatrix} & &
\end{array}
$$

It may be argued, first, that all these changes represent an economy of effort by speakers, since, for example, a simple consonant (C) is 'easier' to produce than a geminate (CC), a voiced intervocalic consonant 'easier' than an unvoiced intervocalic consonant, a continuant 'easier' than a non-continuant: all processes involve a reduction in tension (or 'lenition') in the organs of speech[7]. At the same time, such movement by one member of the plosive system would have meant the loss of a phonemic distinction: thus if -CC- > -C- without $\text{-C}_{[-\text{voice}]}\text{-} > \text{-C}_{[+\text{voice}]}\text{-}$, then the erstwhile -CC-/-C- opposition would have been 'neutralised' as -C-. It would appear, then, that economy of effort is counterbalanced and complemented by the apparent need to preserve a phonemic distinction. Since the pattern of change represented above is evidenced throughout the plosive 'system' (-pp-, -p-, -b- > -p-, -b-, -β- > -p-, -β-; -tt-, -t-, -d- > -t-, -d-, -δ- > -t-, -δ-; -kk-, -k-, -g- > -k-, -g-, -γ- > -k-, -γ-), it becomes easy to conceive of a notion of 'structural pressure' which generalises a type of change to the whole of a sub-system.

The structuralist notions of paradigmatic opposition and system are essential for the presentation of phenomena like the above. Causal mechanisms like structural pressure, preservation of oppositions and analogical patterning cannot otherwise be brought into play. One important theoretical problem also rears its head. The historical linguist embarking on such causal explanations must begin by defining the systems and sub-systems with which he will be dealing. In particular, he must decide which systems are significant in the sense that pressures within such systems can definitely be shown to be of relevance in accounting for diachronic phenomena. The case for the existence of a system is therefore in an important way made through a statement of its proposed effects. It is likely, for instance, that the notion of a 'vowel-system' can be shown to have significance in the history of all the Romance languages: in particular, the notion of symmetry within the system has demonstrable importance (e.g., the idea that changes like diphthongisation affect front and back vowels in parallel).

CHOMSKYAN LINGUISTICS AND THE DIACHRONIC PERSPECTIVE

The diachronic perspective was at first subordinate in status for the Chomskyan linguist. J. Harris (1975:537) explains as follows:

> ... language change is of interest to the theoretical linguist to the extent that it is a valuable source of data relevant to the formulation of explanatory theories concerning the general properties of human language and, ultimately, of human cognitive processes in general. In this respect language change takes its place alongside other sources of data, for example, the study of particular synchronic grammars, language acquisition, language disorders, language play, and so on.

It is fair to say, however, that the diachronic plane of investigation has received relatively scant attention despite such potential relevance to the Chomskyan linguist's overall goal. At the same time, investigation on the diachronic plane poses important problems for Chomskyan theory which must somehow be accommodated.

Whilst Chomskyan linguistics supplies a programme for the investigation of the language of living native speakers, its empirical basis must fall when the object of investigation is a past language for which there are no native speakers available. In historical investigation, therefore, an additional hypothetical level comes into play - the reconstruction of what the competence of the native speakers of a past language might have been. This assumes grotesque proportions of difficulty when we reach a period for which there are few or no texts: even VL, where we have the testimony of literary CL together with many early medieval texts from daughter languages, offers tremendous problems of reconstruction[8]. Even when texts exist in substantial numbers, the situation is only marginally brighter from the empirical point of view. In text-based investigations, the established text, itself often of highly controversial status[9], can only serve as the corpus of performance data, usually inadequately transcribed, from which the hypothetical competence must be inferred. Even if it can be considered that morphological and syntactic phenomena show up fairly well in textual data, the projection of phonetic values and semantic relations from written evidence remain major problems for the historical linguist. Such hypotheses as appear to be necessary in historical linguistics may inevitably be unacceptably weak to the Chomskyan linguist in that they may be totally irrefutable on the basis of the data to hand. Indeed, historical linguistics abounds with hypotheses which rest on the shakiest of criteria, and it is probably only a matter of time before some of the most cherished currency (e.g., the substratist hypothesis[10] and the 'learned borrowing'[11]) is debased to the status of the 'bow-wow' and 'ding-dong' theories of language creation (and, to continue the parallel, before some of the questions they are designed to answer are considered primitively naïve).

Next, I turn to the question of the object of investigation itself. In synchronic linguistics, the Chomskyan definition is clear: we are attempting to describe the competence of the native speaker/hearer. But what should the historical linguist be attempting? Some linguists of the Chomskyan school have been satisfied to limit their task to that of identifying differences between the grammars of two or more stages of a language, so that diachronic linguistics rests firmly on the surer basis of synchronic description. Traditionally, however, historical linguists have seen such a procedure as only a first step in their task, and have considered that the interest of their subject lies in enquiring into the mechanisms of and reasons for language change rather than in a simple cataloguing of observed changes[12]. Delineation of the aims of historical linguistics, and deciding in particular whether these more ambitious traditional goals have anything less than utopian status, provide areas of major difficulty for theorists.

The quest for universals which is such an important feature of the Chomskyan approach can be extended to the data of historical linguistics in the trivial sense that universals can also be sought in past languages and states of languages. Yet some important new dimensions to this quest also arise on the diachronic plane. First, the notion of universals of linguistic change is an appealing one; historical linguists cannot fail to be impressed by the appearance time and time again of the same kind of change in widely different languages or language families, though the formulation of a universal statement is often more elusive than such happy coincidences might suggest[13]. Second, change itself appears to be one of the most intriguing universal features of human language. This leads naturally on to the view that the seeds of change are to be found wherever one looks at language in a synchronic way, and to the realisation that if language is always changing, however slightly, the synchronic perspective may be in an important sense an artifice, since language is never static[14]. If it turns out to be useful to approach language in these terms, diachronic studies will assume a rôle of primary, rather than secondary, importance.

Intertwining with the foregoing discussion is the question of what meaning can or ought to be given to the notion of 'explanatory adequacy' in the context of historical linguistics. We have seen how 'explanatory adequacy' on the synchronic level is bound up with the question of how successfully a particular solution relates to the structure of the language as a whole: hence the premium awarded to solutions which have relevance to areas of language other than those in connection with which they are originally postulated. This kind of 'descriptive explanation' can clearly be paralleled on the diachronic plane: a diachronic rule postulated for one phenomenon may be relevant to the description of another. In synchronic studies, the notion of 'explanation' rigorously excludes diachronic factors;

consideration of historical causation, it can be argued, is irrelevant and indeed may blight the synchronic linguist's appreciation of synchronic phenomena[15]. It is necessary, therefore, in diachronic studies, to draw a distinction between 'descriptive explanation' and 'causal explanation' if the latter is to be admitted as a goal of historical linguistics.

Transposition of the simplicity criterion from the synchronic to the diachronic plane likewise calls for clarification of nature and status. We must first of all take care to distinguish between **simplicity** as a criterion for adequacy in linguistic description and **simplification**, which has been proposed as a cause of linguistic change (see P. Kiparsky (1968: 175-7)). While such a confusion on a theoretical level is unlikely, there is a danger that synchronic linguists trained in the habit of placing maximally simple solutions at the highest premium may transfer this predilection to diachronic studies. Halle's account (1964:347-8) of the Verner and Grimm laws shows how this was done unconsciously even by nineteenth-century linguists[16]. In fact, the simplest explanation may not necessarily be the one that harmonises with the available facts, as may be demonstrated from a brief examination of two fairly recent issues in the history of Sp phonology. The first of these concerns the fact that Sp tends to apocopate final -e in certain contexts during one period of its history; subsequently, it appears to 'restore' the -e in some of these contexts. A straight comparison between CL and MSp would not necessarily show up this feature (see in particular Lapesa (1951 and 1975)). The second concerns the Sp f > h change. A remarkable explanation of this change was put forward by Naro (1972), who suggested that it was the result of an [f] > [ç] palatalisation. Although his postulation commended itself for its 'simplicity', since it was in accord with other patterns of change in Sp and other languages, there is, as his critic Rivarola (1972) pointed out, no evidence for h having a phonetic value [ç] in OSp. In short, the diachronic linguist must insist on the obligatory constraining of any simplicity criterion for historical linguistics by attested external evidence.

THE DISTINCTIVE PROBLEMS OF MORPHOLOGICAL AND SYNTACTIC CHANGE

Gradient and non-gradient change

The neogrammarian account of the mechanism of sound-change was essentially that continuous variation on the phonetic level eventually produces restructuring on the phonemic level. In their review of the neogrammarian position, Weinreich, Labov and Herzog (1968:131) point out the difficulty of building into such a principle any account of morphological change, where the postulation of a continuum is not always possible. If we are faced with a phonetic change such as CL ŏ > Sp ue, it is reasonable to envisage a large number of intervening stages, like Menéndez Pidal's (1929:140) o̜ó̜>o̜̣ó̜>u̯ó̜>u̯á>u̯á>u̯ą́>u̯ẹ́>uẹ́. Similarly with semantic change: thank may be construed as having changed its meaning from "thought" through "favourable thought" and "satisfaction" to "expression of satisfaction" (Lehmann (1962:194)). With a morphological change like CL Future amabit to VL Future amare habet, however, there can clearly be no intervening continuum: one form is replacing another, and the change is non-gradient.

The origins of non-gradient change

The possibility of phonetic change being gradient allows us to view change as a gradual shift on the part of some speakers which may be emulated by others and becomes generalised. Gradient semantic change may similarly be viewed (as, for example, gradual shifting of the reference of a word). Indeed, even non-gradient semantic change is not difficult to envisage in this way: the introduction of a word by coining or borrowing by adventurous speakers is observable in everyday linguistic experience (cf. English gazump, prideful). In morphology and syntax, however, we have to look much farther afield, and to all kinds of complex interweaving factors, in considering how the conflicting variant which eventually replaces the established form originates, and why the established form should have weakened and the new form gained in prestige. To return to our example of CL amabit being replaced by VL amare habet, we may trace factors such as the following: (a) the existence of amare habet as a periphrastic form, probably expressing obligation, in CL; (b) the (universal) semantic association of obligation and futurity; (c) a natural movement towards hyperbole in the expression of future time;

(d) the phonetic weakness of the CL -bit inflection, due to the fall of -t and the uncertainty of -b-; (e) the structural anomaly of future inflections in CL, the first and second conjugations taking a form in -b-, the other conjugations a different form; (f) the possibility of loss of distinctiveness between future and imperfect inflections (amabit (future)/ amabat (imperfect)). Needless to say, the relevance of all these factors is highly contentious. But they give some idea of the distance the historian of morphology must cast his net in order to come up with even tentative suggestions for the origins of non-gradient change.

Data

As far as extracting information from written records goes, historians of morphology and syntax may be at an advantage. Whereas there are major problems in hypothesising phonetic and semantic values on the basis of written texts, morphological and syntactic phenomena are more obviously represented. This does not mean to say there are no problems; we have to judge, for example, whether inconsistencies betoken scribal errors or whether they faithfully reflect alternative possibilities. When variant texts exist, there are often interesting discrepancies between versions which make us wary of taking the evidence at face value. There are also problems in deciding how accurately an author's usage reflects the everyday language of his time, since literary language is often conservative and even deliberately archaic. In poetry, prosodic considerations may influence word order or choice of forms[17].

In Chapters 6 and 7 I have distinguished three principal stages of the history of the Romance languages: CL, early Romance and modern Romance. Details from intermediate stages are filled in from the work of others insofar as such data is available. The VL stage is not made a separate study since the data from this period is scanty; instead, known variations in CL usage in the work of Classical authors and in that of later writers are recorded along with the CL data. For OFr, OSp and OIt I have made the focal point of my study a small number of substantial texts which are spread over a relatively restricted geographical area and chronological period, and which are established in modern critical editions. I have adopted this procedure rather than culling examples more casually from a wider range of texts and periods, as is often done, in order to be able to glimpse profiles of a series of individual competences and to discern clear variation in usage from place to place and time to time. Yet this approach must also be treated as a philological exercise in showing the limitations and possibilities of the searching of texts for syntactic data, and it is for this reason that I have spent time in fairly detailed commentary on the textual examples. For the modern Romance languages, I have introduced written textual material only insofar as it has been appropriate to establish some kind of basis for statistical statement. Although it may be objected that written texts give an artifical picture of modern usage, there are considerable practical advantages to be gained from the manageability and accessibility of such material.

Scope

Perhaps the most daunting aspect of morphological and syntactic change is the breadth of their scope. Since it soon becomes necessary in any investigation to view the position of a particular phenomenon within the language as a whole, the investigator of morphological or syntactic history will always find his interests mushrooming to a point of intractability. When I consider the history of verb-forms, I take account of their paradigmatic structure and their syntactic independence; if I pursue their syntactic properties, I must come to some conclusions on the rules which govern the structures in which they participate. The delimitation of the morphosyntactic historian's scope will always be unsatisfactory in some respect.

Comparative studies

Comparative syntactic studies in the Romance languages are relatively rare. The modern search for language universals has tended to be concerned with fairly deep universals and is not so interested initially in the relatively superficial differences between closely related languages[18]. There is again a problem of scope in deciding how many dialects and stages of dialects to consider in a comparative syntactic study, and the practical difficulty that for many lesser-known dialects, published accounts fall so short in their reporting of even the most distinctive areas of syntax that a truly comparative project is unthinkable without extensive additional field-work. While sketching in such data as I have been able to amass from other Romance languages, where this seemed appropriate, I have attempted to reconcile some of these difficulties by concentrating my attention on the three best documented languages, French, Spanish and Italian, which offer extremely interesting points of similarity and contrast.

NOTES

1. Pike and Bloomfield stand out among the structuralists in their development of the notion of units of syntax (taxemes, tagmemes, etc.) which are comparable with units of phonology (phonemes) and units of morphology (morphemes). Such units, of course, cannot be segmental; they are rather general features of sentences, such as 'order' and 'selection'. In this sense units of syntax are still of a different order from 'lower level' units.

2. See, in particular, Kempson (1975:Chapter 9), who discusses whether pragmatics should be considered as belonging to "competence" or "performance", Weinreich, Labov and Herzog (1968), who argue for the notion of variables in competence, and Campbell and Wales (1970), who distinguish between "communicative competence" and "grammatical competence", the former involving the notion of context in which sentences occur (a dimension totally ignored by Chomsky).

3. This, at least, is the cornerstone of the Popperian view (cf. Popper (1959:41): "... it must be possible for an empirical scientific system to be refuted by experience". Compare, however, the discussion of this approach in Kuhn (1962:145-6), where it is argued that a joint verification-falsification process is a more realistic criterion for the evaluation of a theory.

4. Classic examples are Ross (1970), where the performative hypothesis is justified by fourteen different arguments, and R. Lakoff (1969a:Chapter 5), where the notion of "abstract verb" is supported by data from several clause-types. Compare too the many disparate areas in which "factivity" (Kiparsky and Kiparsky (1971)) and "stativeness" (G. Lakoff (1966) and (1970:115-33)) have been claimed to be important.

5. This is reflected most notoriously in the description of a fairly restricted but certainly problematic corpus of data involving quantifiers and negatives in English, hypotheses concerning which

have been much debated because of their possible relation with rival 'models' of description. See the commentary in Kempson (1975:16-27) and references there.

6. Compare the distinction made by Austin (1962:48).

7. Discussion of the phenomenon and adjudication of rival causal hypotheses is to be found in Martinet (1955:257-96).

8. See Hall (1950), whose theme is more particularly that careful comparative reconstruction of VL (or "proto-Romance") is a task unjustifiably neglected by Romance linguists in favour of philology.

9. See p.162 below, and also Closs Traugott (1972:19-21).

10. Compare Jungemann's careful critique (1955) in which the merits of structuralist accounts of language change are pitted against appeals to substratist influence.

11. Compare Badia's warning (1972) against indiscriminate appeal to the notion of "cultismo" in Hispanic historical linguistics.

12. The reluctance of Chomskyan linguists to dabble with causal reasons for change appears to derive from their unease at the lack of empirical evidence with which historical linguists have to contend: cf. Closs Traugott (1972:13):

> ... we may in fact never be able to reconstruct the full picture of the conditions under which any change or set of changes occurred. This book will therefore not be greatly concerned with particulars of why the language changed...

Even those who have had a great deal of interest in the mechanisms of change have drawn the line at answering the question 'why?'; thus Bever and Langendoen (1971:454) regard as "wildly premature" the question as to what triggers any particular linguistic change.

13. See Hoenigswald (1963:50-1), whose vision of future developments has indeed been borne out by such work as P. Kiparsky (1968a), where universals are expressed as tendencies concerning the organisation of rules rather than as substantive 'laws'.

14. Martinet (1970:176) proposes:

> L'objet véritable de la recherche linguistique sera donc... l'étude des conflits qui existent à l'intérieur de la langue dans le cadre des besoins permanents des êtres humains qui communiquent entre eux au moyen du langage.

15. It cannot be denied, however, that there are interesting and necessary links between the synchronic and diachronic planes. Closs Traugott (1969:2-6 and references) reminds the reader that internal reconstruction would not be feasible unless a language's history were reflected in its synchronic structure. P. Kiparsky (1968a:179-89) suggests that sound-change phenomena supply supporting evidence for the motivation of conventions and levels within synchronic analysis. Furthermore, synchronic linguists may find the historical situation helpful rather than blinding in their consideration of synchronic phenomena: Schane (1973:83) comments with regard to phonology and phonological change:

> Since the alternations found in any contemporary language are the vestiges of historical change, it should not be surprising that underlying representations often coincide with earlier attested forms, and that synchronic phonological rules may (but not necessarily always) recapitulate the actual sound changes.

and Posner (Iordan and Orr (1970:413)) remarks of Schane's earlier work on Fr (Schane (1968)) that "his method, of seeking to resolve morphophonemic anomalies by reference to an underlying form, is virtually identical with that of 'internal reconstruction'".

16. More precisely, Halle argues that the relative chronology of the Verner and Grimm laws can only be fixed, in the absence of independent evidence, by inference from the synchronic ordering of rules.

17. See Foulet (1919:345-74) for an important discussion on this theme.

18. M. Harris (1972a) makes a plea for concentration by historical linguists on changes which might be construed as taking place at an intermediate level of structure; this position marks out an area of interest which is liable to be neglected by both traditional structuralists (who are concerned chiefly with surface patternings) and Chomskyan linguists.

Chapter Two

THE VERB ITSELF: MORPHOLOGICAL, SYNTACTIC AND SEMANTIC PROPERTIES

The description of the verb-forms of Latin and Romance may be seen as an account of the tension which exists between morphological patterning and semantic value (see Imbs (1960:9)). While tense and aspect inflections constitute a fairly transparent system of morphological oppositions, each verb-form has a wide range of semantic values which cannot be so successfully plotted in a systematic way. The functions of different inflections may overlap: in the Romance languages, there is a clear morphological opposition between the Present and Future tenses (Fr _chante_/_chantera_, Sp _canta_/_cantará_, It _canta_/_canterà_), but both may be used to refer to future time (Fr _je chante/chanterai demain_, etc.). Also, a functional similarity may not correspond to a morphological similarity. The It Conditional Perfect tense (less commonly the Conditional - see Lepschy (1977:233-4)) stands functionally in the same relation to the Future as the Imperfect does to the Present, as may be seen from reported speech constructions:

(1) Diceva: "Giovanni viene" ==>
    Diceva che Giovanni veniva
    Diceva: "Giovanni verrà" ==>
    Diceva che Giovanni sarebbe venuto (verrebbe)

but the morphological relation between the tense inflections, even setting aside the presence of the Perfect auxiliary, is not at all similar:

(2)

Present	Imperfect	Future	Conditional
-o	-av-o	-er-ò	-er-ei
-i	-av-i	-er-ai	-er-esti
-a	-av-a	-er-à	-er-ebbe
-iamo	-av-amo	-er-emo	-er-emmo
-ate	-av-ate	-er-ete	-er-este
-ano	-av-ano	-er-anno	-er-ebbero

The purpose of this Chapter is first to examine the morphological structure of Latin and Romance verb-forms and then to establish a framework for the description of their functions.

MORPHOLOGICAL STRUCTURE

It will be advantageous, in the course of this study, to refer to classes of verb-forms which are defined essentially in morphological terms. Since a verb-form may belong to several classes at the same time, one convenient method of structural description which suggests itself for this purpose is that of the distinctive feature matrix, which is a familiar device in phonological descriptions. The tension between form and function immediately becomes apparent in the motivation of these distinctive features, and we must proceed language by language.

In CL, inflected active forms of the verb may initially each be uniquely specified in terms of just four distinctive features; in the following table each form is illustrated by the third person singular and is labelled with its traditional name followed by a mnemonic abbreviation by which it will be referred to henceforth:

(3)

		[Past]	[Fut]	[Perf]	[Subj]
Present (Pres)	amat	−	−	−	−
Imperfect (Imp)	amabat	+	−	−	−
Future (Fut)	amabit	−	+	−	−
Perfect (Perf)	amavit	−	−	+	−
Pluperfect (Plup)	amaverat	+	−	+	−
Future Perfect (FutPerf)	amaverit	−	+	+	−
Present Subjunctive (PresSubj)	amet	−		−	+
Imperfect Subjunctive (ImpSubj)	amaret	+		−	+
Perfect Subjunctive (PerfSubj)	amaverit	−		+	+
Pluperfect Subjunctive (PlupSubj)	amavisset	+		+	+

[+Perf] forms are clearly distinguished morphologically, in the case of -are verbs at least, by the -v- infix. [+Subj] forms have no uniting morphological characteristic, but contract well-known oppositions with the [-Subj] forms. [+Fut] forms are most straightforwardly characterised by their property of expressing reference to future time. The distinction between [-Past] and [+Past] is primarily syntactic, and corresponds to that traditionally labelled 'primary' and 'historic', a categorisation based on sequence of tense rules in complex sentences. It is the Perfect tense (Perf) that presents us with a special problem here. Unfortunately, although Perf is uniquely specified in the above table if it has the value [-Past], this definition of the [Past] feature requires Perf to have both a positive and negative specification, since it is both a 'primary' and a 'historic' form:

(4) Tibi hoc dixi ut veritatem scias (PresSubj, [-Past])
Tibi hoc dixi ut veritatem scires (ImpSubj, [+Past])

"I have told you this so that you may know the truth"/"I told you this so that you might know the truth"

If our notion of the [Past] feature stands (and since it is highly motivated syntactically there is every reason to let it do so), Perf will have to carry a double featural specification; indeed, to avoid confusion, it will perhaps be better if, following the spirit of M. Harris (1970:63), we refer to the Perf which is specified [-Past] as $Perf_1$, and the Perf which is specified [+Past] as $Perf_2$. The problem comes with the specification of $Perf_2$. If it is specified [+Past, -Fut, +Perf], it will not be distinguishable from Plup; if it is specified [+Past, -Fut, -Perf], it will not be distinguishable from Imp. $Perf_2$ cannot be reasonably anything other than [-Fut]. The introduction of a further feature therefore seems inevitable. Since $Perf_2$ and Imp contract a clear aspectual opposition, which is perpetuated in the Romance languages and which will be the subject of detailed discussion below (pp.54-57), it will be fruitful to base the new feature on this opposition: accordingly I introduce the feature Punctual ([Punc]) for this purpose, specifying $Perf_2$ as [+Punc] and Imp as [-Punc]. Despite its morphological form, it seems that $Perf_2$ must also be specified [-Perf] to achieve a contrast with Plup. Support for this specification, which goes against the morphological criterion enunciated earlier, comes from the semantic association of [+Perf] forms with the expression of 'anteriority' to a reference point established either adverbially or by another verb (see below, pp.48-50), a value which is not obviously rendered by [+Past] Perf.

Featural grids based on similar criteria can be drawn up for the inflected verb-forms of the modern Romance languages:

(5) MFr:

		[Past]	[Fut]	[Subj]	[Punc]
Present (Pres)	aime	–	–	–	
Imperfect (Imp)	aimait	+	–	–	–
Future (Fut)	aimera	–	+	–	
Conditional (Cond)	aimerait	+	+	–	
*Preterite (Pret)	aima	+	–	–	+
Present Subjunctive (PresSubj)	aime	–	–	+	
*Imperfect Subjunctive (ImpSubj)	aimat	+	–	+	

*Written forms only

(6) MSp:

		[Past]	[Fut]	[Subj]	[Punc]
Present (Pres)	ama	–	–	–	
Imperfect (Imp)	amaba	+	–	–	–
Future (Fut)	amará	–	+	–	
Conditional (Cond)	amaría	+	+	–	
Preterite (Pret)	amó	+	–	–	+
Present Subjunctive (PresSubj)	ame	–	–	+	
Imperfect Subjunctive ($ImpSubj^{ra}$)	amara	+	–	+	
Imperfect Subjunctive ($ImpSubj^{se}$)	amase	+	–	+	

(7) MIt:

		[Past]	[Fut]	[Subj]	[Punc]
Present (Pres)	ama	–	–	–	
Imperfect (Imp)	amava	+	–	–	–
Future (Fut)	amerà	–	+	–	
Conditional (Cond)	amerebbe	+	+	–	
Preterite (Pret)	amò	+	–	–	+
Present Subjunctive (PresSubj)	ami	–	–	+	
Imperfect Subjunctive (ImpSubj)	amasse	+	–	+	

[+Subj] is construed as for CL; [+Fut] forms are morphologically characterised by the -r- infix, though insofar as Cond in MFr and MSp may have 'relative future' time-reference in reported speech, both Fut and Cond could in these languages be said to have the property of expressing reference to future time: the [Past] feature is once again assigned on the basis of sequence of tense rules, although in MFr and MSp the inflections of the [-Subj] forms (Imp and Cond) are additionally similar from the morphological point of view. In the MSp grid, the -ra and -se forms of ImpSubj are specified identically, satisfying the conventional view that the -ra and -se forms are in free variation in MSp; while Bolinger (1956:345), for instance, argues that this is not the case, it seems that any difference there may be between the forms must be defined according to parameters other than those we have so far considered[1], and that identical specification will allow their correct participation in syntactic rules. The -ra form has not been specified as having a [-Subj] function in MSp; in Peninsular Sp it is certainly obsolete, although Kany's evidence (1951:170-4) suggests that it is still used as an indicative in South American Sp, though with what precise time-reference and aspectual value is unclear[2].

In addition to the inflectional verb-forms, the Romance languages have developed a number of 'periphrastic' forms which are built around the non-finite forms of the verb (the past participle, gerund or infinitive). The historical origins of these periphrastic forms are very often transparent: the Perfect auxiliary Fr avoir Sp haber It avere derives from the CL verb HABERE "to have", and in origin the syntagm HABERE + direct object + past participle had a literal possessive value. It is a short step from this construction to the Romance Perfect of transitive verbs (see Bourciez (1967:116-7)). However, the modern Romance Perfect usually carries no such possessive meaning: in Sp, haber is no longer the verb of possession anyway, having been replaced by tener, and haber has generalised as the Perfect auxiliary of all verbs including intransitives and reflexives. In Fr and It, avoir and avere combine with the past participles of transitive verbs like Fr donner It dare "to give" with which a possessive reading would be impossible. From a strictly formal point of view the Perfect auxiliary, so called, is little more than a prefixed verbal inflection. The 'morphologisation' of a periphrastic form is not at all surprising. We know that some Romance verb-forms that we today regard as inflectional had a periphrastic origin: Fut (Fr *chanterai* and cognates) derives from VL CANTARE HABEO, for example. Indeed, it is tempting to imagine an ever-present cyclical sequence of change in Romance verb morphology by which inflectional forms tend to be replaced by periphrastic forms which then themselves become inflectional; a more recent indication of this process is that in Fr and Sp it seems that the inflectional Future in its purely time-referential sense is being replaced by the periphrastic alternative *aller* + infinitive, *ir a* + infinitive[3].

The principal periphrastic forms of Fr, Sp and It are:

(8)

DESCRIPTION	Fr	Sp	It
Perfect	*avoir/être* + past part.	*haber* + past part.	*avere/essere* past part.
Continuous		*estar* + ger.	*stare* + ger.
Future	*aller* + inf.	*ir a* + inf. *haber de* + inf. (SA)	*avere a* + inf. (SIt)
Immediate Past	*venir de* + inf.	*acabar de* + inf.	
Immediate Future		*estar para* + inf.	*stare/essere per* + inf.

The list is limited to those periphrastic forms which primarily express purely temporal or aspectual value (see below, pp.25-27) and to combinations of an 'auxiliary' verb and non-finite root form (sometimes with an intervening preposition). For these reasons I have not included forms like Fr *avoir à* + infinitive, which is primarily modal (as is Peninsular Sp *haber de* + infinitive) or Fr *être sur le point de* + infinitive, even though this corresponds semantically to Sp *estar para* + infinitive. It must be borne in mind that the lack of a parallel in a language does not mean that the language cannot express the temporal or aspectual notion concerned: Fr has the comparatively infrequent and laborious paraphrase *être en train de* + infinitive which is similar in meaning to Sp *estar* + gerund and It *stare* + gerund; It expresses the notion represented by Fr venir de + infinitive and Sp acabar de + infinitive by an adverb appena. There can also be important differences belying superficial similarities: spoken Fr in particular allows the Perfect auxiliary in compound tenses as well as in simple tenses, so that a set of temps surcomposés or 'supercompound' forms (j'ai eu chanté, etc.) are created; these are unknown in Sp or standard It. The It stare + gerund construction is available only in the Present and Imperfect[4], whereas Sp estar + gerund exists in all tenses.

The periphrastic forms can easily be accommodated within the featural matrices of (5) - (7) above. The Perfect tenses can be specified [+Perf], the Continuous tenses [+Cont], etc. In practice, only [Perf] will concern us, since the parallel between form and function is fairly exact in all the periphrastic forms of Romance with the exception of the [+Perf] ones. It is the Perfect itself (Perf) that poses the real problem, since in MFr and some dialects of MIt Perf has a status similar to that of the CL Perf, and hence in principle a similar descriptive expedient to that taken for CL must be adopted. In MSp, Perf has only [-Past] value; another tense, Pret, carries out the [+Past] functions and is equivalent to CL $Perf_2$. But some Romance languages (the chief examples being standard MIt and Cat) not only preserve Perf in the two functions described ([-Past] and [+Past]), but also have another [+Past] form, cognate with or similar in value to MSp Pret, which is aspectually distinct from Imp. Thus in It, Perf must be subdivided into $Perf_1$ and $Perf_2$, respectively specified [-Past] and [+Past], to account for options in sequence of tense like the following:

(9) Ho detto che Giovanni scrive la lettera
Ho detto che Giovanni scriveva la lettera

Ho sperato che venga
Ho creduto che venisse

It does not seem that we can utilise any of the features so far proposed to effect a distinction between $Perf_2$ and Pret in It. The basis of the distinction must be time-referential, as many Italian grammars make clear (cf. Battaglia and Pernicone (1968:372)), and I shall comment further on this in Chapter 3. Following the usual Italian grammatical terminology, which labels Perf the passato prossimo (implying a relation with the Present) and Pret the passato remoto (implying the lack of such a relation), we might introduce the feature Remote ([Rem]) to distinguish between Perf$_2$ and Pret. [Rem] may also be employed for distinguishing between the *trapassato prossimo* (Pluperfect) and the *trapassato remoto* (Past Anterior), although the distinction in the modern language is entirely syntactic in nature (see Saronne (1970:280-1) and below, p.40). The specification of It past tenses now looks like this:

(10)

		[Past]	[Perf]	[Punc]	[Rem]
Perfect (Perf$_1$)	ha amato	−	+		
Imperfect (Imp)	amava	+	−	−	
Perfect (Perf$_2$)	ha amato	+	−	+	−
Preterite (Pret)	amò	+		+	+
Pluperfect (Plup)	aveva amato	+	+		−
Past Anterior (PAnt)	ebbe amato	+	+		+

Our notion of a 'verb system' for the Romance languages might in principle be construed in one of the following ways: (a) to include only inflectional forms, (b) to include any form, inflectional or periphrastic, that expresses a distinctive temporal, aspectual or modal value, (c) to delimit, by the operation of clear criteria, certain forms as 'systematic' and certain as 'non-systematic'. Many commentators have opted for (c) in that they have included all inflectional forms and some, but not all, periphrastic forms in their study. It seems to be strongly felt that the Perfect tenses should be included in the system, for instance; they undeniably express temporal and aspectual values that are very different from those of the inflectional forms, and they correspond historically to the Perfects of CL, which were inflectional forms. In fact, the behaviour of the clitic pronouns with the Perfect forms provides a criterion for considering these apart from other periphrastic forms. In Fr there appears to be a growing tendency for clitics to be placed immediately before the verb to which they pertain[5], whether this verb is linearly first or second in a surface verb-verb sequence:

(11) a. Je vais le faire
but
b. ?Je le vais faire

But Fr obligatorily moves the clitic pronoun to the left of the *avoir* + past participle group, suggesting that the group is felt to be much more of a unit in itself:

(12) a. Je l'ai fait
     but
     b. *J'ai le fait

In Sp and It, clitic pronoun position is variable in modal auxiliary + verb groups:

(13) Sp: a. Quiero hacerlo
         or
         b. Lo quiero hacer
     It: c. Voglio farlo
         or
         d. Lo voglio fare

but the Perfect only allows preposing of the pronoun:

(14) Sp: a. Lo he hecho
         but
         b. *Helo hecho, *He hécholo
     It: c. L'ho fatto
         but
         d. *Ho lo fatto, *Ho fattolo

The application of this criterion for verb-system membership would mean that Fr periphrastic forms like <u>aller</u> + infinitive and <u>venir de</u> + infinitive were excluded from the system, and in Sp and It <u>estar</u> and <u>stare</u> + gerund, which behave like the expressions in (13), would be excluded. I am not aware of other criteria which might allow other periphrastic forms to be distinguished as 'systematic'. One semantic criterion which is immediately attractive is that a periphrastic form might be regarded as 'systematic' if the semantic value of the auxiliary differs markedly from the value of that verb in other contexts or in isolation. The auxiliary in the Fr <u>aller</u> + infinitive paraphrase, for instance, does not have the "motion" reading that it has in other contexts. This kind of criterion would distinguish clearly between periphrastic verb forms and constructions involving modal auxiliaries, which, as we have seen, cannot be distinguished on the basis of clitic pronoun placement. Yet the question is immediately begged as to what might constitute a significant difference in semantic value: periphrastic forms involving Fr <u>etre</u>, Sp <u>estar</u>, It <u>stare</u>, would be highly problematic, since other usages of these verbs do not yield a picture which is sufficiently uniform semantically to determine with any confidence similarity or dissimilarity of semantic value. Another criterion which achieves some success is that of full paradigmaticity: one characteristic of periphrastic forms like Fr aller + infinitive, Sp ir a + infinitive and It stare + gerund, is that they are only available in a limited number of tenses (Pres and Imp), whereas Fr, Sp and It Perfect auxiliaries are available in every tense. Once again the tension between morphological structure and semantic value may be observed: several periphrastic verb-forms contract important temporal and aspectual oppositions with the inflected verb-forms, and are clearly felt to be part of the 'verb-system'; on the other hand, strict delimitation of the 'verb-system' in formal terms seems to be impossible (cf. Matthews (1974:171-3)). Our notion of a verb-system must therefore be to a certain extent arbitrary, and I shall be approaching the study of verb-form usage both from the point of view of establishing morphological patterns in a language and from the point of view of examining what kinds of temporal and aspectual distinctions the language is capable of making. In practice, however, it will prove most interesting to dwell on the inflectional forms and the Perfect forms, since these are the forms which are semantically multivalent and most frequent in all the Romance languages.

VERB-FORMS AND THEIR FUNCTIONS

I will now elaborate a general framework in terms of which the reference and functions of verb-forms in CL, the Romance languages and English may be described. Semantic categories from now on are labelled in block capitals (e.g., PAST).

TIME-REFERENCE

At the outset, I want to make a clear distinction between the grammatical category of **tense** and the semantic category of **time reference.** The traditional labelling of verb-forms as 'tenses' reflects the view that whatever other syntactic or semantic properties the verb may have, its most basic is that of situating an event or state in time. This is no doubt an intuitive view encouraged by the particular referential structure of verb-forms in many European languages; Whorf (1956:143-5) points out that in Hopi, by contrast, verbs have no 'tense', i.e., the expression of time-reference pure and simple is not an easily separable referential category. But for Romance it is tempting to equate the function or meaning of a verb-form simply with the set of its time-references, and several of the traditional names for verb-forms reflect no more than their distinctive time-references (e.g., the 'Future' refers distinctively to FUTURE time). Some commentators have taken this position to an extreme: Sten (1952: 6), for example, is of the opinion that "les temps de la grammaire servent avant tout à exprimer des notions temporelles", approvingly citing the Brunot and Bruneau position (1949:394) that "les temps francais tendent à ne plus exprimer que la notion de temps". Yet other opinion is fairly solid that it is not so easy to correlate time-reference and tense: Gili Gaya (1948:136) declares that "los tiempos no son... valores fijos", and Price (1971:165) holds that there is no constant relationship between "tense" and "time".

Time-reference may be viewed as **absolute** (definable according to some universal public standard) or **relative** (definable only in relation to another time-reference). The occasions upon which a sentence can be said to refer to a particular point in absolute time are very few; examples involve overt adverbials with a precise time-reference, e.g., I fired the gun at 7 p.m.. Normally, the time-reference of a verb-form is essentially relative to the moment of utterance: the time-reference of a sentence like I am working is a time which refers to the moment of my uttering the sentence, that of I worked a time which is prior to the moment of my uttering the sentence, and so on. It is usual to class time-reference into PAST, PRESENT and FUTURE, which must be taken to imply, respectively, anteriority, simultaneity and posteriority with regard to the moment of speech. Again we must return to Whorf to see that such categories cannot be regarded as universal:

> Imagination of time as like a row harmonizes with a system of THREE tenses; whereas a system of TWO, an earlier and a later, would seem to correspond better to the feeling of duration as it is experienced. For if we inspect consciousness we find no past, present, future, but a unity embracing complexity. (143)

Whorf points out that the verb-systems of many languages primarily express a two-term system based on duration. Since we are going to be dealing with languages for which the PAST, PRESENT, FUTURE distinction is appropriate, however, we can keep these terms, but we must notice that the use of the moment of speech as a reference point and the relative definition of time-reference categories causes problems for the definition of PRESENT. In sentences like Mary is on the phone or John is doing his homework the events be on the phone and do homework strictly have PAST, PRESENT and FUTURE time-reference since they commence before the moment of speech and continue after it. The label PRESENT, if it is to be retained, must accordingly be taken to mean not simply simultaneity with the moment of speech but also 'not exclusively PAST' and 'not exclusively FUTURE'. In this connection, we may compare Prior's rejection (1967) of any theory of time which made PAST, PRESENT and FUTURE mutually exclusive, a conclusion also implicit in the semantically-orientated work of Guillaume (1937) and Bull (1968).

In complex sentences, a secondary time-reference point in addition to the moment of speech is needed. The time-reference of embedded sentence verb-forms may be viewed as relative to that of the corresponding matrix sentence forms, so in [I promised [I would go]] go is posterior to promise, in [I thought [he was deaf]] be deaf and think are simultaneous, and in [I remembered [that he had left]] leave is anterior to remember. In particular, when a sentence is embedded as the complement of a 'reporting' verb, the time-reference of its verb is satisfactorily definable only in this way. In [He said [(that) he would go]] the time-reference of go is posterior to say, which in its turn is anterior to the moment of speech; go relates to the moment of speech in no other way. The notion of a secondary time-reference point has been expressed in various ways. Several linguists, working from morphology to semantics, have proposed a distinction within the verb-system between 'absolute' and 'relative' verb-forms. Kahn (1954) makes a major distinction in his system along such lines. The idea originates in the work of Bally (1933), who described 'relative' forms as those which exhibited implicit comparison with other forms. Gili Gaya (1948:135) regards subjunctive and reported speech clause forms as determined by others. Imbs (1960:14) introduces a notion of "temps de perspective" to account for reported speech clause forms and other sequence-of-tense phenomena.

Bull (1968) regards the reported speech construction as of particular importance; he proposes that the time-reference of all utterances can be defined relative to either the moment of speech or the moment of reported utterance. His overall picture of time-reference is (22) that there are three basic 'axes' along which time-reference can be represented, corresponding to the mental activities of experience, recall and anticipation. He is compelled to establish an additional axis of 'recalled anticipation' to handle the time-reference of verb-forms like *go* in *I promised I would go*. Although it is theoretically possible to project an infinite number of axes in the same way, Bull feels that the moment of speech and the moment of reported utterance are basic in that it is from these that all possible projections stem. 'Recalled anticipation' he therefore associates with the recall axis, and anticipation now takes a parallel place on the experience axis:

(15)

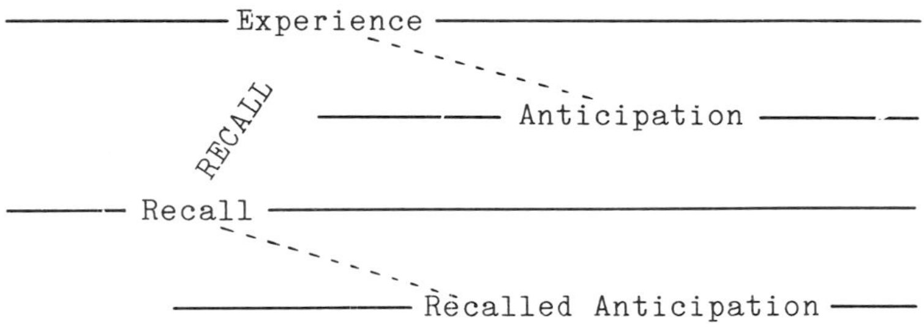

(Simplified from Bull (25))

A weakness of Bull's scheme in my view is that he unites under the notion of 'axis of recall' both one kind of simple PAST time-reference (anteriority to the moment of speech) and 'recalled experience'. I would distinguish between these as respectively (PRIMARY) PAST and TRANSPOSED PRESENT (or TRANSPOSED PAST), the former exemplified by *was leaving* in *he said he was leaving*. This distinction can be shown to have important syntactic implications: the latter sentence is ambiguous as a reporting of either *I am leaving* or *I was leaving*, and the representation of its 'transpositional history' by the use of the terms TRANSPOSED PRESENT and TRANSPOSED PAST facilitates the description of its time-reference in a way that its construing simply as 'recall' will not.

In my terminology, the notion of TRANSPOSITION has been used exclusively in respect of a PAST reference point. It is clear that TRANSPOSED time-reference could be thought of as pertaining to the FUTURE as well. In the sentences:

(16) a. I will go after he has arrived
b. He will tell me that she will leave the next day

the event arrive is anterior to go and leave is posterior to tell. It would be logical to think of arrive and leave as having FUTURE-TRANSPOSED PAST and FUTURE-TRANSPOSED FUTURE time-reference respectively, and to make a distinction between FUTURE-TRANSPOSITION and PAST-TRANSPOSITION. Indeed, this kind of viewpoint is essentially the one taken by Reichenbach (1947:290), who distinguishes, as I am doing here, between 'point of event', 'point of speech' and 'point of reference', and allows the 'point of reference' to be anterior to, simultaneous with or posterior to the 'point of speech'. But there is a general semantic difference between FUTURE-TRANSPOSITION and PAST-TRANSPOSITION: in (16a-b) arrive and leave can still be defined with respect to the moment of speech and are FUTURE, whereas in I promised I would go there is no means of relating go to the moment of speech - it could be PAST (I promised (last Tuesday) I would go (next Friday)), PRESENT (I promised I would go (right now)) or FUTURE (I promised I would go (next week)). On the other hand it is unequivocally PAST-TRANSPOSED FUTURE. There is no way the time-reference of go can be plotted otherwise than relative to a PAST reference point. Equally there is no way that any FUTURE-TRANSPOSED form can be anything other than FUTURE, and a reading for (16a) like I will go (tomorrow) after he has arrived (just now) is anomalous; indeed, any FUTURE-TRANSPOSED time-reference which was not also FUTURE would violate Reichenbach's principle of the permanence of the reference-point (293). This referential asymmetry has its parallel in the morphology of the Romance verb: while PAST-TRANSPOSITION reference often corresponds to morphological modification of the verb-form:

(17) Fr: Il a dit: "Je viendrai"
==> Il a dit qu'il viendrait

FUTURE-TRANSPOSITION reference does not:

(18) Fr: Il dira: "Je viendrai"
==> Il dira qu'il viendra

Once again, since we are dealing with Romance and not seeking to establish a universal system of time-reference, I propose not to establish a category of FUTURE-TRANSPOSITION in my time-reference scheme, but to use the term TRANSPOSITION to indicate PAST-TRANSPOSITION.

A verb-form may express more than one time-referential category: the Fr Pres may have PRESENT reference, as attend in il vous attend maintenant, or FUTURE reference, as vient in il vient demain, and the Fr CondPerf may have TRANSPOSED FUTURE reference, as aurait fait in il m'a dit qu'il l'aurait déjà fait, or PAST reference, as aurait vu in il m'aurait vu hier. There is nevertheless often quite a good correspondence between the morphological structure of the verb-forms and the time-referential categories in which they have been placed: the 'future' infix -r- (Fr chante-r-ai, Sp canta-r-ía, It cante-r-ai) is regularly associated with FUTURE reference, and the 'imperfect' inflections (Fr -ais, etc., Sp -aba, -ía, etc., It -ava, etc.) are regularly associated with TRANSPOSED reference forms.

A further category of time-reference that must be distinguished here is that illustrated by bark in dogs bark. Such reference is associated with neither PRESENT, PAST nor FUTURE time-reference exclusively, but may be said to be UNIVERSAL in nature. Bull (68) considers that such sentences refer to an 'axis-free continuum'. UNIVERSAL reference can also be TRANSPOSED, as in he said that dogs barked, and may be restricted to PAST or FUTURE time, as in Summers used to be hot (PAST UNIVERSAL) and Summers will be hot again (FUTURE UNIVERSAL).

Time-reference is expressible in Romance not only by the inflection of a verb-form but also by an adverb or phrase. This is an aspect which has been rather neglected in structural studies of the verb, where the verb has been considered very much as an independent unit. If we consider the Fr sentences in (19), we see that the time-reference of Pres is apparently determined exclusively by the overt temporal adverb:

(19) a. Il part demain (FUTURE)
b. Il part maintenant (PRESENT)
c. Et alors il part pour la bataille (PAST)

Where such temporal adverbs are absent, there is potential ambiguity of time-reference:

(20) a. Il va au théâtre
(i) = est en train d'aller (PRESENT)
(ii) (demain) (FUTURE)
(iii) (tous les soirs) (UNIVERSAL)

b. Le train sera parti
(i) (quand nous arriverons) (FUTURE)
(ii) = doit être parti (PAST)

There may also be quite a precise relation between verb-form and adverb. I will examine in more detail (p.47) the close links between verb-form selection and temporal adverb selection in connection with the explanation of the differences in usage between Perf and Pret in MSp and English. In MSp, adverbials like ayer, la semana pasada, hace dos años, etc., occur with Pret but not with Perf; adverbials like ahora and no...todavía occur with Perf but not with Pret.

The cooccurrence of verb and adverbial performs several different kinds of function. First, the adverbial may simply make reference within one category of time-reference more specific: in John will arrive tomorrow, tomorrow specifies the area of the FUTURE to which the verb-form refers, whereas in isolation John will arrive has general FUTURE reference. Secondly, the adverbial may limit the reference of a multivalent form, as we have seen in the sentences of (19); equally, the adverbial itself may have vague time-reference or be multivalent from the time-reference point of view - today may cooccur with Pret, Pres or Fut (he did it today, he is doing it today, he will do it today) and the sentences so formed have respectively PAST, PRESENT and FUTURE time-reference. Thirdly, the verb-adverbial group may effectively signal that the verb has more than simple temporal value: in John will have arrived yesterday the adverb has PAST value which is not among the normal range of temporal possibilities for FutPerf, which is typically FUTURE; accordingly, Fut Perf is interpreted in its modal function of "must have arrived".

This third use of the verb-adverb combination brings us to a difficult question concerning the relation between tense and time-reference. It seems that the 'modal' interpretation of John will have arrived yesterday is brought about by the impossibility of giving the sentence a purely temporal reading; this in turn is the consequence of a lack of congruence between the time-reference of the verb-form and that of the adverbial. This suggests that tenses have a 'residual' or 'unmarked' time-reference beyond the limits of which variation by the adverb cannot apply, except that some combinations which are not permissible from the point of view of time-reference will have a 'marked' non-time-referential value. If this is so, it remains to establish the 'unmarked' time-reference of each tense. Crystal (1966:18-19) suggests that notions of 'marked' and 'unmarked' cooccurrences can be linked to frequency, the 'marked' combinations being the least frequent. This principle seems to work up to a point; looking at Klum's (1961) statistical study of verb-adverb cooccurrence in French, we find that cooccurrence of Fut with a PRESENT adverbial like maintenant, with which it would have a 'marked' reading of "supposition", has a frequency of only 2.9% compared with the 55% scored by cooccurrence with a FUTURE adverbial like demain (174). But what do we make of the profile for Cond, where no cooccurrence with a precise time-referring adverb scores more than 7.5% (205)? A more obvious and rigorous descriptive criterion is needed here. We may start by looking at combinations which are not permissible, a procedure by which Crystal (19) sets little store. In Table 2.1 I summarise the cooccurrences observed by Klum, classified according to the referential categories I have introduced above. We may immediately note the following restrictions: (a) Fut does not cooccur with PAST, TRANSPOSED PAST or TRANSPOSED PRESENT adverbs, (b) Perf, Imp, Plup and Pret do not cooccur with FUTURE adverbs, (c) Pres and Fut do not cooccur with TRANSPOSED PRESENT or TRANSPOSED PAST adverbs, (d) Pret does not cooccur with adverbs which have reference to a period immediately surrounding PRESENT. Unfortunately, the picture gained from a corpus-based account such as Klum's cannot be complete. Figures for FutPerf, CondPerf and PAnt are so small as to yield next to no information about their cooccurrence possibilities. The lack of cooccurrence of Pres with the PAST adverbials la semaine passée and l'autre jour must be fortuitous, since the possibility of Pres cooccurring with a PAST adverb is shown by its attestation with hier. Hornstein (1977), working in a generativist framework and with Reichenbachian semantic representations, comes nearer to a method which will give a complete principled account of such restrictions for English. He characterises temporal adverbs as well as tenses according to the relations which are contracted between the moment of speech (S), the moment

Table 2.1: Verb-adverb ccocurrence in MFr (from Klum (1961))

	Pres	Perf	Fut	FutPerf	Imp	Plup	Pret	PAnt	Cond	CondPerf	Pres aller + inf.	Imp aller + inf.	Pres venir de + inf.	Imp venir de + inf.
PAST:														
Hier	*	*			*	*				*				
La semaine passée		*			*		*							
L'autre jour		*			*	*	*							
FUTURE:														
Demain	*		*	*					*		*			
La semaine prochaine	*		*											
PRESENT:														
En ce moment	*				*	*			*					
Maintenant	*	*	*		*	*			*		*	*		
'Extended' PRESENT:														
Ce matin	*	*	*		*	*			*	*				
Ce soir	*	*	*	*	*				*		*			
Aujourd'hui	*	*	*		*				*		*			
PAST:														
Tout à l'heure	*	*	*		*	*			*		*		*	
Alors	*	*	*		*	*	*		*	*				
A ce moment	*	*	*		*	*	*	*						
PAST or TRANSPOSED PRESENT:														
La veille					*	*	*							*
La semaine précédente						*				*				
Quelques heures plus tôt		*			*	*	*							
PAST or TRANSPOSED FUTURE:														
Le lendemain	*	*	*		*	*	*		*		*	*		
La semaine suivante		*	*		*		*					*		
Quelques heures plus tard	*	*	*		*	*	*		*			*		
Indeterminate:														
Après	*	*	*		*	*	*		*	*				
Bientôt	*	*	*		*	*	*	*	*		*	*		
Plus tard	*	*	*		*	*	*		*			*		
Dates	*	*	*	*	*	*	*		*		*	*		*

of the event (E) and the reference point (R), and then draws up restrictions on what he calls 'basic tense structure' (TS), which is in fact the tense structure of the verb. TS is not maintained (a) if the adverb requires any of S, R and E to be 'associated' (i.e., contemporaneous) differently from the way in which they are associated in the semantic representation of the verb, (b) if the linear order of S, R and E is not the same for verb and adverb in their semantic representations. Thus, for example, John came home is specified E, R ___ S (E and R are associated and are prior to S), but now is contemporaneous with S, so requiring the specification E, R, S (E, R and S are all associated and contemporaneous). To reconcile the two would mean changing the pattern of association in one or the other specification, and so *John came home now is impossible. Another example: John is coming is specified S, R, E (the arrow above the E signifies the progressive form) and tomorrow is posterior to S; the two give a derived TS S ___ R, E. This is allowable since linear order is preserved and no different association is involved. Hornstein observes that That will be Max at the door now must be impossible in a purely temporal interpretation, since That will be Max must be specified S ___ R, E, whereas now is contemporaneous with S; the derived TS would be S, R, E, which requires a new association of S with R, E. He solves the problem of giving the sentence an interpretation by specifying Fut alternatively as (m) S, R, E, where (m) stands for a 'marked' reading, in which it is of course not consistent with the specification for now (536). Hornstein's concept of a 'marked' value for a tense-and-adverb combination is simply that of a value which his temporal specifications do not permit but which nevertheless turns out to be acceptable. This would be valuable if some sort of naturalness or universality could be claimed for his descriptive system, but unfortunately the whole method turns out to have serious deficiencies. Hornstein sets great store, as we have seen, by the linear ordering of S, R and E. He explicitly states (523) that only S, R, E is to be taken as the specification of Pres, despite the semantic equivalence of S, R, E and E, R, S and S, E, R. This perplexing requirement derives from a peculiarity of English by which Pres and the Present Continuous (PresCont) are able to combine with FUTURE adverbs: if PresCont were specified E, R, S, the derived specification of John is coming home tomorrow as S ___ R, E would require a change in the linear order and hence incorrectly predict that the sentence was unacceptable. Hornstein thus conveniently represents the asymmetry in the verb-adverb cooccurrence system of English by which Pres can cooccur with a FUTURE adverbial but not with a PAST adverbial, but the insistence on linear ordering is essentially an ad hoc constraint and has no independent motivation. We may also ask how Hornstein's system would apply to other languages. Sp has a PresCont form which in many respects is similar to that of English (John is working = Juan está trabajando), but it does not share with English PresCont the ability to combine with a FUTURE adverbial (John is coming tomorrow ≠ *Juan está viniendo mañana), although Pres in the two languages is similar in this respect (John comes tomorrow = Juan viene mañana). If we were to adopt Hornstein's system for Sp, then, some means would have to be found of blocking the cooccurrence of the Pres estar + infinitive form with a FUTURE adverb. Both Hornstein and Reichenbach have difficulties with the specification of English Perf. Reichenbach has recourse to the rather feeble principle of the 'positional use of the reference point' (295) to provide for complex sentences which have non-contemporaneous reference points, and appeals to this principle to explain the use of the English Simple Past (Pret) in the sentence This is the man who drove the car, where is and drove need two different reference points in their specifications and contrast with German Dies ist der Mann, der den Wagen gefahren hat, where Pres and Perf relate to the same reference point. He also notes (292-3) the English use of Pret with ago adverbials (I saw him ten years ago) by contrast with German and Fr - the cooccurrence cannot therefore be similarly dealt with in the three languages. Hornstein is perplexed (525) by the doubtful status of ??John has come home right now, since a PRESENT adverbial should be permissible with Perf (specified E ___ S, R - the adverb referring to the reference point). Hornstein also notices that Perf can cooccur with PAST adverbs which will refer to the moment of the event (John has eaten cake in the past) but fails to distinguish these adverbs satisfactorily from other PAST adverbs like last Thursday which will not combine with Perf even though these should be permissible combinations in his system. In short, Hornstein's notion of 'markedness' is enshrined in a descriptive system that is language-specific and far from complete. Moreover, it is not obvious that the notion of 'markedness' ought to be reserved only for those 'modal' readings which break the acceptable time-reference combination rules. The sentence John comes tomorrow, for instance, has the 'modal' overtone of "John is due to come tomorrow", and might therefore be said to be 'marked' by comparison with John is coming tomorrow or John will come tomorrow.

Another approach we might adopt towards the question of the 'markedness' or 'unmarkedness' of time-reference values for verb-forms is to consider 'unmarked' values as those which the verb-form has in isolation and 'marked' values as those which can be achieved only by the verb-form being combined with an overt adverbial context. However, the contextless use of a verb-form is impossible to achieve, since at the very least the verb-stem must be lexicalised - a verb inflection cannot exist in isolation. The following two English sentences could scarcely be more minimal in context, for instance:

(21) a. He'll go
     b. He'll be there

and yet they are quite different in their possibilities of interpretation. (21a) is likely to be read as a straightforward FUTURE, while (21b) could have a FUTURE reading or a PRESENT 'modal' reading. The ambiguity of (21b) can be resolved only by adverbial modification (he'll be there tomorrow, he'll be there now). (21a) cannot be made PRESENT by any kind of adverbial modification. The difference between the two sentences depends on the aspectual value of the verb-stems go and be (see below, pp.54-56). It seems that PRESENT 'modal' readings for Fut are only available with durative expressions: note how (21a) could be made to have PRESENT reference by making the verb PresCont, which is typically durative - he'll be going now. The method has severe limitations, therefore, and it is interesting to note that it does not distinguish between the 'modal' and 'temporal' readings of Fut in terms of markedness.

I propose, therefore, to leave the question of markedness in abeyance and to recognise that different combinations of verb-forms, verb-stem and adverb will yield different readings, and that the possibilities of combination and interpretation may vary from language to language.

ASPECT

Perhaps the most controversial parameter of all those I shall discuss is the somewhat maverick category known broadly as aspect. Several discussions of the subject (e.g., Klum (1961), Reid (1970)) have taken Vendryes' (1942-5:84) review of Holt (1943) as their starting-point:

> Il n'y a guère en linguistique de question plus difficile que celle de l'aspect, parce qu'il n'y en a pas de plus controversée et sur laquelle les opinions divergent davantage... On n'est d'accord ni sur la définition même de l'aspect, ni sur les rapports de l'aspect et du temps, ni sur la façon dont l'aspect s'exprime, ni sur la place qu'il convient de reconnaître à l'aspect dans le système verbal des différentes langues.

The chief problem is that linguists have seen the question of aspect in varying ways, and generally from differing points of view; discussions have consequently lacked consistency in definition of terms. Definitions of aspect fall into what we might call the 'subjective' and the 'objective' schools of thought. The 'objectivists' attempt to define the nature of aspect in neutral semantic terms: thus Lucot (1956:447) speaks of "... le rapport d'une notion verbale à l'idée de durée", and Pohl (1964:177) of "... toute référence, positive ou nulle, au début ou à la fin d'un procès...". The 'subjectivists' define aspect in terms of the attitude of the speaker: thus Rallides (1971:9) says that aspect "... refers to forms whose content is the speaker's point of view", and Gili Gaya (1948:131) that "estas maneras distintas de mirar la acción expresada por un verbo... se llaman aspectos de la acción verbal". The 'subjectivist' view can often be qualified in more 'objective' terms. Rallides, for example, further refines (10) his position as follows:

> The SPEAKER'S POINT OF VIEW may be that he views a given event as extended over a period of time, or within defined limits of time, or within an open or closed context of time, etc.

'Aspectual' distinctions can in many cases be seen purely as functions of time-reference. It is usual to assert that in Sp Imp and Pret contrast in 'aspectual' value. Yet explanations of this contrast are often given in time-referential terms: Ramsden (1959:§55) gives the following pedagogical rule-of-thumb:

> The imperfect considers verbal action in its duration, without indication of beginning or end (a state of mind free of time limits, for instance, or an action repeated an indeterminate number of times); the preterite, on the other hand, presents verbal action in its completeness, ascribed to a particular moment or to a definite period of time.

Similarly, the distinction between [+Perf] and [-Perf] forms in the Romance languages and English has been considered as an aspectual phenomenon, although it may be handled in essentially time-referential terms. (Reid (1970:154) proposed a parameter of "stage", neither time-referential nor aspectual in nature, to distinguish between such pairs.) Members of the [+Perf] paradigm often occur in subordinate clauses where they express anteriority to the main clause verb-form:

(22) English: When John arrives, Mary <u>will have left</u>
Fr: Quand Jean arrivera, Marie <u>sera partie</u>
Sp: Cuando llegue Juan, María <u>habrá salido</u>
It: Quando Giovanni arriverà, Maria <u>sarà partita</u>
English: When they <u>had finished</u>, they left
Fr: Quand ils <u>avaient</u> (<u>ont eu</u>) <u>fini</u>, ils sont partis (spoken)
Quand ils <u>eurent fini</u>, ils partirent (written)
Sp: Cuando <u>hubieron terminado</u>, salieron
It: Quando <u>avevano finito</u> (finirono), sono partiti (partirono) (spoken)
Quando <u>ebbero finito</u>, partirono (written)

The necessity for a 'reference point' in sentences containing [+Perf] forms is demonstrated by the fact that in isolation [+Perf] forms may not have a simple time-referential reading:

(23) English: Mary will have left
Fr: Marie sera partie
Sp: María habrá salido
It: Maria sarà partita

would most spontaneously be interpreted modally as Futures of supposition with PAST reference. To distinguish [+Perf] forms from [-Perf] forms, then, we could simply establish the essentially time-referential category of ANTERIORITY, and describe Plup as capable of PAST ANTERIOR reference, FutPerf of FUTURE ANTERIOR reference and CondPerf of TRANSPOSED FUTURE ANTERIOR reference. Perf itself is something of a problem: PRESENT ANTERIORITY being time-referentially much the same thing as PAST. In several Romance languages the simple expression of PAST is indeed one of the functions, if not the chief function, of Perf. In languages which preserve an opposition between Perf and another PAST-referring form, however, preserving a semantic label like PRESENT ANTERIOR as opposed to PAST is not a bad way of describing the value of Perf. In these languages, Perf usually carries some notion of reference to the moment of speech or a more extended PRESENT time, or it is used to refer to events in the 'recent past', usually with adverbials which are vague in time-reference and can include PRESENT, or which contain some deictic marking (e.g., the 'first person' demonstrative this, etc.) which relate to PRESENT. A comparison amongst Sp, Ptg, Cat and a variety of It which preserves the distinction is shown below:

(24)	Sp	Ptg	Cat	It
"yesterday"	le vi ayer	vi-o ontem	el vaig veure ahir	l'ho visto ieri
"this morning" (moment of speech later than "this morning")	le vi esta mañana	vi-o esta manhã	l'he vist aquest matí	l'ho visto stamane
"last year"	le vi el año pasado	vi-o o ano passado	el vaig veure l'any passat	lo vidi l'anno scorso
"yet"	todavía no han llegado	embora não têm chegado	encara no han arribat	non sono ancora arrivati

The development of Perf in Fr to the function of a simple PAST-referring form sheds interesting light on the relation between tense and aspect, since it shows how a primarily aspectual value can become a primarily time-referential value through the close relation between 'aspect' and time-reference. It also very clearly demonstrates how the morphological system of a language and a proposed referential system are not necessarily parallel. It is inappropriate to regard Fr Perf as expressing only PRESENT ANTERIOR reference just because it is formally parallel to FutPerf and Plup, which may appropriately be said to have respectively FUTURE ANTERIOR and PAST ANTERIOR reference.

Morphological Aspect

Imperfective and Perfective. In the foregoing discussion of the relation between time-reference and aspect, we have identified two kinds of aspectual opposition which are represented morphologically in all the Romance languages. The first is that between Imp and Pret (or Perf where this functions as a simple Past), which we may label IMPERFECTIVE/PERFECTIVE. This is essentially the same kind of opposition that is encountered in the verb-systems of the Slavonic languages; the description given by Ramsden of the opposition in Sp corresponds almost exactly to that described by Isachenko (see Murphy (1963:21)) for Russian:

> Where the imperfective aspect is used to express the idea of an action in progress... the speaker is as it were himself fully immersed in the current of this process. He can see neither the beginning nor the end of it and hence is unable to express the process as a completed action seen as a complete entity... Where the action is expressed by forms of the perfective aspect..., the speaker is standing outside the action expressed by the verbal form and therefore surveys the action as one whole...

The second kind of aspectual opposition to be considered is that between [+Perf] and [-Perf] forms. Despite the traditional labelling of the [+Perf] forms, it is not appropriate to consider them as entering into an opposition of a PERFECTIVE/IMPERFECTIVE nature with their [-Perf] counterparts. This is clear if we examine the relation between Fut and FutPerf in English and the Romance languages - Fut is aspectually neutral, so that I will sing may be construed as either PERFECTIVE or IMPERFECTIVE in the senses we have already established for these terms (PERFECTIVE: I will sing for an hour this afternoon - action viewed as a whole; IMPERFECTIVE:

I will sing while ever she is there - action viewed as being in progress). The distinctive value of Fut Perf similarly appears to have nothing primarily to do with the PERFECTIVE/IMPERFECTIVE opposition: in I will have sung, FutPerf simply indicates termination of singing prior to some FUTURE reference-point. It is therefore necessary to give a label other than PERFECTIVE/IMPERFECTIVE to the aspectual opposition between [+Perf] and [-Perf] forms, and I propose to use the terms COMPLETIVE/NON-COMPLETIVE. However, for the most part there is little difference between the aspectual notion of COMPLETIVE and the temporal one of ANTERIOR, and I will accordingly use chiefly the latter in the characterisation of the [+Perf] forms.

Generative grammar and the Perfect. Bearing in mind that the value of Perf varies considerably from language to language, and that it can be considered as contracting oppositions of an aspectual and time-referential nature with simple verb-forms, I would like to digress for a moment to examine a more syntactically-orientated account of English Perf which has been offered by generative grammar.

Chomsky (1957:39) proposed that have + the past participle inflection -en should be considered as a single constituent belonging to a different category from the verbal stem: hence have + -en was to be dominated by the category AUX(iliary) and the verb stem by V(erb). His auxiliary rewrite rule handles the English Continuous verb-forms and Passive as well as the modal auxiliaries:

(25) AUX ⟶ Tense (Modal) (have + -en)(be + -ing)
(be + -en)

This separation was challenged by Ross (1969), whose position that there was not necessarily a distinction between auxiliaries and main verbs was developed in detail for the have auxiliary by McCawley (1971). McCawley proposed that all occurrences of the auxiliary have were to be derived from a Tense node (itself to be construed as a verb) developed as PAST, a view also put forward in Hoffman (1966). Hoffman had considered only the non-finite uses of the have auxiliary: the perfect infinitive and gerundive complements and the non-finite form which superficially follows a modal. In such cases, the have form clearly functions as a PAST-referring element, contracting a time-referential opposition with the non-perfect finite form, as may be shown by adverb cooccurrence phenomena:

(26) a. Peter is thought to have kept ferrets in his larder { last year / *at the moment }

Peter is thought to keep ferrets in his larder { *last year / at the moment }

b. Peter's having kept ferrets in his larder { last year / *at the moment } shocks me

Peter's keeping ferrets in his larder { last year / at the moment } shocks me

c. Peter may have kept ferrets in his larder { last year / *at the moment }

Peter may keep ferrets in his larder { *last year / at the moment }

(The simple gerundive complement form in (26b) appears to be unmarked for time-reference.) Following McCawley's examples (100), it is easy to show that such instances of non-finite auxiliary <u>have</u> appear in contexts where finite auxiliary <u>have</u> cannot:

(27) a. John is believed to have arrived at 2 p.m. yesterday

but

b. *John has arrived at 2 p.m. yesterday

c. John is believed to have already met Sue when he married Cynthia

but

d. *John has already met Sue when he married Cynthia

If the <u>have</u> auxiliary is to be regarded as a unitary phenomenon, therefore, some reconciliatory solution must be found. McCawley opts (150) for taking the non-finite PAST-referring value as basic and attempts to adapt this to suit the finite forms too:

> ... all... these senses of the present perfect correspond to semantic representations in which something that provides the source of a past tense is embedded in something that provides the source of a present tense, and... accord-

> ingly, deletions can give rise to a structure of the type proposed above [i.e., John has arrived would have the structure $[_{S_1}[_{S_2}$John arrive$]_{S_2}$ Past$]_{S_1}$].

It is in this way that McCawley attempts a more exact representation of the 'PAST reference with PRESENT relevance' property traditionally associated with Perf[6], the most obvious manifestation of which is what he labels the "stative" use of Perf (where a state commences in PAST time but continues through the moment of speech), e.g.:

(28) a. I've caught 'flu (=imp= "and I've still got it")

versus

b. I caught 'flu (=imp= "but now I've recovered")

Let us now examine the consequences of such a description of Perf from the point of view of the elucidation of the opposition between Perf and Pret (= English Simple Past). If the element PAST underlies surface have exclusively, it is not clear how Pret is to be generated. McCawley effectively removes Pret from serious consideration by claiming (110) that "a past tense normally requires an antecedent", and concluding that the sentence The farmer killed the duckling is unacceptable unless there is a discourse context which sets a time to which killed can refer. The context may consist of a temporal adverbial or of a more complex structure perhaps involving another verb-form:

(29) a. (Last night), the farmer killed the duckling

b. The farmer (took his gun and) killed the duckling

McCawley suggests that there is a relation akin to pronominalisation between Pret and its 'antecedent' time-reference[7].

Apparently, the price we must pay for an exclusive underlaying of have by PAST is a complete dissociation of PAST from Pret and the generation of Pret by a totally different kind of rule - in other words, a complete loss of paradigmatic relation between Pret and Perf.

Anderson (1973:335) proposed a more complex description of Perf which sought to capture the 'PRESENT relevance' value of the form. One well-known property of English Perf, for instance, is that its subjects must continue to exist, or be alive, or be of some relevance to, the moment of speech: thus the sentence

(30) *Einstein has visited Princeton

is unacceptable since it implies that Einstein is still alive at the moment of speech; the sentence

(31) Princeton has been visited by Einstein

on the other hand, is acceptable, since it implies that Princeton continues to exist at the moment of speech. Anderson introduces a constraint that

> ... the existential tensing of an argument agrees with that of the tensed predicate it is most immediately subordinate to, unless it is 'present'.

and provides structural descriptions for sentences (30) and (31) as follows:

(32) a.

b.

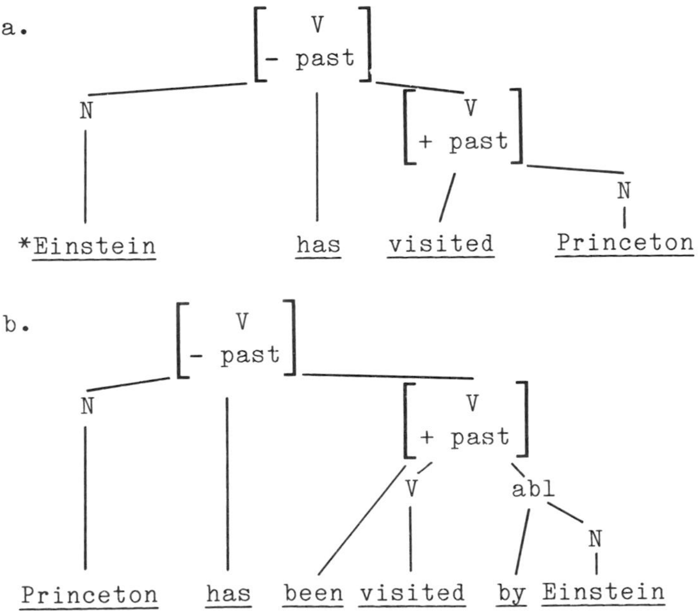

Einstein is to be construed as 'non-present'; it is accordingly acceptable under the immediate domination of a [+past] node, though not under a [-past]

node; Princeton, on the other hand, being 'present', is unacceptable under both a [+past] or a [-past] node. In this proposal, the relation of Perf to PRESENT emerges forcefully, and Perf is not regarded as a 'Past' verb-form; also, the auxiliary have is dominated by a [-past] node, which is morphologically more satisfactory. I have already suggested that Romance Perf, even in languages where it functions as a Simple Past, must have [-Past] as one of its specifications, and this is true also of English Perf, which in reported speech constructions may be transformed in the complement of a [+Past] verb into Plup, which must be taken as its [+Past] counterpart:

(33) [He said$_{[+Past]}$ [He has$_{[-Past]}$ gone]]
     === He said he had gone

Of the many factors which appear to be associated with the distinction between English Perf and Pret, one is adverb cooccurrence. In British English, for example, yet and already cannot cooccur with Pret, and ago-adverbials cannot occur with Perf:

(34) a. I {have seen / *saw} the film already

b. I {haven't seen / *didn't see} it yet

c. I {lived / *have lived} there five years ago

To the class of adverbials cooccurring with Pret but not Perf (I will call this set /PRET/) belong many other expressions of 'defined PAST time': last week, last year, yesterday, etc. Yet and already belong to a much smaller set (/PERF/) of expressions of 'relevance to the moment of speech'. It is likely that these classes are both 'marked'; many adverbs cooccur with both Perf and Pret, e.g., today, this week, this year, etc.[8] There is evidence to suggest that adverb cooccurrence may in some instances be the unique determining factor in a choice between Perf and Pret; in (35), for example, the time-reference of the verb see and the reference of the nominals in the context of which it occurs are identical, and only the adverbial qualification differs from sentence to sentence:

(35) I {have seen / *saw} the film already - I {saw / *have seen} it yesterday

It would therefore be most unsatisfactory if in the generation of (35) Perf and Pret were introduced (as McCawley suggested) in two completely different ways, since it can be argued that Perf is just as much dependent upon an 'antecedent' adverbial context as Pret, and so just as much a candidate for introduction by 'pronominalisation'.

Setting the evidence of the Romance languages side by side with that of English, it is easy to see that /PRET/ and /PERF/ have no natural or 'universal' definition (cf. M. Harris (1982:43-4)), but vary considerably from language to language. But the existence of an opposition definable in terms of adverb coocurrence strongly suggests that Pret and Perf should be considered as unitary terms of a paradigmatic contrast. It is quite mistaken to regard them as essentially different in nature, despite their superficial syntactic dissimilarity and the possibility that the have auxiliary of Perf has properties in common with other auxiliaries.

Nevertheless, some attention must be given to Perf as a member of the [+Perf] paradigm. I suggested above that the have auxiliary could be considered as a marker of ANTERIORITY, a property made clear by the ability of the [+Perf] forms to cooccur with adverbials which overtly mark anteriority to a stated or unstated moment of time:

(36) a. I will have done it by then
b. I will have done it by the time you arrive
c. I had done it when he arrived
d. He thought he would have finished by Thursday

I will call the set of such adverbials /ANT/ adverbials; the absence of an overt /ANT/ adverbial sometimes results in a [+Perf] form having a strange, incomplete value:

(37) a. !I will have done it
b. !I had done it
c. !He thought he would have finished

We have already discussed the desirability of describing Perf as having PRESENT ANTERIOR reference. Certainly Perf can be regarded in this way for some of its functions in English and the Romance languages, and may, for instance, cooccur with an /ANT/ adverbial referring to the moment of speech:

(38) He surely { has done } it by now
{ *did }
{ *does }

Yet sentences in which Perf is the verb-form are quite natural without the cooccurrence of an overt /ANT/ adverbial, e.g.:

(39) He has done it

This apparently exceptional state of affairs no doubt has a natural explanation. The moment of utterance occupies, as we have seen, a unique place in a time-referential scheme, since it is an unequivocal, universal reference point. Its overt expression is most likely redundant. Thus it is reasonable to suggest that in (39) reference to the moment of speech is implicit and need not be overtly expressed. If this is correct, then Perf can without difficulty take its place beside other members of the [+Perf] paradigm, and we may describe the time-reference it exhibits in sentences like (39) quite accurately as ANTERIORITY to PRESENT.

The question of non-finite *have* must now be considered. The view that Pret and Perf can be regularly related to their cooccurring adverbials leaves the question of the behaviour of non-finite *have* somewhat in the cold, since, as we have seen in examples like (27) above, non-finite *have* can cooccur with /PRET/ adverbials. In fact, the Perfect infinitive in English and Romance is the surface manifestation not only of Perf and Pret, but also of Plup, as the following sentences show:

(40) a. He is believed to have left by now (He has left by now)
b. He is believed to have left three years ago (He left three years ago)
c. He is/was believed to have left by six o'clock (He left/had left by six o' clock)

Such a multiplicity of values is scarcely surprising when it is considered that in contrast to the many finite verb-forms of English and Romance there are only two infinitive forms (English *leave*, *have left*, etc.). The Perfect Infinitive (named in accordance with its morphological form, but not with its syntactic and semantic function) does triple duty, corresponding to the [-Past, +Perf], [+Past, +Perf] and [+Past] form; in other words, it expresses PASTness as well as ANTERIORITY, and hence is not always specified [+Perf]. This is not the only point in these languages where a superficially [+Perf] form is the marker of PASTness rather than ANTERIORITY: we shall see in Chapters 4 and 6 how in the conditional sentence tense-sequences [+Perf] forms (Plup, PlupSubj, CondPerf) are regularly employed in the formation of PAST COUNTERFACTUAL conditionals. The relation between ANTERIORITY and PASTness is a close one, as we are by now well aware, and a [+Perf] form is the first natural candidate for the expression of PASTness if for any reason a distinctive [+Past] form is not available.

Progressive and Non-progressive. There is a third kind of aspectual distinction that we must consider as relevant to the morphology of such languages as Sp, Ptg and It, namely, that which exists between the simple forms of the verb and the corresponding 'progressive' or 'continuous' forms (Sp estar haciendo, Ptg estar a fazer, It stare facendo). This seems to be a relatively straightforward match between morphological and semantic category and can be labelled aspectually PROGRESSIVE/NON-PROGRESSIVE.

Lexical Aspect

I wish now to make a fundamental distinction between the **morphological aspectual** properties I have discussed in the preceding section and the aspectual properties which are inherent in verb-stems themselves, which may be termed **lexical aspectual.** The first linguist to have brought this interesting property of verb-stems to light is generally reckoned to be Herman (1933), who distinguished between Aspekt ('morphological aspect') and Aktionsart ('lexical aspect') (the latter later to be Gallicised as mode d'action).

The study of lexical aspect has proved highly controversial. It was encouraged by work on the Slavonic languages, where it is often possible to pair up verbs which differ only in aspectual value, and where a system of prefixation and suffixation on the verbal stem produces aspectual oppositions. In Russian there are such pairs as on stučal ("he knocked" = "he was knocking") and on stuknul ("he knocked" = "he knocked once"), videt' ("see") and uvidet' ("see momentarily"), govorit' ("talk") and skazat' ("say"). Yet Forsyth (1970) suggests (Chapter 3) that the problem is not quite so straightforward, and that there is a good deal of debate concerning the validity of such pairings. Romance linguists have observed parallels in the languages with which they are familiar, although the formal relationship is generally absent even if the semantic relationship can be established[9]. Taking as an example a putative aspectual relation between Fr dormir and s'endormir, where the prefix s'en- could be construed as a marker of 'incipient' aspect, it may be noted that the pattern s'en + verb with a corresponding 'incipient' reading is paralleled in the forms s'enamourer, s'endurcir, s'engraisser, s'enfuir and s'ensuivre. Of these, a corresponding *amourer does not exist, durcir is transitive unlike dormir, and fuir and suivre are verbs of motion. Graisser is not obviously semantically relatable to s'engraisser. Other verbs formed with s'en- and having more or less 'incipient' meaning are based on adjectives (s'enhardir) or nouns (s'enraciner, s'enrhumer, s'enrôler). S'en- may be more properly regarded in some instances as a marker of position (s'enferrer, s'enfoncer) or of reciprocal relation (s'encorder, s'enchevêtrer). It becomes exceedingly difficult, therefore, to make any useful structural statement about a proposed aspectual relation between s'endormir and dormir.

Sifting through the various kinds of aspectual distinction that have been made and the terminology employed to label them is a bewildering exercise. The basic distinction observed is between what, following Comrie (1976:414), I propose to call 'PUNCTUAL' and 'DURATIVE' aspect. PUNCTUAL events may be characterised as not necessarily having duration (be born, die, etc.), whereas DURATIVE events and states do normally have duration (see, hear, etc.). Amongst the different labels given to this distinction, it is interesting to note that of Sten (1952) and Klum (1961), who call the distinction 'perfectif'/'imperfectif'. The relation with the morphological category is plain: PUNCTUAL, like PERFECTIVE, involves the notion of an act complete in itself, while DURATIVE, like IMPERFECTIVE, focuses on duration. However, as we shall see, it is certainly possible for DURATIVE events and states to be seen as PERFECTIVE: in Sp quedó allí dos horas, quedar is DURATIVE, but the action as a whole is seen as PERFECTIVE, as a completed whole. Hence I shall continue to use different sets of terms for the morphological aspectual and the lexical aspectual categories. Other kinds of lexical aspectual category, somewhat different in nature from PUNCTUAL and DURATIVE, have been proposed. Schogt (1968:4), for example, characterises verb-stems as 'telic' or 'atelic' (those expressing a 'goal', e.g. drown, which necessarily implies the completion of the event, and those which do not express a 'goal', e.g., play[10]). Bull (1968: 44-5) similarly distinguishes between 'cyclic' events, the termination of which is implied, e.g., get up, and 'noncyclic' events, which carry no such implication, e.g., sleep. He also distinguishes (but incorporates into the 'cyclical' category) a verb-stem like Sp girar "turn, revolve", which represents a series of 'cyclic' events.

Bull points out that while the action represented by comer una manzana is cyclic, that represented by comer manzanas is non-cyclic. Gili Gaya (1948:31) notices too that aspect will vary according to context: thus he firmado la carta and he firmado de 11 a 12 are aspectually different. Sten (1952:8-9) follows Hanckel's (1929:31-2) view of 'Verben mit imperfektivischer Tendenz' and 'Verben mit perfektivischer Tendenz'. Reid (1970:150) agrees that:

> It is certainly mistaken, as is sometimes done, to divide all French verbs into two objective and mutually exclusive classes called respectively imperfective and perfective or durative and punctual verbs.

Verb-stems, in short, appear to be marked or unmarked for lexical aspect. In the preceding discussion, I have deliberately selected stems which are aspectually marked - indeed, most commentators do, and this is possibly one source of confusion in presentations of aspectual phenomena. We may contrast with verbs like arrive (inherently PUNCTUAL) and sleep (inherently DURATIVE) a stem like stand up. In isolation, without adverbial qualification, the sentence he stood up is aspectually ambivalent; only the cooccurrence of a PUNCTUAL or DURATIVE adverbial ensures a unique aspectual value (he stood up suddenly, he stood up for a long time). A great many verb-stems appear to be aspectually unmarked in this way. In fact, it rapidly becomes apparent that in assigning lexical aspectual properties to verb-stems, we are in reality doing no more than systematising our expectations about normal behaviour. Although we may claim that a verb like arrive is in some sense PUNCTUAL, a sentence like he arrived all week can certainly be given some kind of interpretation (an ironic answer to the question When did he arrive?, perhaps). Unusual aspectual readings should therefore be marked with the ! of semantic deviance rather than with the ? or * of syntactic unacceptability.

I propose to add to my list of lexical aspectual categories that of REPETITIVE. This is necessary for the characterisation of events which inherently occur more than once, e.g., revolve and flash. Furthermore, verb-stems which are not inherently REPETITIVE may often come to have REPETITIVE aspectual value in certain contexts, e.g., arrived in he arrived at the same time every day. REPETITIVE may be seen as a subcategory of DURATIVE in that the repetition of an action necessarily has duration.

The study of lexical aspect has brought to the fore the fact that aspectual distinctions, like time-reference distinctions, are represented not only in verb inflections but in other elements in the sentence as well. Since verb-inflection and verb-stem are inseparable, the relation between morphological and lexical aspect is crucial to an understanding of the expression of aspect in English and the Romance languages. Even Gili Gaya (1948:131), who considers that lexical and morphological aspect can be parcelled up into the realms of 'meaning' and 'grammar' respectively, thereby abdicating all responsibility for a study of lexical aspect in his grammar, nevertheless mentions the well-kncwn connection between lexical aspect and morphological aspect in the Sp Past tenses. A DURATIVE verb-stem in combination with Pret in Sp will tend to have a reading which may be described as one of 'initiative phase'[11]. Thus leí in entonces leí el periódico may be considered to represent first and foremost the beginning of the action of reading. This phenomenon often poses interesting problems of translation from Sp to English. The sentence conocí a este hombre en Madrid must be rendered in English with a PUNCTUAL verb-stem (I met this man in Madrid) whereas conocer with an Imp inflection will be rendered by the English DURATIVE verb-stem know (conocía a este hombre en Madrid = I knew this man in Madrid) - the aspectual distinction which is made morphologically in Sp must be made lexically in English.

In fact there are three points at which aspectual values may be introduced into the verb phrase, namely, the verb-stem, the verb-inflection and the modifying adverbial. Adverbials may easily be assigned lexical aspectual values: PUNCTUAL (e.g., at two o'clock), DURATIVE (e.g., for two hours) and REPETITIVE (e.g., every day). The full importance and necessity of the REPETITIVE category may now be appreciated, for while there are relatively few verb-stems which are inherently REPETITIVE in value, there are a good number of adverbials which exhibit this property.

It is worth examining in some detail the possibilities of cooccurrence between verb-stem, verb-inflection and adverb in Sp Past tenses. There appear to be at least five classes of verb-stem which yield different patterns of semantic interpretation when they cooccur with the Imp and Pret inflections and PUNCTUAL, DURATIVE and REPETITIVE adverbials: (a) stems which are basically unmarked aspectually, e.g., mirar; (b) stems which are basically PUNCTUAL, are nevertheless compatible with REPETITIVE adverbials, but which can only in some cases be interpreted as DURATIVE, e.g, llegar; (c) stems which are basically DURATIVE and are compatible with REPETITIVE adverbials; (d) stems as in (b), but which in combination with DURATIVE adverbials yield a reading which represents a time-interval between the end of the event they represent and the beginning of some 'converse' event, e.g., salir (converse regresar); (e) stems which have no REPETITIVE interpretation but which are unmarked for PUNCTUAL and DURATIVE, e.g., morir. We will now look at all the possibilities of stem + inflection + adverbial combinations:

(a) Unmarked stems

Miró (Pret) a su hermano a las dos (PUNCTUAL)

Overall PUNCTUAL interpretation: "He looked at his brother at two"

Miraba (Imp) a su hermano a las dos (PUNCTUAL)

Overall DURATIVE or REPETITIVE interpretation: "He was in the process of looking at his brother at two / He used to look at his brother at two"

Miró (Pret) a su hermano largo rato (DURATIVE)

Overall DURATIVE interpretation, with action viewed as a whole: "He looked at his brother for a long time"

Miraba (Imp) a su hermano largo rato (DURATIVE)

Overall DURATIVE: "He was looking at his brother for a long time"

Miró (Pret) a su hermano todos los días (REPETITIVE)

Overall REPETITIVE, though must be understood as a series of events viewed as a whole: "He used to look at his brother every day (for a period of time)"

Miraba (Imp) a su hermano todos los días (REPETITIVE)

Overall REPETITIVE: "He used to look at his brother every day"

(b) Basically PUNCTUAL stems

Llegó (Pret) a las dos (PUNCTUAL)

Overall PUNCTUAL interpretation: "He arrived at two"

Llegaba (Imp) a las dos (PUNCTUAL)

Overall DURATIVE or REPETITIVE interpretation: "He was in the process of arriving at two / He used to arrive at two"

!Llegó (Pret) largo rato (DURATIVE)

Unacceptable

Llegaba (Imp) largo rato (DURATIVE)

Overall DURATIVE, though slightly odd: "He was arriving for a long time"

Llegó (Pret) todos los días (REPETITIVE)

Overall REPETITIVE, though odd without further adverbial modification, especially an adverb which would 'limit' the duration of the event to a fixed period: "He would arrive (at the same time) every day (that week)"

Llegaba (Imp) todos los días (REPETITIVE)

Overall REPETITIVE interpretation: "He arrived every day"

(c) Basically DURATIVE stems

Durmió (Pret) a las dos (PUNCTUAL)

Overall interpretation is the 'initiative phase' of the DURATIVE event, which is itself PUNCTUAL: "He went to sleep at two"

Dormía (Imp) a las dos (PUNCTUAL)

Overall DURATIVE: "He was sleeping at two"

Durmió (Pret) largo rato (DURATIVE)

Overall DURATIVE interpretation, with state viewed as a whole: "He slept for a long time"

Dormía (Imp) largo rato (DURATIVE)

Overall DURATIVE: "He was sleeping for a long time"

Durmió (Pret) todos los días (REPETITIVE)

Overall REPETITIVE, though must be understood as a series of states viewed as a whole: "He used to sleep every day (for a period of time)"

Dormía (Imp) todos los días (REPETITIVE)

Overall REPETITIVE: "He used to sleep every day"

(d) Special PUNCTUAL stems

As (a), except:

Salió (Pret) largo rato (DURATIVE)

The duration is that of the interval between <u>salir</u> and <u>regresar</u>: "He went out for a long time"

Salía (Imp) largo rato (DURATIVE)

Normally has a REPETITIVE interpretation; again the duration refers to the interval between <u>salir</u> and <u>regresar</u>: "He used to go out for a long time"

(e) Non-REPETITIVE stems

As (c), except:

!Murió (Pret) todos los días (REPETITIVE)

Impossible in normal circumstances

!Moría (Imp) todos los días (REPETITIVE)

Impossible in normal circumstances

The influence of the adverbials in the above examples is fairly easy to characterise. <u>Todos los días</u> is basically REPETITIVE and a sentence in which it appears has an overall REPETITIVE interpretation too. <u>A las dos</u> cooccurring with a PUNCTUAL expression pinpoints the time at which the event takes place; with a DURATIVE expression it states the time at which the event or state is in progress - a PUNCTUAL adverbial seems therefore not to affect positively the overall aspectual reading. <u>Largo rato</u>, which is basically DURATIVE, admits only an overall DURATIVE or REPETITIVE reading. The effect of the verb-inflection on overall aspectual value clearly varies with the aspectual class of the verb-stem and the modifying adverbial. In no verb-stem + adverbial cooccurrence category are the Imp and Pret inflections synonymous.

It will be remembered that time-reference adverbs appear to dominate verb-form inflections in that in the event of a conflict between the two, it is the time-reference of the adverb that prevails.

Thus Fr *il sera venu hier* must be interpreted as overall PAST in accordance with the adverb *hier*, despite the FutPerf tense, which is normally FUTURE. However, in aspectual combinations, the verb-inflection seems to be of relatively more weight; the aspectual distinctions made between Pret and Imp earlier are always of relevance in giving a semantic interpretation to the sentence. In particular, lexical aspect is often susceptible of modification by the aspectual value of the verb-inflection: inherently PUNCTUAL verbs like *llegar* can be 'stretched' to become DURATIVE by the Imp inflection, as in the examples above.

The importance of lexical aspect can also be seen in other areas. The interpretation of Sp sentences containing an *until*-adverbial may hinge on the lexical aspect of the verb-stem, for instance. When the verb-stem is DURATIVE or is susceptible of a DURATIVE reading, surface negation of the verb implies either negation of the sentence as a whole or that the initiative phase of the event represented by the verb commences at the time referred to by the adverbial. Thus:

(41) No trabajó hasta las seis
 = NEG [Trabajó hasta las seis]
 or
 = Comenzó a trabajar a las seis (no antes)

When the verb-stem is PUNCTUAL, however, surface negation of the verb can imply only that the event occurred at the time referred to by the adverbial:

(42) No llegó hasta las seis
 ≠ NEG [!Llegó hasta las seis]
 but
 = Llegó a las seis (no antes)

Another area of Spanish in which lexical aspect turns out to be of importance is in the syntax of *estar*. The past participle of a PUNCTUAL verb may combine with *estar* to represent a DURATIVE state which results from a PUNCTUAL event, e.g.:

(43) La puerta está abierta
 =imp= Alguien abrió la puerta

(43) cannot, however, contain an agentive phrase:

(44) *La puerta está abierta por Juan

The same kinds of process applied to a transitive DURATIVE event, on the other hand, will yield the previously inadmissible pattern of (44):

(45) La chica está acompañada
=imp= Alguien acompañó a la chica
and
La chica está acompañada por su padre
=imp= El padre acompañó y acompaña a la chica

I have limited my attention in this section to those lexical aspectual distinctions which seem to be crucial to the overall aspectual interpretation of the verb-phrase, but there are many other possible aspectual subcategorisations of lexical verb-stems which are of importance in a complete account of the relation between verb-stem, verb inflection and adverbial. G. Lakoff (1970:121-2) demonstrated the significance of the STATIVE/NON-STATIVE distinction for the English Progressive verb-forms, and the English situation is paralleled in Sp and It: a non-stative stem combines with the Progressive whereas a stative stem does not:

(46) English: I'm looking at the pictures
*I'm knowing John went there
Sp: Estoy mirando los cuadros
*Estoy sabiendo que Juan fue allí
It: Sto guardando i quadri
*Sto sapendo che Giovanni è andato là

Bertinetto (1981) has shown the syntactic relevance of a number of other lexical aspectual distinctions in Italian. Although many of the categories he proposes are subsumable under the major divisions of PUNCTUAL and DURATIVE, he points to the interesting distinction between TELIC and ATELIC stems (see above, p.52), which cut across the PUNCTUAL/DURATIVE division. Only telic stems are compatible with <u>in X time</u> adverbials:

(47) Giovanni è partito in mezzora; direi che si è sbrigato più del solito (PUNCTUAL, TELIC)
Giovanni, a quella vista, è trasalito in due minuti (PUNCTUAL, ATELIC)
Giovanni ha pulito la vasca dei pesci in due ore (DURATIVE, TELIC)

*Giovanni ha passeggiato lungo il viale in mezzora (DURATIVE, ATELIC) (49-50)

Stems Bertinetto characterises as PERMANENT are not susceptible of any limiting time-adverbial modification:

(48) *Domani Giovanni discenderà da una famiglia nobile, suppongo (41)

MOOD

Just as we have distinguished between **tense** and **time-reference** and **morphological** and **lexical** aspect, so it is necessary to distinguish between **mood**, the morphological marking which amongst other things may express modal values, and **modality**, the corresponding semantic category. We may observe that several forms of the simple verb paradigm may have the same time-referential and aspectual values; in the following Fr examples:

(49) a. Je le ferai demain
b. Je le ferais demain
c. Faites-le demain!
d. Je veux qu'il le fasse demain

all the underlined forms are FUTURE-referring and aspectually unmarked. The four verb-forms have all been considered at some time as exemplifying different types of mood, namely, indicative, conditional, imperative and subjunctive. It is not at all easy to establish definite values for these moods, since there is nothing so obligingly definite as a time-referential scheme on which to plot their semantic readings. At first sight, only the imperative has a discrete and easily characterisable function as the expression of a command. The indicative may be taken as the 'unmarked' term of the series as the form which expresses simple assertion, negation and question; conditional and subjunctive have special 'overtones' which depart from these functions.

Of the non-indicative types, the conditional is perhaps the most controversial, there being a considerable corpus of literature devoted to the case for and against it being thought of as a separate mood at all. In general, the more formally orientated schools have come down on the side of a purely temporal value for Cond: Togeby (1965:8), in the spirit of the Copenhagen school, concludes that from a functional point of view the form cannot be divided, and that since morphologically it has all the indications of being a 'tense', it will be considered as such. A dichotomous view of Cond is given by Nyrop (1930:§291):

> [Le conditionnel] présente en même temps une valeur temporelle et une valeur modale; il appartient aussi non seulement à l'indicatif, mais aussi au subjonctif dans les cas où il exprime la possibilité d'une action conditionelle ou l'incertitude d'une action.

Other commentators lean to one side or the other. Frei (1929:261-2) sees Cond as primarily a 'tense', though modal in some respects:

> Le conditionnel, employé au propre, n'est pas un mode, comme le désigne le grammaire traditionnelle, mais un temps relatif. Il fonctionne dans une proposition conséquentielle faisant pendant à une conditionnelle: <u>Si j'étais venu, il serait parti</u>. Mais par figure il peut s'employer absolument, et exprime alors une valeur modale: <u>Il serait parti</u> (sens dubitatif, éventuel).

Kahn (1954:44) sees Cond as predominantly modal:

> Que la forme en -<u>rait</u> soit précédée d'une conjonction de subordination comme <u>que</u> ou <u>quand</u>, qu'elle soit déterminée par une hypothèse ou non, sa marque modale de non-réel l'oppose à l'indicatif, sauf dans la phrase hypothétique non-réelle - où il y a neutralisation -, et dans les expressions figées comme <u>on dirait que</u>, <u>j'aimerais</u> + inf. ou <u>que</u> où le temps correspondant de l'indicatif a un sens tout différent.

The issue has long preoccupied French linguists[12]. The fascination exercised by the form on structural linguists is due to the clear impossibility of finding for it anything approaching a unitary value. My own view is that a largely spurious problem has been created with regard to the description of Cond, and I will defer full discussion of the question of its status (see below, p.94).

Although the [+Subj] forms raise even more problems of description, linguists at least appear to be agreed on the complexities of subjunctive usage, and it is an old riddle how the many apparently disparate usages can be related to the few subjunctive forms. It is not my purpose here to make casual generalisations on a topic which has received careful and extensive treatment by many scholars[13], but I will briefly review here some approaches to the problem. It is clear that a purely morphological account of the subjunctive will not get us very far; subjunctive usage is determined by a whole range of extraverbal factors which are apparently both syntactic (insofar as there appear to be elements like Fr avant que which invariably require the verb-form following to be in the subjunctive) and semantic (insofar as there is sometimes a choice available as to whether subjunctive or indicative forms are used, as in Sp after aunque) in nature. So at one end of the scale we could use the ad hoc device of simply marking subjunctive-requiring elements as such, and at the other end we might envisage the more explanatory solution of discovering a general feature or property for subjunctive-requiring elements on the basis of which a predictive hypothesis as to when subjunctive forms will be required can be framed. The latter solution would be the more highly valued and is the more diligently sought[14], and at least an approach to it can be discerned in sections of the Sp data. I have already noted that after aunque either subjunctive or indicative forms can occur. The first kind of approach I have mentioned might well do no more than state that aunque is an element which optionally requires the subjunctive. A closer examination of the data, however, reveals that use of the subjunctive or the indicative is closely related to presuppositions concerning the truth of the proposition in the aunque clause. The two sentences

(50) a. Aunque viene, no le diré nada
b. Aunque venga, no le diré nada

differ semantically in expectations concerning venir. In (50a), the event is certain, or highly probable; (50a) might follow in discourse a statement to the effect that the person in question was indeed coming. In (50b) the event is more of a contingency or a conjecture. Rough English translations are, respectively:

(51) a. Although he's coming, I won't tell him anything
b. Although he may be coming, I won't tell him anything

This account of the choice of verb-form after aunque is given an extra boost when it is further discovered that exactly parallel considerations appear to affect the choice of verb-form after tal vez, acaso, quizá(s) and a lo mejor, which may be taken as forming a natural class with regard to subjunctive usage. As an example of a more syntactically motivated usage of the subjunctive, we may take another natural class, that of verbs of opinion (e.g., creer, pensar, parecer, etc.). The verb-form in the complement of these verbs is normally in the indicative, whether the complement contains a negative or not:

(52) {Creo / Pienso / Me parece} que (no) tiene razón

In Spanish, the negative may be moved out of the complement sentence and into the matrix sentence when the matrix sentence contains one of these verbs; however, when it is moved in this way, the complement sentence verb-form must be put into the subjunctive:

(53) No {creo / pienso / me parece} que tenga razón

Note that the sentences of (52) (with no) and those of (53) are synonymous.

However, although we may achieve a limited success in grouping together some usages of the subjunctive under common semantic headings, it would be mistaken to think that in any Romance language subjunctive usage can be described according to a unified general principle. What kind of principle, for instance, could link the subjunctive usages I have just examined with the subjunctive of indirect commands or the subjunctive of FUTURE-referring temporal clauses in Sp? The subjunctive forms in Romance, like many tense forms, are multivalent.

As with the comparison of the time-referential values of cognate tense-forms in the Romance languages, so comparison of the use of the subjunctive is an extremely subtle matter. As a particularly complex example, we might consider the use and value of the subjunctive in the complement of verbs of thinking. In Fr and Sp, the indicative is normally used in the complement sentence of a positive affirmative verb of thinking; in It, on the other hand, the subjunctive is regularly found. With the 'raising' of the negative (see (53) above), the subjunctive is likely in Fr, well-nigh obligatory in Sp and It. With the thinking verb in the interrogative, Fr has either indicative or subjunctive, Sp indicative, It subjunctive:

(54) Fr	Sp	It
je crois qu'il est ici	creo que está aquí	credo che sia qui
je ne crois pas qu'il soit ici	no creo que esté aquí	no credo che sia qui
croyez-vous qu'il soit ici?	crees que está aquí?	credi che sia qui?

However, modification of the mood is often possible, with definite semantic import. In Fr, the indicative can be used to express the reality of the complement:

(55) Il ne croit pas qu'on a pu réussir cette opération
Croyez-vous que j'ai peur?
(Grevisse (1964:§999a))

Similarly, Sp allows variation of mood:

(56) Max no cree que la CIA participó en el golpe chileno (Lleó (1979:4))
(Speaker is convinced that the CIA was involved)

It seems that in neither Fr nor Sp do <u>croire</u>/<u>creer</u> as affirmatives accept the subjunctive, although <u>paraître</u>/<u>parecer</u>, which are closely related semantically, do:

(57) a. Il paraît bien qu'à la fin de sa vie, il ait joué un double jeu (Grevisse (1964:§998b))
b. Parece que tenga mucho dinero (Lleó (1979:4))

Both the examples in (57) imply that the complement of <u>paraître</u>/<u>parecer</u> is known not to be true. With (57b) may be contrasted the It <u>Pare che tenga molto denaro</u>, which carries no such presupposition. In It, the indicative may be used after <u>credere</u> to express a presupposed certainty about the truth of the complement sentence: <u>credo che verrà domani</u> implies that he will indeed come tomorrow. In the three languages the same general characterisation of the presuppositions associated with the indicative/

subjunctive choice applies, therefore: indicative is associated with reality; subjunctive with doubt, at least in 'marked' contexts. But the choice of mood in the 'unmarked' context differs considerably from language to language. This in itself should warn us against any generalisation concerning the Romance subjunctive and the establishing of any unified semantic value for the mood, and convince us that mood and modality, like tense and time-reference, are not in a simple relationship.

One modality that is expressed by both indicative and subjunctive forms in Romance is that of 'politeness' or 'attenuation'. A request for a beer might be framed in one of the following ways:

(58) Fr: Je veux une bière (Pres)
Je voulais une bière (Imp)
Je voudrais une bière (Cond)

Sp: Quiero una cerveza (Pres)
Quería una cerveza (Imp)
Querría una cerveza (Cond)
Quisiera una cerveza (ImpSubj^{ra})

It: Voglio una birra (Pres)
Volevo una birra (Imp)
Vorrei una birra (Cond)

There are, to be sure, many other ways of expressing this modality in the Romance languages which do not involve the use of vouloir/querer/volere at all. If we restrict our attention just to the sentences of (58), it may be noted that several verb-forms are available, but that there is not strict synonymy among them. At the same time, while Imp, Cond and (in Sp) ImpSubj^{ra} are usually reckoned more 'polite' than Pres, it is not easy to detect finer gradient distinctions. Fr Imp and Cond, Sp Imp, Cond and ImpSubj^{ra} and It Imp and Cond appear regularly as markers of 'attenuation'; representative examples are:

(59) Fr:

Sauriez-vous me dire pourquoi nous nous sommes arrêtés?
"Could you tell me...?"

Est-ce que tu me cherchais?
"Were [= are] you looking for me?"

Sp:

¿Tendría Vd. la bondad de contestar?
"Would you be kind enough to answer?"

Me preguntaba si le gustaría bailar
"I was wondering [= wonder] if you would like to dance"

¿Adónde fuéramos esta noche? (South American, in Kany (1951:183))
"Where should we go this evening?"

It:
Io direi che farebbe meglio a lavorare sodo
"I would say [= am saying] that he would do better to work harder"

Mi premeva di sapere se Giovanni è partito
"I wanted [= want] to know if John has left"

Another interesting modality is expressed by Imp, particularly in French, where it has been termed the 'hypochoristic' Imp. This use of Imp is usually cited as being typical of children's make-believe worlds, e.g.:

(60) Il faisait de grosses misères à sa maman, le vilain garcon[15]
"He's worrying his poor mother, isn't he, the naughty boy" (Damourette and Pichon (1936: §1746))

VERB-FORMS AND NON-VERBAL ELEMENTS

The semantic interpretation of a verb-form may sometimes depend upon elements in the same sentence which are not part of the verb-phrase. In the sentences:

(61) a. Fr: Je parle trois langues
Sp: Hablo tres idiomas
It: Parlo tre lingue

b. Fr: Je parle avec tout le monde
Sp: Hablo con todo el mundo
It: Parlo con tutti

c. Fr: Je parle d'un point de vue tout à fait original
Sp: Hablo desde un punto de vista bastante original
It: Parlo da un punto di vista abbastanza originale

the semantic value of the verbs varies considerably. In the sentences of (61a), je parle/hablo/parlo has the meaning of je sais parler/sé hablar/so parlare;

in (61b), j'ai la coutume de parler/suelo hablar/ parlo di solito. In both cases, the time-reference is of a UNIVERSAL kind. In (61c), on the other hand, parle/hablo/parlo is almost a lexicalised speech-act verb with the meaning je suis en train de parler/estoy hablando/sto parlando. The choice of verb-stem has been in all cases the same; there are no adverbials or syntactic factors which might demand one reading rather than another. We are bound to conclude that it is the non-verbal context (object NP and Prepositional Phrase) which determines the value of the verb-form.

The nature of the subject NP may also cause variation in the semantic interpretation of the verb. The sentences

(62) a. Fr: Le chien aboie
Sp: El perro ladra
It: Il cane abbaia
b. Fr: Les chiens aboient
Sp: Los perros ladran
It: I cani abbaiano

have different time-references depending entirely on the reference of the subject NP. When the reference of the subject NP is specific, the time-reference of the verb is PRESENT; when it is generic, the time-reference of the verb is UNIVERSAL.

UNDERLYING AND SURFACE VERB-FORMS

Some simple sentence functions of verb-forms which in some structuralist accounts of verb-form usage have often stood out as special cases receive a more natural explanation if they are compared with similar usages in complex sentences where the verb-form of an embedded sentence may clearly be seen to be syntactically determined. In the terminology of generative grammar, we may say that such verb-forms are the **surface** manifestations of different **underlying** forms, and their value is therefore not necessarily comparable with other usages of the same verb-form.

A clearcut example of this phenomenon concerns the description of verb-form function usually known as indirect style or style indirect libre. In explaining my notion of TRANSPOSED time-reference (see above, p.31), I outlined a rule whereby a [-Past] verb-form in the complement of a [+Past] verb-form also became [+Past]. This rule, which I shall from now on call [Past]-AGREEMENT, has its most obvious manifestation in reported speech structures:

(63) Fr: [Il a dit[+Past] [Je le vois[-Past]]]
==> Il a dit qu'il le voyait[+Past]
Sp: [Dijo[+Past] [Le veo[-Past]]]
==> Dijo que le veía[+Past]
It: [Ha detto[+Past] [Lo vedo[-Past]]]
==> Ha detto che lo vedeva[+Past]

though it also appears to apply in all <u>that</u>/<u>que</u>/<u>che</u> + S complements:

(64) Fr: [Il paraît[-Past] [que tu viendras[-Past]]]
but [Il paraissait[+Past] [que tu viendrais[+Past]]]
Sp: [Parece[-Past] [que vendrás[-Past]]]
but [Parecía[+Past] [que vendrías[-Past]]]
It: [Pare[-Past] [che venga[-Past]]]
but [Pareva[+Past] [che venisse[+Past]]]

Some form of the rule may also cover those cases referred to earlier in which a verb-form which has 'unmarked' or UNIVERSAL reference 'agrees' morphologically with a 'marked' form which appears elsewhere in the sentence, e.g.:

(65) Fr: C'est[-Past] mon frère que je vois [-Past]
but C'était[+Past] mon frère que j'ai vu[+Past]
Sp: Es[-Past] mi hermano a quien veo[-Past]
but Fue[+Past] mi hermano a quien vi[+Past]
It: È[-Past] mio fratello che vedo[-Past]
but Era[+Past] mio fratello che ho visto[+Past] [16]

Sentences in indirect style may be conveniently viewed as being yielded by the deletion of the matrix clause of sentences like those in (63), the surface products of which would be

(66) Fr: Il le voyait
Sp: Le veía
It: Lo vedeva

In support of this hypothesis two main arguments may be adduced. First, there is a clear semantic parallel between the sentences of (66) and (63). Speakers tend to feel that sentences like (66) are incomplete, and explanation of the incompleteness usually involves the reconstructions of the deleted matrix clause. Secondly, sentences like (66) are ambiguous in two respects. In the first place, there is ambiguity between an indirect style reading and a straightforward PAST time-reference reading, e.g., from the Fr data:

(67) Il le voyait (mais... pourquoi avait-il peur? - s'est-il demandé)
     Il le voyait (quand il m'a rencontré - vous dis-je)

In the second place, there is potential ambiguity as to the 'original' reported verb-form, which may be [-Past], as in the examples given so far, or [+Past], as in:

(68) [Il a dit$_{[+Past]}$ [Je le voyais$_{[+Past]}$ hier]]
     $\Longrightarrow$ Il a dit qu'il le voyait$_{[+Past]}$ hier/la veille

The setting up of underlying structures in which, for example, (63) is represented in the way suggested, will describe appropriately such ambiguities.

So-called 'main clause subjunctives' in the Romance languages present a phenomenon analogous to that of indirect style, the hypothesis being that all 'main clause subjunctives' are derived from subordinate clauses in underlying structure. As an example, I will consider the 'third person imperative' in Spanish; I suggest that the structure

(69) Que lo hagan ellos mismos

is related in underlying structure to an indirect command like

(70) {Digo / Mando / Pido} que ellos lo hagan ellos mismos

Verbs of command like Sp <u>decir</u>, <u>mandar</u> and <u>pedir</u> belong to a class that may be labelled /IMPER/; a more abstract representation of the underlying structure common to (69) and (70) would be (71), from which (70) is generated by lexicalisation of /IMPER/ and

(69) by its deletion:

(71) [(Yo) /IMPER/ [ellos mismos lo hacer]]

A broad justification for this hypothesis can be given as follows. First, the presence of the complementiser que in the surface structure of (69) strongly suggests that we have to do with a subordinate structure that is 'incomplete' in nature. Secondly, the semantic similarity between (69) and (70) is suggestive of some underlying relationship between the sentences. Lastly, that the sequence-of-tense in (70), where PresSubj in the complement is [-Past] in agreement with the Pres form digo, is paralleled in (69), can be seen by the strangeness of ImpSubj rather than PresSubj in both constructions:

(72) ?Que lo hicieran ellos mismos
and
?Digo que lo hicieran ellos mismos

To my knowledge, there is no account of the so-called 'Future of supposition' and its [+Past] counterpart the 'conditional of supposition' (Cond Perf in It[17]) which goes any further than regarding the usage as a noteworthy curiosity. Curious it is indeed, or rather, structurally odd, since, atypically, Fut is used with PRESENT reference and Cond with PAST reference: this may be shown by the following adverbial-verb cooccurrence patterns:

(73) Fr: Il sera 8h. maintenant
Il serait 8h. quand il est arrivé
Sp: Serán las 8 ahora
Serían las 8 cuando llegó
It: Saranno le 8 adesso
Sarebbero state le 8 quando è arrivato

Consider now the following examples, in which the sentences of (73) are embedded as complements of a number of verbs:

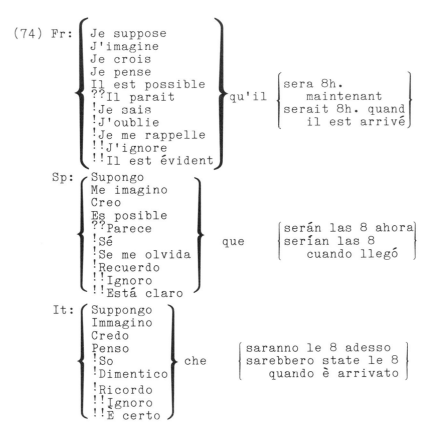

(74) Fr: { Je suppose / J'imagine / Je crois / Je pense / Il est possible / ??Il parait / !Je sais / !J'oublie / !Je me rappelle / !!J'ignore / !!Il est évident } qu'il { sera 8h. maintenant / serait 8h. quand il est arrivé }

Sp: { Supongo / Me imagino / Creo / Es posible / ??Parece / !Sé / !Se me olvida / !Recuerdo / !!Ignoro / !!Está claro } que { serán las 8 ahora / serían las 8 cuando llegó }

It: { Suppongo / Immagino / Credo / Penso / !So / !Dimentico / !Ricordo / !!Ignoro / !!È certo } che { saranno le 8 adesso / sarebbero state le 8 quando è arrivato }

On the basis of this data, it would appear that the Fut and Cond of supposition are permitted only in the complements of non-factive verbs of supposition, a class I will label /SUPP/. /SUPP/, like /IMPER/, may be taken as a speech-act verb[18]; in the first person singular it is, like other speech-act verbs, insusceptible of anything but a positive truth-value, as may be seen from the unacceptability of tag-questions formed on it:

(75) Fr: !Je suppose qu'il sera 8h. maintenant, n'est-ce pas?

Sp: !Supongo que serán las 8 ahora, ¿verdad?

It: !Suppongo che saranno le 8 adesso, vero?

It should be noted that Cond and CondPerf in (74) are not the result of [Past]-AGREEMENT but mark the PAST time-reference of the complement of /SUPP/.

The marking of PAST time-reference by a [+Past] verb-form is typical of the complement of a speech-act verb. I propose that the sentences of (73) and the acceptable sentences of (74) are related at underlying level and that the abstract underlying structure corresponding to both is

(76) [je/(yo)/(io) /SUPP/ [être 8h./ser las 8/essere le 8 Adv]]

/SUPP/ is either lexicalised as supposer/suponer/supporre, etc., or is left unlexicalised and deleted. The specification of the verb-form of être/ser/essere appears to be optionally [+Fut] when /SUPP/ is lexicalised:

(77) Fr:
Je suppose qu'il [{est / sera} | {était / serait}] 8h. [maintenant | alors]

Sp:
Supongo que [{son / serán} | {eran / serían}] las 8 [ahora | entonces]

It:
Suppongo che [{sono / saranno} | {erano / sarebbero / state}] le 8 [adesso | allora]

and obligatorily [+Fut] when /SUPP/ is not lexicalised. This provisional account of the Fut, Cond and CondPerf of supposition is not claimed to be a regularisation of the phenomenon - it remains just as curious as before. What I wish to insist upon is that the problem is not an isolated one, but can be situated within a broader syntactic dimension of verb-form usage.

Finally, I turn to a phenomenon of ambiguity that reflects two functions of Cond[19]. Sentences consisting of a Cond verb-form with minimal additional context, e.g.

(78) Fr: Il partirait
Sp: Saldría
It: Partirebbe

may be interpreted either as examples of 'style indirect', as in the extended examples of (79), or as what immediately seems to be some kind of conditional structure, as in the extended contexts of (80):

(79) Fr: Il partirait - il ne voulait rester là.
     Sp: Saldría - no quería quedar allí.
     It: Partirebbe - non vorrebbe rimanere là.

(80) Fr: Je sais ce qu'il ferait (s'il pouvait) - il partirait.
     Sp: Ya sé lo que haría (si pudiera) - saldría.
     It: So quello che farebbe (se potesse) - partirebbe.

Accordingly, we would expect to postulate two contrasting underlying structures for the two readings of (80), the first of which will be a structure like those of (63) above with the matrix clause deleted, and the second of which will be that of a conditional sentence with the protasis deleted[20].

EXTRALINGUISTIC PARAMETERS

In his examination of the parameters of verb-form description, one of the first distinctions Imbs (1960:12) makes is that between 'détermination interne' and 'détermination externe'. Many scholars have called attention to the importance of 'external' or extralinguistic factors in the choice of verb-forms. Bull (1968:57) points to the importance of the context of discourse or situation in his account of what he calls 'desynchronization' (that is, when a verb-form becomes associated with an axis other than its 'normal' one - for example, when Pres has FUTURE rather than PRESENT time-reference):

> The fact that all the prime tenses may be orientated to any axis of orientation creates circumstances in which the axis involved in any given speech situation is ambiguous. The Spaniard... resolves this ambiguity in two fashions. He states explicitly, using some non-verb form, the axis being used. The more common resolution, however, is based on the assumption that both the speaker and hearer are aware of the immmediate life situation at the moment of speaking, that they are in some degree of common focus which helps define the axis.

We may state the second recourse described by Bull by saying that situational or discourse context will lead the hearer to choose the intended interpretation of a potentially ambiguous utterance. For example, the utterance me caso con Silvia is potentially ambiguous between PRESENT and FUTURE time-reference. Unless pronounced during an actual wedding ceremony, it will be FUTURE, but in both cases the situation will make its time-reference clear without the need for disambiguating adverbials.

However, the fact that situational context is capable of imposing an interpretation on a verb-form does not absolve us from the task of specifying the range of possible interpretations available. It does not seem possible or proper to incorporate into our linguistic description of the semantic values of verb-forms any statement about the likelihood of choice among available interpretations according to extralinguistic situation. We should also, I believe, be chary of reducing some semantic values of verb-forms to the doubtful status of extralinguistic determination. It seems to me that Imbs (1960:17) comes close to this when he speaks of the transposition of time-reference as being the result of 'stylistic' considerations, on a par with the figurative use of language. The examples he considers are the 'historic' Present (Pres with PAST time-reference) and the FutPerf of 'supposition'. These time-references for Pres and FutPerf are however by no means odd or unusual, and I see no reason for not incorporating them into a purely linguistic account of normal verb-form usage, despite the difficulty encountered in doing this.

Description of the pragmatic factors involved in the determining of verb-form usage can nevertheless be done with some exactness, as the work of R. Lakoff (1970) showed. She observed (842) that there is a choice in English between Pres and Pret in the sentence

(81) The boy you spoke to {has / had} blue eyes

and tried to determine what might be responsible for the choice of one verb-form or the other by placing each sentence in a context in which only one form is acceptable:

SITUATION I:
Speaker 1. When I was with you today, I spoke to a boy, but I don't remember what color

eyes he had.

Speaker 2. I remember. The boy you spoke to had/*has blue eyes.

SITUATION II:

Speaker 1. I spoke to a boy on the phone today, but I don't rememember what color eyes he had.

Speaker 2. Well, I'm sure I don't know either.

Speaker 1. Maybe you know him... his name is Harry Smith.

Speaker 2. Oh, Harry Smith! The boy you spoke to has/?had blue eyes.

Lakoff comments:

> In both [Situations I and II], Speaker 2 is speaking of the knowledge of the color of the boy's eyes from the point of view of the time at which he acquired the information that enables him to give Speaker 1 the answer. In Situation I, Speaker 2 acquired the knowledge prior to his conversation with Speaker 1: he has not, at the time of this utterance, been given any new information by Speaker 1 that affects his ability to make his report. But in Situation II, it is new information introduced virtually contemporaneously to Speaker 2's speech act that enables him to identify the boy's eye color, rather than anything that happened previously. So, for Speaker 2, the color of the boy's eyes is a new fact, since not all the necessary knowledge was available to him previously. Hence, he may use the present tense.

It follows from this that a full account of verb-form usage in sentences like (81) can only be achieved by taking into account the pragmatic notion of 'speaker's point of view'.

A similar notion can, it seems to me, be of great value in accounting for the choice of verb-forms available in the complement clause of a verb of reporting. When the reporting verb is [+Past], a [-Past] verb-form may be reported in the complement clause as either [+Past] or [-Past][21]: the statement I am leaving this evening by an original speaker (OS) may be reported by a reporting speaker (RS) in either of the following ways:

(82) a. OS said that he was leaving that evening
b. OS said that he is leaving this evening

A slightly extended context makes the basis for choice clear:

(83) a. I saw OS last week and OS said that he was leaving that evening
b. I saw OS last week and OS said that he is leaving this evening
c. I saw OS today and OS said that he is leaving this evening
d. ?I saw OS today and OS said that he was leaving that evening

Only (83a and c) report OS's quoted statement. (83b) reports something like I am leaving on Tuesday evening of next week, and (83d) something like I am leaving on the evening you have in mind. It is particularly obvious that the choice of adverb depends entirely on the point of view of RS with regard to OS's proposed time of leaving: if for RS it is PAST, then that evening is required; if for RS (as always for OS) it is FUTURE, then OS's original this evening can be used. When OS's this evening and RS's this evening are identical, then (83c) is appropriate; when OS's this evening and RS's that evening are identical, then (83a) is appropriate. (83b and d) meet neither of these conditions. Similar considerations may now be seen to govern the choice of verb-form. When the reported event or state is PAST for OS, a [+Past] verb-form must be used:

(84) OS said that he {was / *is} leaving that evening

When the reported event or state is FUTURE for OS, then a [+Past] verb-form may (even in conjunction with the adverb this evening), but need not, be used:

(85) OS said that he {was / is} leaving this evening

Such interplay between the viewpoints of OS and RS is well-known to those who have worked on the phenomenon of reported speech[22], and clearly forms an essential part of any rule for determining the verb-form of the complement clause of a reporting verb.

NOTES

1. Thus Bolinger (ibid.): "'Si yo (1) fuera (2) fuese usted [en este momento], no lo haría'. No. 2 suggests less authority than No. 1; 2 is advice, 1 is recommendation." Many speakers would not acknowledge this distinction, in fact.

2. Kany gives examples of the -ra form functioning as a Pluperfect, an Imperfect, a Preterite and a Perfect. We might speculate that in some areas of South America the form has lost its distinctive aspectual value to become a Past tense (Preterite or Imperfect) and that in others it has preserved the aspectual value but lost its distinctive time-reference (Perfect). The data offered does not permit a consistent interpretation, unfortunately.

3. See Fleischman (1982:101-2).

4. There are also lexical restrictions on the It construction: see Marchand (1955:50).

5. See Grevisse (1964:§483) for a detailed account of the behaviour of clitics in such constructions, and, for a thorough specialist study with a principled solution, Kayne (1975).

6. Representative views are Jespersen (1933: 243): "... the Perfect is a retrospective present, which connects a past occurrence with the present time, either as continued up to the present moment... or as having results or consequences bearing on the present moment", and Palmer (1965:72): "... the perfect is used to indicate a period of time that began before, but continued right up to, a point of time (either present or past, according to the tense)".

7. Indeed, McCawley makes out a convincing parallel with the pronominalisation procedure elaborated in Langacker (1969).

8. /PRET/ adverbials correspond to class C3(a) established in Crystal (1966), /PERF/ adverbials to class C3(b). Today is class C4 and this week, this year class C5.

9. See Reid (1970:147-8) and for a generativist approach to related MSp data, Bosque (1976).

10. See also Comrie (1976:44-8).

11. I use the term 'phase' to refer to the stages of an event or state. I should point out that the term has been used in a number of different ways in the past (see, for example, Joos (1968: 138ff.), Fourquet (1966)); my usage is not to be confused with these, and in particular I am not representing 'phase' as a systematic grammatical cate-

gory.

12. Amongst many references, see, for example, Clédat (1910) and (1927), Pignon (1942), Yvon (1946), (1952) and (1958) and Tassie (1963). On the cognate MSp form, see Alarcos (1959).

13. See, for example, Imbs (1955) and Cohen (1964).

14. An interesting episode in this search appeared in _Hispania_ in the shape of a debate between Lozano (1972) and (1975) and Bolinger (1974). Despite his 1972 title, Lozano proposed a reduction of the functions of the MSp subjunctive to two basic types: "optative", the model for which is the indirect command, and "dubitative", the model for which is the complement of a verb like _dudar_. Lozano argued that all subjunctive-requiring elements could be specified in terms of the features [+optative] and [+dubitative] which reflected these contexts. Bolinger, on the other hand, took a more semantically-orientated approach, claiming that there are no rules as such for the subjunctive, but that choice of subjunctive or indicative is always dependent on a speaker's attitude.

15. Scholars have gone to great lengths to explain this usage, which is a considerable inconvenience in any purely 'semantics-orientated' model of verb-form usage. See in particular Wilmet (1968) and the references there.

16. The precise form of this rule will vary from language to language. Sp appears to require the clefting copula to have an identical morphological specification to that of the main verb; Fr and It appear able to use Imp as the form of the clefting copula for any [+Past] main verb.

17. Just as in It CondPerf is preferred in reported speech constructions as the [+Past] equivalent of Fut, so it is parallel to Fut in the expression of supposition. Cond may also express supposition, but usually, as an alternative to Fut, with exclusively PRESENT reference with a DURATIVE verb-stem: _Sarebbero stanchi_ ("They must be tired (now)").

18. It will be noted that _suppose_ does not fulfil the "hereby-test" proposed by Ross (1970) for performatives and semantically does not represent (as do _declare_ and _name_, for instance) the 'performance' of any action. R. Lakoff (1969c:179) is apparently happy, however, to regard English _suppose_ as a performative; a reading of Austin (1963) and Searle (1970:23) confirms this view. Since _suppose_ can be associated with a distinctive kind of speech-act which is represented superficially by a distinc-

tive kind of syntactic structure (the tag question), it seems logical to overlook the tests for 'performatives' that it fails. It is for such reasons that I prefer to use here the more neutral term 'speech-act verb' for all such verbs.

19. This phenomenon was described by Clédat (1927):

> Si, d'une phrase prononcée près de nous, les seuls mots 'il réussirait' parviennent jusqu'à nos oreilles, la flexion du verbe suffit à nous indiquer que l'action de réussir ou bien <u>était considérée dans le passé</u> comme devant se produire (c'est le sens étymologique de 'futur dans le passé' de l'indicatif: on savait qu'<u>il réussirait</u>), ou bien est <u>considérée par celui qui parle</u> comme pouvant ou ayant pu se produire (c'est la valeur modale, dite du 'conditionnel': <u>il réussirait</u> que nous n'en serions pas étonnés. - Est-ce <u>qu'il réussirait</u> vraiment? - S'il avait été plus habile, ou s'il était plus habile, il réussirait.).

20. Cf. Imbs (1960:77): "L'idée de conditionnement peut cependant être suggérée par le contexte: <u>j'irais volontiers</u> peut être compris: 'j'irais volontiers, <u>si c'était possible</u>'..."

21. <u>Pace</u> the Kiparskys (1971:359), who claim that with a non-factive reporting verb the conversion of [-Past] to [+Past] is obligatory. It was my observation that data from my own English did not tally with theirs that put me on the track of the more general pragmatically-based rule.

22. See, among recent studies, Verdín Díaz (1970:61ff.) and Banfield (1973:17-25).

Chapter Three

THE VERB ITSELF: IMPLICATIONS FOR THE DESCRIPTIVE MODEL

We have now established that at least the following elements are crucial to the expression of time-reference, aspect and modality in a sentence:

A. The verb inflection itself, which bears a 'residual' range of meaning;

B. The verb-stem, which has important lexical aspectual properties;

C. Temporal adverbials, which may limit the range of meaning of the verb inflection;

D. Aspectual adverbials, which interact with the aspectual properties of verb-stem and verb inflection;

E. The syntactic context, which may 'modify' the morphological specification of verb-forms in a purely formal way;

F. The pragmatic context, which is particularly important for the signalling of some speaker-presuppositions and modalities.

The purpose of this Chapter is to discuss briefly how these various factors are to be represented in a generative grammar; to show how the pattern of verb-form usage in one of the Romance languages may be successfully described using the devices developed, and finally to compare the implications of the generativist devices proposed with pre-generative accounts of verb-form usage.

GENERATIVE GRAMMAR AND VERB-FORM USAGE

Temporal Adverbials

I have already introduced the notion of an 'abstract adverbial' in my representation of the Pret/Perf distinction in English and Romance in Chapter 2. The possibility of ambiguity of reference in sentences like (20) in Chapter 2 suggests further the need to assume the presence of an adverbial in underlying structure even when there is no overt adverbial in the corresponding surface structure. Such 'abstract adverbials' represent classes of surface adverbials which in certain circumstances need not be lexicalised[1].

Should verbs be selected in terms of adverbs, or adverbs in terms of verbs? Gallagher (1970), making a similar proposal concerning underlying adverbials, assumed that adverbs of time predict the tense of verbs. Klum (1959), to whose work I have already referred, is, as far as I am aware, the only scholar to have tackled this problem head-on, though not within a generative framework. He proposes a solution based on linear conditioning (i.e., that the leftmost element in the surface determines the semantic properties of the verb-phrase). This view is no doubt valid from a perceptual point of view, in that a hearer perceives the meaning of a sentence by using clues which appear 'first', but seems otherwise a red herring, since adverb position is frequently optional (Je l'ai vu hier or Hier je l'ai vu)[2]. In support of the hypothesis that verb-forms are dependent upon adverbs, it might be argued that since time-reference is a determining factor in the choice of verb-form, the choice of verb-form should be dependent upon the adverb as the constituent which is responsible for the precise and often overt expression of time-reference. In favour of the hypothesis that adverbs are dependent upon verb-forms, we may adduce (a) the optional nature of the adverb in surface structure, as a result of which it is not prima facie clear whether the adverb is an obligatory category of underlying structure or not; (b) the wide range of surface adverbials, contrasting with the relatively small number of available verb-forms; (c) the 'unmarked' nature of many adverbs (i.e., their ability to cooccur with several verb-forms). The introduction of the device of an abstract adverbial would of course reduce the significance of these last factors, since it would (a) give expression to the optional surface realisation of adverbs, (b) enable generalisations to be made concerning class-membership of adverbs, and (c) provide naturally for the participation of adverbials in more than one abstract class. A less problematic alternative which the notion of abstract syntax makes possible is to regard verb-form and adverbial as belonging to the same plane of analysis, both being selected in terms of a category associated with the verb-phrase of a higher clause (or indeed with the highest clause). Thus the general form of the underlying structure of a sentence like

(1) Il partira

could be construed as:

(2)

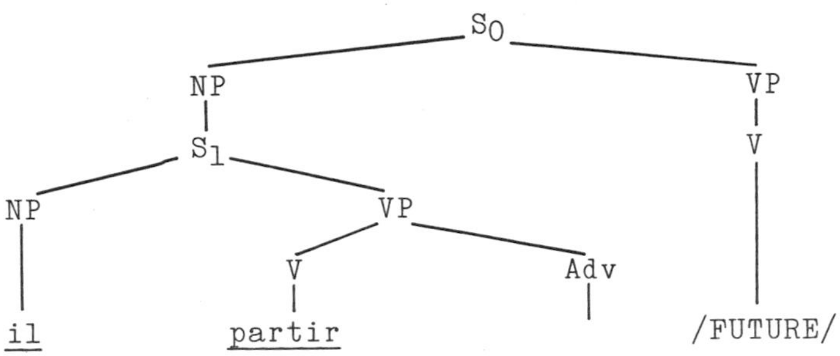

V and Adv (the latter if lexicalised) in S_1 are required to be congruent with /FUTURE/. In one possible surface realisation of (2), Adv would be lexicalised by a member of the abstract adverbial /FUTURE/ and V would either be marked for [+Fut] or would be realised as Pres in the absence of other determining factors[3]. This treatment of time-adverbials has several other advantages. First, it makes the treatment of time-adverbials consistent with proposals for other adverbials (e.g., G. Lakoff (1970:Appendix F)); secondly, it provides naturally for the rather vague time-reference of a sentence which has no overt time-adverbial, since the time-reference of such a sentence could only be said to be of a certain class. Thirdly, the placing of the time-reference higher rather than lower in the tree facilitates the 'tensing' of truth-values associated with the sentence[4]: for example, the sentence

(3) John was an engineer

has associated with it a truth-value which may be stated as follows:

(4) It is true that in the PAST [John be an engineer]

and which maps on to an underlying structure for (3) which is of the same type as (2):

(5) John be an engineer /PAST/

A provisional list of abstract time-adverbials will include /FUTURE/, /PRESENT/ and /PAST/ (or posteriority, simultaneity and anteriority relative to the moment of utterance); there would also need to be an unmarked adverbial (i.e., a zero development of the V in S_0 of (2)) which would provide for cases in which verb-forms cannot be said to refer to a specific time - this will also cover some of the cases I have qualified as having UNIVERSAL time-reference. Gallagher (1970) provided for this possibility by suggesting that when there was no time adverb in underlying structure then there was "no tense". For English and MSp, /PAST/ will have the marked subsets /PRET/ and /PERF/, and other subdivisions which turn out to be advantageous may be introduced without difficulty. /ANT/ may be introduced additionally, as suggested in Chapter 2, for instance, to characterise the reference of several of the functions of the [+Perf] forms and their congruent adverbs. For example, the sentence

(6) Il avait fini

may be construed as having the structure

(7)

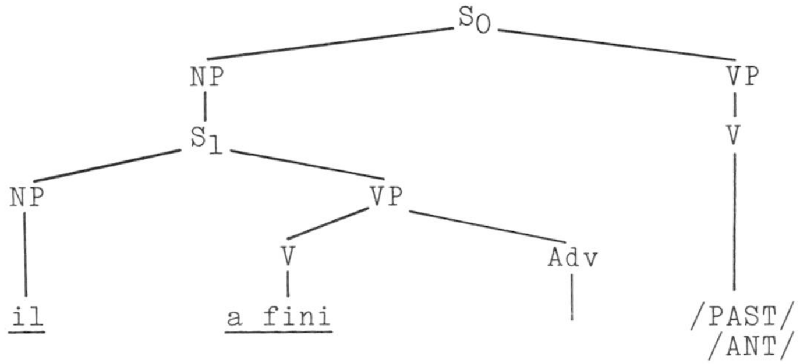

The surface structures corresponding to (7) are (6), in which Adv is not lexicalised at all, (8), in which /ANT/ is lexicalised as déjà, (9), in which /PAST/ but not /ANT/ is lexicalised, and (10), in which the adverbial avant samedi matin seems to lexicalise /PAST/ and /ANT/ simultaneously:

(8) Il avait déjà fini

(9) Il avait fini hier

(10) Il avait fini avant samedi matin

Aspect Adverbials

At first sight, the kinds of consideration which led us to propose abstract temporal adverbials in underlying structure might also encourage us to envisage abstract adverbials of aspect. A sentence like MSp

(11) Durmió

is ambiguous between the readings of 'initiative phase' (durmió (a las dos)) and 'fixed term durative' (durmió (una hora)). The underlying structures corresponding to these readings could accordingly be construed as

(12) a. (Él) durmió /PUNCTUAL/
     b. (Él) durmió /DURATIVE/

Similarly,

(13) Salía

is ambiguous between the readings of 'durative' (salía (a las dos)) and 'repetitive' (salía (cada día)) and might be construed as having the underlying structures

(14) a. (Él) salía /DURATIVE/
     b. (Él) salía /REPETITIVE/

However, as we saw in Chapter 2, there is no requirement that verb-stem, verb inflection and aspectual adverbial shall be 'congruent' with regard to aspect: the underlying structure of

(15) Dormía a las dos

is hence not appropriately

(16)

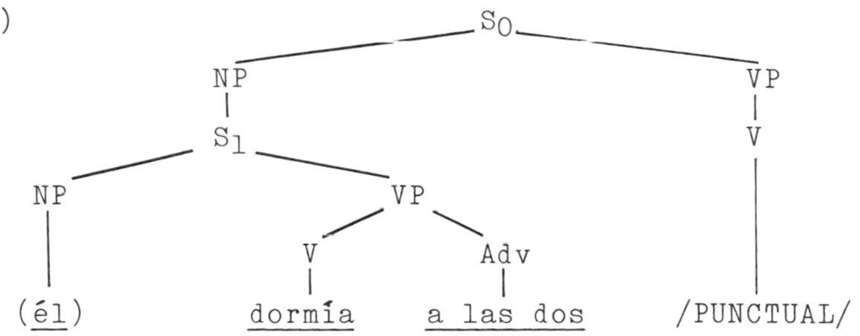

since it is only the Adv that is /PUNCTUAL/: the verb-stem and inflection are DURATIVE and the overall aspectual value is, if anything, DURATIVE. The introduction of abstract categories for verb-inflections is pointless, since they would only duplicate the inflectional categories. Stems will belong simultaneously to a number of different classes, including classes that may with advantage be labelled /PUNCTUAL/ and /DURATIVE/; but I have already mentioned in Chapter 2 the difficulty of assigning stems uniquely to aspectual categories. In fact, as we have seen, stems, inflections and adverbials of different aspectual classes appear to combine fairly freely, and anomalous combinations are usually interpretable by 'forcing' the stem into the required category. Thus apparently anomalous combinations like

(17) a. He died every night (/NON-REPETITIVE/ stem + /REPETITIVE/ Adv
b. She is being happy (/STATIVE/ stem + [+Cont] inflection)

tend to be interpreted as if, in the case of (17a), die was /REPETITIVE/ ("He died (metaphorically) every night" or "He acted a death every night") and, in the case of (17b), as if be happy were /NON-STATIVE/ ("She is pretending to be happy"). It seems, therefore, that relations between verb-stem, verb inflection and aspectual adverbial are most appropriately handled in the grammar by rules of semantic interpretation, and not by allowing stem, inflection and adverb to be generated freely. This view is encouraged by the impossibility of categorising the overall aspectual interpretation of the sentence in such a way that it is easily associable with a sentence constituent (as overall time-referential categories are associable with temporal adverbs).

Syntactic Rules

In Chapter 2 I proposed a number of syntactic rules which led to the correct specification of verb-forms in certain contexts. They were: (a) [Past]-AGREEMENT, which accounted for the appearance of [+Past] verb-forms in the complements of [+Past] reporting verbs; (b) a rule for introducing [+Subj] forms in the complements of /IMPER/ verbs, and (c) a rule introducing [+Fut] forms in the complements of /SUPP/ verbs. The apparent contradiction which exists between the /PRESENT/ adverb and the [+Fut] verb-form in a sentence like

(18) Jean sera [+Fut] ici maintenant /PRESENT/

can now be explained by viewing this as the surface product of an underlying structure like (78) in Chapter 2:

(19) [je /SUPP/ [Jean être ici /PRESENT/]]

where être has the specification [+Fut] solely because of its rôle in the complement of /SUPP/; in the underlying structure it would still be congruent with /PRESENT/.

Gallagher (1970) also demonstrates the rôle of purely syntactic rules in the generation of verb-forms. In the sentences of (20), for instance, the form of the second verb seems to depend on that of the first:

(20) a. John said the Washington Monument was heavy
b. The man who answered the phone was my brother

Verb-adverb cooccurrence properties in the corresponding simple sentences reveal that the second verb in these examples is not a primary PAST-referring form:

(21) a. !The Washington Monument was heavy in 1948
b. !The man was my brother yesterday

Gallagher's proposal is that these verbs are given no cooccurring time adverb in underlying structure and are regarded as "tenseless"; "tenseless" verbs, in the absence of other determining factors, would be realised as Pres. That this is appropriate in the case of the sentences of (21) is shown by the unacceptability of other verb-forms in the same context:

(22) a. The Washington Monument !will be/!had been heavy
b. The man !will be/!had been my brother[5]

The tense of the second verb in the sentences of (21) is hence an exclusively syntactic phenomenon, and the [+Past] form is therefore not, in my terms, to be associated with a /PAST/ adverbial.

<u>Pragmatic Factors</u>

The incorporation of pragmatic factors into a grammar is a very general theoretical problem with which we need not become embroiled here. Suffice it to say that the grammar must provide some mechanism for the association of verb-forms with pragmatic factors like the speaker-presuppositions involved in (83) and (84) in Chapter 2, and the modalities associated with sentences like those of (58), (59) and (60) in Chapter 2. For present purposes, the generation of the appropriate verb-form in such contexts can be seen as essentially a syntactic matter in the sense that a particular presupposition or modality index will 'trigger' the insertion of the corresponding verb-form specification.

POLYVALENCY OF VERB-FORMS

The upshot of the foregoing observations is that verb-forms will be generated in the grammar and associated with semantic interpretations in a number of different ways. A natural corollary of this is that verb-forms which are superficially identical will hence be perceived as having a multiplicity of functions as the products of different rules. The range of verb-form values available in the Romance languages can be judged from Imbs' (1960) account of the indicative verb-forms of MFr, examples from which I now examine, offering indications as to how the values of the verb-forms are to be accounted for within the framework of a generative grammar. For each example I will show (a) the modality, (b) the abstract temporal adverbial, (c) the lexical aspectual and other properties of the verb-stem, (d) the abstract aspectual adverbial, (e) the syntactic context, (f) the pragmatic and discourse context where these interact with the verb-inflection in the determination of time-referential, aspectual and modal readings for the sentence. Hence not every category of (a) to (f) will be described for every example.

Elements in parentheses, e.g., (/PAST/), refer to abstract elements in underlying structure which have no overt surface realisation.

I use Imbs' list since it is one of the most complete offered, but it must be remembered that his examples are partly his own invention and partly quotations from literary texts. Some of the latter type of examples refer implicitly to a point of reference that has been already established in the discourse, so that they are incomplete when taken in isolation. Example (63), for instance, falls into this category; the use of Plup implies reference to a previous event or state to which the event or state represented by the verb inflected for Plup is ANTERIOR, and it is impossible to describe the time-reference of Plup here without comparison with the preceding discourse.

Pres

(23) Je constate que tout est fini (22)

(b) (/PRESENT/)
(c) PUNCTUAL, speech-act verb
(f) First person subject

(c) and (f) establish a performative status for the verb-stem constat-; it accordingly has a time-reference that is strictly contemporaneous with the moment of speech.

(24) Quelle est cette fièvre d'écrire qui me prend aujourd'hui? (22)

(b) /PRESENT/

(25) D'habitude, à ce moment précis,... Jeanne avale, debout, la dernière goutte de son café au lait (23)

(d) /R/

The REPETITIVE adverbial d'habitude establishes unambiguously UNIVERSAL reference.

(26) Il parle cinq langues

(c) DURATIVE: the stem parl- has at least two readings: (i) "be speaking", (ii) "be able to speak"
(f) Plural object NP (cinq langues)

The UNIVERSAL reference here depends upon reading (ii) for the verb-stem parl-. A non-UNIVERSAL reading is also possible with reading (i), but (f) makes this unlikely (the impossibility of speaking five languages at once).

(27) Les femmes, c'est quelque chose de compliqué (27)

(f) Generic topic NP (les femmes)

The UNIVERSAL reference depends upon (f).

(28) Le mariage a lieu dans trois jours

(a) (/INTENT/)
(b) /FUTURE/
(c) PUNCTUAL

The possibility of Pres having FUTURE reference has been mentioned at several points, and hitherto the distinction, if any, between Pres and Fut with FUTURE reference has been ignored. The choice between Pres and Fut is not optional, since speakers perceive a difference in meaning between the two tenses which, however, has nothing to do with time-reference but is rather a difference of modality. In MFr, as well as in other Romance languages and to a certain extent in English (although the rôle of PresCont complicates the position there) Pres with FUTURE reference implies an intention or prearrangement: (28) accordingly has the full meaning of "The marriage is due to take place in three days". Representation of this modality must therefore be provided for in the grammar, and has been labelled /INTENT/. It is unlikely, however, that in the spoken language, /INTENT/ is always necessary for the understanding of Pres as a FUTURE-referring form.

(29) Si jamais je suis libre demain, je viendrai... (35)

(b) /FUTURE/
(e) Conditional protasis (see Chapter 4)

(30) ... le duc entre dans l'antichambre, salue les huit (33)

(b) (/PAST/)
(f) Discourse context of /PAST/

This usage is often termed the 'historic present'. Discourse context must establish the PAST reference, for in isolation this sentence could be a commentary on a scene contemporaneous with the moment of speech, and hence have PRESENT reference. /PAST/ must therefore be seen as strictly congruent with Pres, although it is likely that this usage is limited to particular styles or registers (literary and colloquial, for example) of French and the other Romance languages.

(31) Je <u>sors</u> de l'ambassade de Serbie (34)

(b) (/PAST/) (/PERF/)
(c) PUNCTUAL
(f) First person subject

(f) renders strict PRESENT reference unlikely here. A number of stems of PUNCTUAL aspectual tendency, especially with first person singular subjects, seem capable of expressing 'immediate PAST' reference with a Pres inflection: another example given by Imbs is <u>J'apprends à l'instant que...</u> (34). The time-reference of the verb-forms in these examples is that of congruency with /PERF/ rather than with /PRET/.

<u>Fut</u>

FUTURE reference can be expressed with (32) or without (33) an overt adverbial:

(32) Tu crois qu'il <u>marchera</u>? (43)

(b) (/FUTURE/)

(33) Il <u>adviendra</u> dans l'avenir que le mont du Temple de Yahvé sera établi au sommet des montagnes... (42)

(b) /FUTURE/

The expression of a modality may also be involved in the use of Fut with FUTURE reference:

(34) Vous <u>quitterez</u> cette femme (50)

(a) /IMPER/
(b) (/FUTURE/)

This sentence may be construed as declarative, but is more usually interpreted as an imperative, with Fut having the force of <u>quittez</u>.

(35) Vous prendrez bien une tasse de thé avec moi? (50)
(a) (/INVIT/)
(b) (/FUTURE/)

Again, although this could be a straightforward question, it is most normally interpreted as an invitation. /INVIT/ is related to, though not identical with, /IMPER/.

(36) Ce sera pour Madame Rousseau (53)
(a) (/SUPP/)
(b) (/PRESENT/)

This type has already been discussed in detail.

(37) Je ne vous cacherai pas que je suis guère satisfait (52)
(a) (/ATTEN/)
(b) (/PRESENT/)

I have already drawn attention (see above, p.64) to ATTENUATION (/ATTEN/) as a determining factor in verb-form usage. Strict FUTURE reference with neutral modality is also possible here.

(38) Le 21 juin (1848), la fermeture des ateliers nationaux est décidée: les ouvriers de 18 à 25 ans s'enrôleront dans l'armée... (43)
(b) (/PAST/)
(f) Discourse context establishes /PAST/ (overtly in the adverbial of the first of the sentences in this example)

This usage of Fut is parallel to that of the 'historic present' exemplified in (30).

(39) A l'égard des voleurs on ne sera jamais assez prudent (47)
(b) /UNIVERSAL/
(f) Generic NP (les voleurs)

Imp

The Imp inflection is normally inconsistent with an overall PUNCTUAL aspectual reading, and the usual overall aspectual values encountered are DURATIVE (40) or REPETITIVE (41):

(40) Numa Roumestan <u>avait</u> vingt-deux ans quand il vint terminer à Paris son droit, commencé à Aix (90)
(b) /PAST/
(c) DURATIVE
(d) /P/ (<u>quand...</u>)

(41) Généralement, les pensionnaires externes ne s'<u>abonnaient</u> qu'au dîner (96)
(b) (/PAST/)
(d) /R/

When a verb-stem of PUNCTUAL aspectual tendency combines with the Imp inflection, it must be interpreted either as overall DURATIVE or has having a kind of TRANSPOSED FUTURE reference; thus <u>sortais</u> in

(42) Vous avez de la chance de me rencontrer: je <u>sortais</u> (92)
(b) (/PAST/)
(c) PUNCTUAL
or (b) (/FUTURE/)
(c) PUNCTUAL
(e) Complement of verb of 'imminence' (surface <u>aller</u>, <u>être sur le point de</u>, etc.)

means "was in the process of going out" or "was about to go out".

Discourse context in some styles of written French sometimes requires an overall PUNCTUAL interpretation, strictly speaking, although it is likely that authors employ the combination of a stem of PUNCTUAL tendency and the residually DURATIVE Imp inflection to suggest an overall DURATIVE reading, so presenting the action as in progress at a point in PAST time:

(43) Tous deux se saluèrent. L'instant après, le Dr Velpeau <u>quittait</u> la cellule... (93)
(b) /PAST/
(c) PUNCTUAL
(f) Discourse context (here a 'sequential' adverb (<u>l'instant après</u>) and Pret in the preceding sentence)

(44) Pour le moment, j'agis comme si je <u>prenais</u> au sérieux certain problème (99)
(b) /PRESENT/
(e) Complement of 'world-creating' expression (<u>comme si</u>) (see below, p.115)

(45) Je voulais te dire quelque chose pendant que nous sommes seules (97)
(a) (/ATTEN/)
(b) /PRESENT/ (pendant que...)

A similar example was discussed above (p.64).

(46) Si je pouvais demain regarder partir cet homme, il me semble que je serais sauvée (98)
(b) /FUTURE/
(e) Conditional protasis (see Chapter 4)

Imp may have a 'tenseless' value:

(47) Je croyais que c'était mon négro (94)
(e) [Past]-AGREEMENT with matrix-clause verb (croyais)

(48) Elle a des yeux bleus, que votre mari n'avait pas (97)
(f) Presupposition concerning subject (votre mari)

The presupposition is that the husband of the addressee no longer exists, or (as is in fact the case) that he is a former husband.

(49) Il faisait de grosses misères à sa maman, le vilain garçon (97)
(a) (/HYPO/)
(c) (/PRESENT/)

The HYPOCHORISTIC modality (/HYPO/) has been introduced above, p.65.

Pret

All the examples in Imbs' list have PAST reference. The distinctions he makes in the use of Pret have regard to aspectual phenomena which I have described for MSp in Chapter 2. Thus, the combination of Pret with a PUNCTUAL tendency verb-stem yields an overall PUNCTUAL reading, as in (50); the combination of Pret with a DURATIVE tendency verb-stem yields either an overall 'fixed term' DURATIVE reading with a DURATIVE adverbial, as in (51), or an 'initiative phase' reading with a 'sequential' adverbial as in (52); the presence of an overt REPETITIVE adverbial, as in (53), yields an overall 'fixed term REPETITIVE' reading:

(50) Stéphane Mallarmé... <u>naquit</u> le 18 mars 1842, à Paris (83)
- (b) /PAST/
- (c) PUNCTUAL
- (d) /P/
- (f) Presupposition concerning subject (<u>Mallarmé</u>, who is dead, suggests /PRET/ rather than /PERF/ in written French)

(51) L'entretien <u>dura</u> environ deux heures (86)
- (b) (/PAST/) (/PRET/)
- (c) DURATIVE
- (d) /D/

(52) Plus tard elle <u>aima</u> l'histoire de la fille de Jephté (86)
- (b) (/PAST/) /PRET/ ('sequential' adverb <u>plus tard</u>)

(53) Quatre fois de suite le père Roland <u>fit</u> stopper (86)
- (b) (/PAST/) (/PRET/)
- (c) PUNCTUAL
- (d) /R/

<u>Perf</u>

Imbs ignores the use of Perf in spoken MFr; but since Perf has replaced Pret totally here, we would simply add to the functions outlined below those of Pret above. In written MFr, the use of Perf with PAST reference is always distinct from Pret, the difference being very similar to that we have observed for MSp and English Pret and Perf. Thus

(54) L'Europe des patries <u>a remplacé</u> l'Europe des hautes autorités (101)
- (b) (/PAST/)
- (f) Presupposition concerning subject (<u>l'Europe...</u>, which continues to exist at the moment of speech, suggests /PERF/)

(55) Le plus agité, le plus bruyant de tous, c'est Roumestan. Il <u>a</u> déjà <u>prononcé</u> deux discours depuis la rentrée. (102)
- (b) (/PAST/) /ANTERIOR/ (<u>déjà</u>)
- (f) Discourse context of /PAST/

This usage is parallel to the 'historic present' and 'historic future' usages exemplified in (30) and (38) above.

Just as Pres can be used with FUTURE reference, as an equivalent of Fut, so Perf has a usage as the equivalent of FutPerf. The use of Perf with this value in (56) also foregrounds the completion and hence suddenness of the action, and it may be appropriate to render this notion by the adverbial /COMPLETION/, here overtly represented by <u>dans un instant</u> (cf. (70) below):

(56) J'<u>ai fini</u> dans un instant (101)
     (b) (/FUTURE/) (/ANTERIOR/)
     (d) /COMPLETION/

(57) Un malheur <u>est</u> vite <u>arrivé</u> (101)
     (b) (/PAST/) (/PERF/)

or
     (d) /COMPLETION/ (<u>vite</u>)
     (f) Discourse context of UNIVERSAL reference

The context of discourse must establish the UNIVERSAL reference; in isolation, (57) could be read with simply PAST (/PERF/) meaning.

<u>Cond</u>

In both the following examples, Cond has TRANSPOSED FUTURE reference:

(58) Je pensais qu'il <u>viendrait</u> (62)
     (b) (/FUTURE/)
     (e) [Past]-AGREEMENT with matrix-clause verb (<u>pensais</u>)

(59) Elle poussa le portail qu'<u>ouvrirait</u> Raymond, dimanche, pour la première fois (65)
     (b) (/FUTURE/)
     (e) [Past]-AGREEMENT with deleted matrix-clause verb

(59) is an example of <u>style indirect</u> (see above, p. 66).

(60) Si tu m'écrivais, je te <u>répondrais</u> (72)
     (b) (/FUTURE/)
     (e) Conditional apodosis (see Chapter 4)

(61) J'<u>aurais</u> du plaisir à le revoir (77)
(b) (/FUTURE/)
(e) Deleted conditional apodosis (see p.60 above)

(62) Je ne <u>saurais</u> rien dire... (78)
(a) (/ATTEN/)
(b) (/PRESENT/)

Examples of this kind have been discussed above, p. 64.

<u>Plup</u>

(63) Tous s'<u>étaient agenouillés</u> dans les ténèbres de la chapelle (124)
(b) (/PAST/) (/ANTERIOR/)
(f) Discourse establishes point of reference

(64) Mais déjà il <u>avait rejoint</u> le peloton des autos (127)
(b) (/PAST/) /ANTERIOR/ (<u>déjà</u>)

Plup may have TRANSPOSED PRESENT ANTERIOR reference, for example, in <u>style indirect</u> (cf. (60) above):

(65) Pourquoi donc n'<u>avait</u>-elle pas, comme celle-là, <u>résisté</u>, <u>supplié</u>? (128)
(b) (/PAST/) (/PERF/)
(e) [Past]-AGREEMENT with deleted matrix-clause verb

(66) Non, je serais mort sans connaître le bonheur, si vous n'<u>étiez venue</u> me voir dans cette prison (129)
(b) (/PAST/)
(e) Conditional apodosis (see Chapter 4)

(67) Enfin, elle répondit: - Je m'en <u>étais</u> toujours <u>doutée</u> (129)
(a) (/ATTEN/)
(b) (/PRESENT/)

or

(b) (/PAST/) (/ANTERIOR/)

For the second of the readings we must understand an adverbial like <u>jusqu'aujourd'hui</u>, and the implication that the state of <u>s'en douter</u> ceases at the moment referred to; for the first reading, the implication is that s'en douter continues (with the grounds confirmed). Without overt adverbial modification, the first reading appears to be the more likely.

(68) Comment qu'il l'avait mis, son papa! (129)
(a) (/HYPO/)
(b) (/PRESENT/)

This usage is parallel to the HYPOCHORISTIC modality associated with Imp (see (49) above).

PAnt

(69) Après qu'il eut bien constatée qu'au fond de cette situation il y avait ce jeune homme... il regarda en lui-même... (123)
(b) (/PAST/) (/ANTERIOR/)
(e) Temporal subordinate clause with Pret as the matrix-clause form (see Chapter 5)

PAnt may be used, like Perf (cf. (56) and (57) above) to mark the sudden completion of an action:

(70) D'un seul regard, le prisonnier eut embrassé l'appartement dans ses moindres détails (122)
(b) (/PAST/)
(d) /COMPLETION/ (d'un seul regard)

Other forms
Imbs considers FutPerf and CondPerf, and a number of periphrastic forms like se mettre à + infinitive and finir par + infinitive. These periphrastic forms are omitted from consideration for the reasons given in Chapter 2; the description of the other [+Perf] forms does not necessitate the introduction of any descriptive devices other than the ones I have discussed so far. I will therefore end my examination of Imbs' data here.

STRUCTURALISM REVISITED

I return now to the question of whether the notion of 'verb-system' can have anything exceeding purely morphological significance. The presentation of data in the preceding section will discourage facile equations of verb-form with function, or even with a range of functions; but the weaker position of associating each verb-form with a characteristic 'value' may still be tenable. Indeed, 'values' may be hierarchised, the totality of values for each verb-form supplying the necessary distinctive patterning: Schogt (1968:19-20), for example, toys with Jakobson's notion of Gesamtbedeutung versus Hauptbedeutung (global versus principal meaning) in characterising verb-form function. There is the converse possibility of shaving away all factors which may induce variation in the value of a verb-form until its 'residual' value, or value in isolation, is reached (see Garey (1955)).

If I attempt to redefine these aspirations in the light of the overall model of verb-form usage presented in this Chapter, I believe that their respective strengths and weaknesses will emerge more forcefully. We must scrutinise most carefully first of all the notion of the 'value' of a verb-form. We have seen how the verb-form inflection itself is no more than one element, though an obligatory element, to be sure, in the establishing of the time-reference, aspect and modal semantic readings for a sentence. We must be careful not to confuse the 'value' of the verb-form with the semantic reading of the sentence as a whole. It is commonly asserted (and indeed a useful abbreviation), for instance, that Pres has PAST reference in a sentence like (30) above; but strictly it is the sentence as a whole that has PAST reference; Pres is no more than congruent with the discourse context of /PAST/. The 'value' of the verb-form, then, might be seen as amounting to no more than the range of contexts in which it may occur. Any comparison of verb-forms as regards such a concept of their 'value' must take place entirely at surface level, for I have suggested that many verb-forms are derived in the course of the application of syntactic rules. The functions of Cond, for instance, suggest that this verb-form could never be construed as 'basic'; it is always introduced by some syntactic rule such as [Past]-AGREEMENT or the rule which applies to the complements of /SUPP/. Since by definition all the 'values' of any verb-form are available only in surface structure, any hierarchisation of these 'values' poses problems. We might propose that the 'principal meaning' of a verb-form was that under which it had the simplest derivational history, so that, for instance, the principal meaning of Fut was

FUTURE-referring rather than PRESENT-referring with a 'supposition' reading, the latter involving its generation through its syntactic context as part of the complement of /SUPP/. But what then happens in the case of Cond? Which of its several functions, all the results of different derivational routes, could be considered 'principal'? There are also problems with a multivalent form like Pres, which may be congruent with a /PRESENT/, /FUTURE/ or /UNIVERSAL/ adverbial; how is a 'principal' value to be decided upon here? I leave the problem here, because I believe it is in fact a spurious one: our prime task is to establish a complete account of all the 'values' of every verb-form, and it seems sheer sophistry to insist on a hierarchisation which is not going to have any demonstrable linguistic significance.

The question of a characteristic 'residual' value for a verb-form is a more tantalising one, in my view, since it can be presented in hard and fast terms. The examples presented in the previous section clearly show that the overt specification of some of the constituents which are potentially important in the establishing of time-referential, aspectual and modal values for a sentence is often redundant, since verb-forms in isolation may imply values for other constituents. Fut in isolation, for example, appears to imply invariably a FUTURE time-reference, and so the /FUTURE/ temporal adverbial need not be lexicalised. So it might be thought that on the basis of the values verb-forms have in what we might call a zero surface context, we could build up a system of distinctive values to characterise each one. The first problem which besets such a task is that reduction in surface context often leads, as I have shown in several examples in this Chapter, to ambiguity: Imp in isolation could be ambiguous between readings of simple PAST reference, UNIVERSAL PAST reference, or <u>style indirect</u> usage, for instance. We would therefore have to characterise each verb-form in terms of a range of values rather than as having a single distinctive value. Moreover, these values might overlap: both Pres and Fut in isolation can be FUTURE-referring, for example. Yet there is a more serious objection to the setting up of 'residual' values. The verb-inflection which identifies the verb-form is a bound morpheme which must always be attached to a lexical stem - and we have seen the importance of this lexical stem in determining the semantic interpretation of the sentence as a whole. In MFr, a subject must also appear with the verb-form, an element which can also affect the time-referential or aspectual reading of the sentence. For 'verb-form in isolation', we must therefore understand, 'verb-form in the context of a verb-stem and (indefinite) subject noun-phrase, in a simple sentence, and not in the context of any obligatorily overt adverbial or other context'. Yet it is only fair to point out that within these carefully defined terms of reference, the notion of 'residual' value is an intuitively attractive one: in Chapter 2, I noted how several of the traditional names for verb-forms evoke such values; cases of multivalency are resolved by selection of a property which implies a structural opposition, so although Pres may be FUTURE-referring, it is still opposed to Fut, which is FUTURE-referring and not (in isolation) PRESENT-referring, and Imp and Pret are named for their aspectual properties, which are different, rather than for their time-referential properties, which are similar. This kind of simple statement is, however, about as far as the 'residual value' approach can take us; it provides little basis for an extension of an account of verb-form usage to cover the exceedingly complex range of values exhibited by verb-forms. 'Residual value' must also be selected on the grounds of structural convenience rather than according to independent criteria.

The notion of opposition which is crucial to a structuralist view can most certainly be used in a description of the verb-system, but it must be made clear in what contexts contrasts between verb-forms are set. I believe that a great deal of confusion has arisen, first, through the lack of insistence on comparison of verb-form functions in like contexts, and, second, through the failure to recognise that there can be no such thing as a 'zero context'. The aspiration to hierarchise verb-form functions appears to ignore comparison of like contexts altogether; the 'residual value' approach compares particular like contexts, but not all. When we begin to examine verb-forms in many types of context, then we lose the possibility of structural tidiness and apparently verge on an unstructured taxonomy. But in reality the taxonomic nature of such a task is avoided when, as with the Fr data examined, the study of verb-forms is integrated into a broader syntactic and semantic view of the expression of time-reference, aspect and modality.

NOTES

1. The notion is parallel to that of the 'abstract verb', developed in R. Lakoff (1969a).

2. In Klum's larger study (1961), some of the results of which have been seen in Table 2.1, I believe that his failure to distinguish sufficiently between instances (a) in which an adverb disambiguates a potentially ambiguous verb-form, (b) in which it establishes a TRANSPOSED time-reference, and (c) in which it is in fact redundant in establishing the verb-form's time-reference (where the verb-form has its 'residual' time-reference, e.g, FUTURE for Fut), tends to limit the usefulness of an otherwise interesting statistical survey.

3. Examples in which single determining factors can be isolated are in fact extremely difficult to find; while this is in accordance with with my ultimate conclusions, it can complicate the presentation of strands of the contributory arguments. The choice between Fut and Pres in the surface form of (2) is not in fact optional, since speakers perceive a difference in meaning between Fut and Pres (see above, p.88). But the basis for choice is nothing to do with time-reference pure and simple.

4. Langer (1927) pointed out the importance of the verb as an introducer of truth-value. While the precise logical form of 'tensed' truth-values is an issue in itself (see, for example, Prior (1968: 117ff.)), elementary meaning-relations should be easily set up for surface forms (a task to which Gili Gaya (1972) draws attention).

5. It is interesting that the sentences of (21) and (22) are semantically strange even though logically correct. Indeed, if placed in a 'logical' context they are perfectly acceptable:

> The fact that the Washington Monument is heavy now implies that the Washington Monument was heavy in 1948, etc.

The source of the strangeness in a 'neutral' context seems to lie in the pragmatic expectation that "heaviness" as a property of the Washington Monument and "being a brother" as a property of an individual are UNIVERSAL and not time-specific. There is not always the same expectation on these properties, as the following examples show:

> My uncle was heavy in 1948 (but now he has lost weight)
>
> That man was my brother yesterday, but today he is my enemy (figurative)

Chapter Four

THE VERB AS CONSTITUENT: CONDITIONAL SENTENCES

The Romance languages have several different ways of expressing conditional sentences. The condition may be represented (a) by a clause introduced by _si_, etc., (b) by a clause introduced by a conjunction other than _si_, etc., e.g. Fr _supposé que_, _à condition que_, _pourvu que_, _bien que_, _quand même_, Sp _a condición de que_, _siempre que_, _con tal que_, _aunque_, _aun cuando_, It _supposto che_, _a condizione che_, _purché_, _a patto che_, _benché_, (c) an infinitive construction:

(1) Fr: A savoir cela, il n'y aurait pas de problème
Sp: De saber eso, no habría problema
It: A saperlo, non ci sarebbe problema

(d) by an imperative:

(2) Fr: Ecoutez et je vous le dis
Sp: Escuche y se lo digo
It: Ascolti e glielo dico

(e) more marginally, by a declarative sentence,

(3) Fr: Vous écoutez: je vous le dis
Sp: Usted escucha: se lo digo
It: Lei ascolta: glielo dico

Of these, type (a) is especially interesting from our point of view because the choice of verb-forms in the constituent clauses is closely constrained. This type is also the most versatile in semantic range, as we shall see.

_Si_, etc., has a number of other functions that must be carefully separated from that of conditional conjunction. They are:

A. Indirect question complementiser, e.g.:

(4) Fr: Je lui ai demandé s'il avait fini
Sp: Le pregunté si había terminado
It: Gli ho domandato se aveva (avesse) finito

In this category may be also be included a MFr and MIt usage which may be construed as an indirect question with the matrix-clause deleted, but often has the value of an exclamation, e.g.:

(5) Fr: Si j'ai bien dormi![1]
(= (Vous me demandez) si j'ai bien dormi!)
It: Se sono stanco? Certo!
(= (Mi domanda) se sono stanco?)

An extension of this kind of usage is probably responsible for the regular use, in colloquial MSp, of <u>si</u> as the marker of an exclamation, e.g.:

(6) ¿Tú te das cuenta de cómo eres? ¡Si eres tú el que no escuchas más que aquello que te interesa de escuchar! Y yo, porque te digo las verdades, ya por eso soy yo que desvía las conversaciones. ¡Si además ya lo sé, si te conozco, hijo mío, te conozco!
(R. Sánchez Ferlosio, <u>El Jarama</u>, 165)
"... It's you that never listens to anything but what you happen to be interested in!... I know all about it; I know you of old..."

B. In OSp and OIt, the function of intensifier in optative expressions, e.g.:

(7) 'Merçed, ya rey; si el Criador vos salve!'
(<u>Cid</u>, 3045)
"'Thanks, O King; may the Creator save you!'"

(8) E se tu mai nel dolce mondo regge,
dimmi...
(<u>Inf</u>, 10.82-3)
"And that you may [as you hope to] return to the sweet world, tell me..."

SEMANTIC READINGS FOR CONDITIONAL SENTENCES

I shall initially examine only conditional sentences formed with a clause introduced by <u>si</u>, etc., and I shall refer, as is customary, to this clause as the

protasis and to the other clause as the **apodosis.** In the first place, a major distinction may be drawn between those conditional sentences whose protasis has a positive truth-value and those whose protasis has a negative or indeterminate truth-value. The former type I shall refer to as 'pseudo-conditionals', since while they have the superficial form of a conditional sentence, they do not express a genuine hypothesis and hence are inadmissible as conditional sentences proper. I shall discuss these briefly first of all.

<u>Pseudo-conditional sentences</u>

I shall describe these according to the truth-value of the 'protasis' as FACTUAL, and according to the time-reference of the protasis as PRESENT or PAST (FACTUAL) and FUTURE (ANTICIPATED FACTUAL). English examples of these types are:

(9) a. If John was angry when he broke his glasses, he's livid now (PAST FACTUAL)
b. If Harry is in the library he must be working hard (PRESENT FACTUAL)
c. If Tom will be here in ten minutes, I'll go now (FUTURE ANTICIPATED FACTUAL)

Pseudo-conditionals fall into a number of syntactico-semantic types, a provisional list of which I give below. The Romance data is parallel to the English.

A. Sentences in which the 'protasis' strongly resembles a forward-extraposed complement, e.g.:

(10) If John was angry when he broke his glasses it wasn't surprising
(= [The fact that John was angry when...] wasn't surprising)

This category may be called EXTRAPOSING.

B. Sentences which appear to be related to cleft structures, e.g.:

(11) If I left early, it was because I was bored
(= I left early because I was bored)

C. Sentences in which the 'protasis' is contrasted with the 'apodosis', which I shall call CONTRASTIVE, e.g.:

(12) If John was angry, Sheila was silent

C. Sentences which are paraphrasable by a concessive structure. The paraphrase-equivalent for "If X, then Y" in this type of pseudo-conditional is "Although it is true that X, Y", e.g.:

(13) If he knew, he didn't say

The 'protasis' of CONCESSIVE pseudo-conditionals is often qualified by <u>even</u> (Fr <u>bien</u>, Sp <u>incluso</u>, It <u>bene</u>).

E. Sentences for which "If X, then Y" is paraphrasable by "Since it is true that X, Y", e.g.:

(14) If you're so clever, why don't you know the answer?

This type may be labelled RATIONAL.

It should be noted that, just as in the case of (6b), it is possible to envisage a genuine conditional reading for some of the sentences in (10)-(14). For example, (12) appears to be ambiguous, shorn of any clarifying context, between the readings

(15) a. Whenever John was angry, Sheila was silent (PAST UNIVERSAL, Genuine)
b. John was angry, but Mary was silent (PAST, CONTRASTIVE, Pseudo)

CONCESSIVES may also be genuine conditional types, e.g.:

(16) Even if he had known (but he didn't), he wouldn't have said

Pseudo-conditionals may be envisaged as having underlying non-conditional structures which show superficial constructional homonymy with genuine conditionals, and this would be an attractive means of distinguishing them from genuine conditionals. Yet it is doubtful if in fact the distinction can be so clearcut, and there is some evidence that pseudo-conditionals do have some subsidiary genuine conditional value. We may note the commentary of the Le Bidois (1938:332) on an example of what is apparently a MFr EXTRAPOSING pseudo-conditional, <u>Si tu me retrouves ici, c'est merveille</u>:

> ... sa valeur [de si], en pareil cas, est à peu près celle de quand (ou plus exactement celle du quod lat[in] au sens de le fait que..., quant au fait que...); toute la différence, c'est que si présente le fait réel d'une façon moins catégorique que ne le ferait quand. Sans qu'il y ait ici d'hypothèse, une légère coloration hypothétique s'imprime pourtant dans la phrase pour en amortir le ton.

It may be more appropriate, then, to view 'pseudo-conditionals' rather as 'weak conditionals' which share an attenuated conditional force with 'genuine conditionals' but lie in closest semantic proximity to non-conditional sentence types as identified above.

Genuine Conditionals

Genuine conditionals may also be classified according to their time-referential properties as PRESENT, PAST or FUTURE. Additionally, we must consider the truth-value of the protasis event or state, a parameter which is reflected in the traditional distinctions made for CL conditionals between "Realis", "Potentialis" and "Irrealis" types, which have often been carried forward to apply to English and the Romance languages. Grevisse's description of MFr conditionals (1964:§1037) is along these lines; he distinguishes "l'hypothèse pur et simple":

(17) a. Si tu admettais cette opinion, tu as tort
b. S'il pleut demain, je ne sortirai pas

from "potentiel":

(18) Si (un jour) tu admettais cette opinion (tu l'admettras peut-etre, cela se pourrait), tu aurais tort

and "irréel", which may be PRESENT-referring:

(19) Si (en ce moment) tu admettais cette opinion (mais tu ne l'admets pas), tu aurais tort

or PAST-referring:

(20) Si (l'an dernier) tu avais admis cette opinion (mais tu ne l'as pas admis), tu aurais eu tort

This traditional account may be refined and simplified, however. It would appear that a systematic opposition is made between protases which have a negative truth-value (false-presupposing or COUNTERFACTUAL) and those the truth value of which is not known, but could be either positive or negative (OPEN). So there is a clear contrast between the pair of PRESENT-referring conditional sentences:

(21) a. Si vous pensez cela, vous aurez tort (OPEN)
b. Si vous pensiez cela, vous auriez tort (COUNTERFACTUAL)

Unfortunately, time-referential properties slightly complicate this picture. An event or state is in principle verifiable and susceptible of bearing a truth-value when it is PRESENT or PAST, but when it is FUTURE, it is non-verifiable, and its truth-value cannot be ascertained. Although there is a morphological opposition between the pair of sentences:

(22) a. S'il pleut demain, je ne sortirai pas
b. S'il pleuvait demain, je ne sortirais pas

there can in fact strictly be no contrast in the truth-value of the protases, since both are FUTURE-referring and potentially true or false. The discrimination of (22a) and (22b) and their cognate forms in the Romance languages and English is a more delicate matter. Once again I turn to the Le Bidois (1938:539-40) for an account of the difference:

> 'S'il vient demain, je lui parlerai' est la forme ordinaire de la supposition relative à l'avenir. Mais elle est quelquefois présentée autrement: 'S'il venait demain, je lui parlerais'. Le sens est le même; toute la différence est dans la nuance de pensée: avec le présent, s'il vient, la supposition se présente de la façon la plus directe, la plus franche, c'est la forme que la langue emploie spontanément; s'il venait implique dans la pensée, non pas exactement un doute, mais un peu de retenue, de réserve; modalité psychologique qui amène, dans l'expression de la conséquence, le mode de l'éventualité, le conditionnel...

The expectation concerning the truth-value of the protasis of a sentence like (22b), whilst not being absolutely negative, seems to have more of the negative than the positive about it. The expectation in (22a), on the other hand, seems to be fairly neutral.

I propose to label the type exhibited by (22a) an OPEN conditional, in line with (21a), and the type exhibited by (22b) an ANTICIPATED COUNTERFACTUAL conditional, since while not absolutely COUNTERFACTUAL, it has more to do with COUNTERFACTUALity than with OPENness. This categorisation allows us to describe conditional sentences in terms of just two parameters, those of **time-reference** and **presupposition**, whilst at the same time capturing something of the insight of those who distinguished between 'unreal' (demonstrably false-presupposing) and 'potential' (not demonstrably false-presupposing, but not neutral) classes.

Genuine conditionals, like pseudo-conditionals, contract paraphrase-relations with other kinds of structure. Since it is often difficult for speakers to say which of several paraphrase types is the most appropriate reading for a given conditional sentence, it is probably more accurate to regard some conditional sentences as having overlapping semantic readings rather than as exhibiting ambiguity. Yet on the other hand, many genuine conditional sentences will admit only certain types of paraphrase and exclude others, so that there are cases in which paraphrase types can be mutually exclusive. Overall there seem good grounds for supposing that surface conditional sentences may represent several covert underlying types.

A provisional list of paraphrase-types is as follows:

A. CONSEQUENCE. "If X, then Y" = "The consequence of X is Y", e.g.:

(23) If you do that again, I'll punish you = The consequence of your doing that again will be that I'll punish you

B. CONDITION. "If X, then Y" = "Y on the condition that X", e.g.:

(24) If you give me ten pounds I'll go away = I'll go away on condition that you give me ten pounds

C. IMPLICATION. "If X, then Y" = "X implies Y", e.g.:

(25) If a person is breathing, he's alive = A person breathing implies he's alive

This kind of conditional sentence is often used to demonstrate the absurdity of a hypothesis by supplying an absurd implication:

(26) If Beethoven had written his last string quartet in 1870, he would have been a hundred at the time = Beethoven writing his last string quartet in 1870 implies he was 100 at the time

D. PROVISION. "If X, then Y" = "Y, provided that X", e.g.:

(27) If you admit the charge, you are free to go = You are free to go provided that you admit the charge

This paraphrase type is also appropriate to a special class of genuine conditionals which may be conveniently referred to as 'presupposition conditions', e.g.:

(28) The President will no doubt tell you so, if we still have a President = Provided that we still have a President, he will tell you so

In such sentences as (28), the protasis makes explicit a presupposition associated with the apodosis, that is, it lays down the conditions for the appropriateness of the apodosis statement.

E. CONCESSION. "If X, Y" = "Y even if X; Y if X and Y if not X", e.g.:

(29) (Even) if he knew the answer, he wouldn't say anything = He wouldn't say anything in any case, whether he knew the answer or not (but in fact he doesn't know the answer)

The apodosis of a CONCESSIVE conditional is always asserted as a fact, and is not the consequence of the protasis; and the protasis does not set any condition; in fact, a CONCESSIVE conditional implicitly denies that the protasis is a condition for the apodosis. CONCESSIVE conditionals therefore contrast with other genuine conditional sentence-types in having different truth-value presuppositions associated with protasis and apodosis. Compare the following CONCESSIVE conditionals

(30) (Even) if he did know (OPEN), he didn't say (FACTUAL)

Even if he had come (COUNTERFACTUAL), he wouldn't have said anything (FACTUAL: he didn't)

with similar CONSEQUENCE conditionals:

(31) If he didn't know (OPEN), he didn't say anything (OPEN)
If he had come (COUNTERFACTUAL), he would have said something (COUNTERFACTUAL)

Some of these paraphrase-types are incompatible with one another, as may be seen from the following examples:

(32) If you do that again, I'll punish you
= The consequence of your doing that will be that I'll punish you (CONSEQUENCE)
≠ !I'll punish you on condition you do that again (CONDITION)
≠ !Provided you do that again I'll punish you (PROVISION)
≠ Your doing that again will imply that I'll punish you (IMPLICATION)

(33) I'll give you ten pounds if you leave
= I'll give you ten pounds on condition that you leave now (CONDITION)
= I'll give you ten pounds provided you leave now (PROVISION)
≠ Your leaving now will imply that I'll give you ten pounds (IMPLICATION)

(34) If a person is breathing, he's alive
= Provided a person is breathing, he's alive (PROVISION)
≠ !On condition that a person is breathing, he's alive (CONDITION)

It is difficult, however, to find principles that will link genuine conditional sentences in a regular way with their appropriate paraphrase type or types. Very general semantic relationships can be put up as a rough guide only: it seems, for instance, that a CONSEQUENCE paraphrase is preferred when the apodosis event or state is posterior to the protasis event or state, and that an IMPLICATION paraphrase is usual when the apodosis event or state is simultaneous with or anterior to the protasis event or state. Thus:

(35) If she shouts he will come
= The consequence of her shouting will be that he will come (CONSEQUENCE)
(Apodosis event posterior to protasis event)

(36) If the gun goes off he will have pulled the trigger (IMPLICATION)
(Apodosis event is anterior to protasis event)

(37) If the red flag is flying, they will be shooting
= The red flag flying implies that they are shooting (IMPLICATION)
(Apodosis event simultaneous with protasis event)

Nevertheless, there are sentences in which the apodosis event or state is posterior to the protasis event or state, which can be considered to have an IMPLICATION reading:

(38) If a black cloud appears on the horizon, it will rain
= A black cloud appearing on the horizon implies that it will rain
and
= The consequence of a black cloud appearing on the horizon is that it will rain (CONSEQUENCE)

Returning briefly to the alternatives to si, etc., for the expression of conditionality in the Romance languages, we can see that not all are as potentially multivalent as si, etc., from the semantic point of view. Other conjunctions are usually restricted to just one of the paraphrase-types identified, e.g., Fr à condition que, Sp a condición de que, It a condizione che (CONDITION), Fr pourvu que, Sp con tal que, It purché (PROVISION), Fr quand meme, Sp aun cuando, It benché (CONCESSION). The infinitive, imperative and conjoined structures do not appear to accept CONCESSIVE readings, another fact that sets CONCESSIVE conditionals apart from other types. Sentences like (1), (2) and (3) above cannot be paraphrased by any CONCESSIVE reading, e.g. (from MFr):

(39) Même si nous savions cela, nous n'irions pas là
≠A savoir cela, nous n'irions pas là

Même si vous écoutez bien, vous n'allez pas comprendre
≠ (Vous) écoutez bien et vous n'allez pas comprendre

THE SYNTACTIC STRUCTURE OF CONDITIONAL SENTENCES

Conditionals as matrix-and-subordinate structures

The hypothesis that conditional sentences are matrix-and-subordinate structures, with if/si/se being an alternative lexicalisation of the conjunctions listed at the beginning of this Chapter is immediately suggested on semantic grounds.

On the syntactic level, initial support for such a hypothesis may be drawn from such well-known constraints on pronominalisation as formulated by Langacker (1969). Consider the following sentences:

(40) a. If John had known that, he wouldn't have gone
b. If he had known that, John wouldn't have gone
c. John wouldn't have gone if he had known that
but
d. *He wouldn't have gone if John had known that

Assuming for a moment a matrix-and-embedded clause structure for these sentences, their underlying structure will be of the following form:

(41) a.
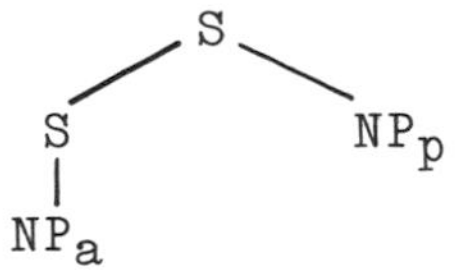

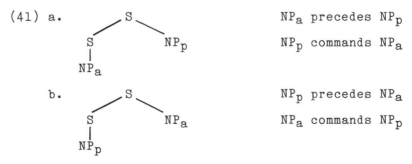

NP_a precedes NP_p
NP_p commands NP_a

b.
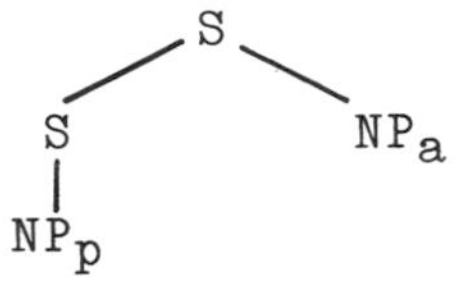

NP_p precedes NP_a
NP_a commands NP_p

c. 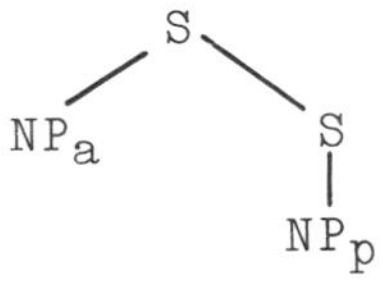

NP_a precedes NP_p

NP_a commands NP_p

d. 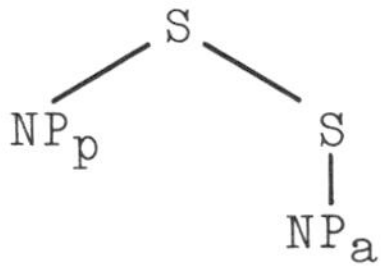

NP_p precedes NP_a

NP_p commands NP_a

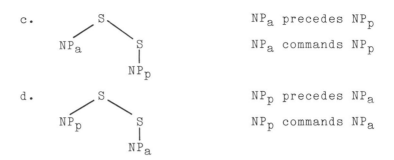

I follow Langacker's terminology and symbolisation: NP_a stands for the antecedent NP (i.e., the NP which is not pronominalised), NP_p stands for the pronominalised NP; "precedes" means "stands to the left of in surface structure", and the notion of "command" is defined thus: a node A commands a Node B if (a) A does not dominate B and B does not dominate A, (b) A is in the structure of an S node, and (c) this S node dominates B. (So, for example, NP_p commands NP_a in (41a).) The constraint on pronominalisation can now be stated as follows: NP_a may be used to pronominalise NP_p unless (a) NP_p precedes NP_a and (b) either (i) NP_p commands NP_a or (ii) NP_a and NP_p are elements of separate conjoined structures. This constraint correctly predicts the acceptability of (40a–c) and the unacceptability of (40d) when these sentences are construed as having the structures (41a–d). Notice, however, that if (40b) were construed as a conjoined structure of the form

(42) 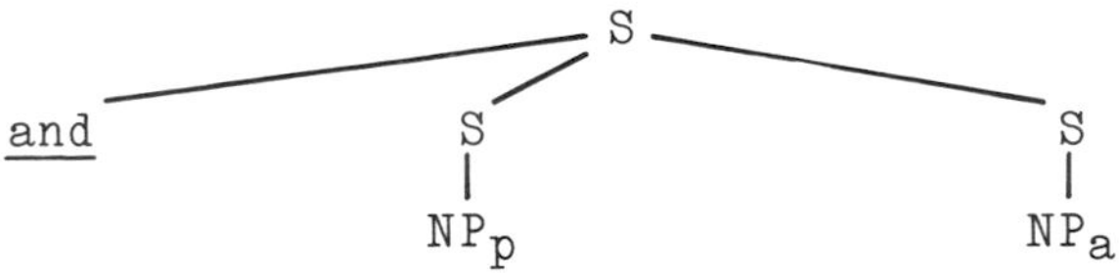

conditions (a) and (b(ii)) would be satisfied, and the constraint would incorrectly predict that (40b) was unacceptable.

The matrix-and-subordinate hypothesis is not without its difficulties, however. If conditional sentences are to be viewed as matrix-and-subordinate in nature, they will differ in important ways from other matrix-and-subordinate structures. In the first place, for many matrix-and-subordinate structures embedding does not appear to change the truth-value or the speech-act type of the constituent clauses. The two constituent clauses of (43a), for example, shown in (43b), are both declarative sentences with a presumed positive truth-value:

(43) a. There is the boy I saw
     b. [There is the boy_i [I saw the boy_i]]

But now consider the conditional sentence

(44) If he had arrived earlier he would have seen the professor

which may be taken to consist of the propositions <u>He arrived earlier</u> and <u>he saw the professor</u>. When they are synthesised into (44) their presupposed truth-value becomes negative, and they are no longer declarative in nature. Furthermore, their verb-forms bear little resemblance to simple sentence usage; (44) cannot derive from the simple sentences <u>He had arrived earlier</u> and <u>He would have seen the professor</u>. Also, the constituent sentences of (43) were semantically satisfactory in isolation; but if the apodosis of a conditional sentence (the supposed 'matrix-clause') occurs in isolation with the Cond Perf verb-form it has in (44), it is felt to be incomplete without a protasis, which no doubt follows from the very close semantic relation which, as we have seen, exists between apodosis and protasis.

A second property of many matrix-and-subordinate structures is that elements of the matrix-clause may determine features of the subordinate clause. In the Romance languages, subjunctivisation (or the possibility of subjunctivisation) of the verb in a subordinate clause often depends on the choice of a matrix-clause verb; the rule of [Past]-AGREEMENT for a subordinate clause verb is formulated in terms of the matrix-clause verb-form marking. I am not aware of any claims that the reverse situation, the determining of features of the matrix-clause verb by elements involved in the subordinate clause, obtains. While rules for conditional sentences which would make the verb-form of the protasis dependent on the verb-form of the apodosis could obviously be formulated, such a recourse seems not altogether satisfactory. There is such a closely constrained relationship between the verb-forms of protasis and apodosis that it would be equally possible to formulate such a rule in the reverse manner, making the apodosis verb-form dependent on that of the protasis - indeed, from a perceptual or production point of view, there is a good deal to commend this, since the protasis is frequently encountered (again unlike many matrix-and-subordinate structures, in which the subordinate clause exceptionally precedes the matrix-clause) as the leftmost surface clause[2].

Conditionals as Coordinate Structures

I now turn to an alternative hypothesis concerning the structure of conditional sentences, namely the suggestion that apodosis and protasis may be coordinate in nature. From the outset it is clear that a conditional sentence will have to be a coordinate structure of a rather special kind, since there is normally no limit that can be set on the number of sentences which may be conjoined by coordinating conjunctions, the general underlying structure of such sentences being of the form:

(45)

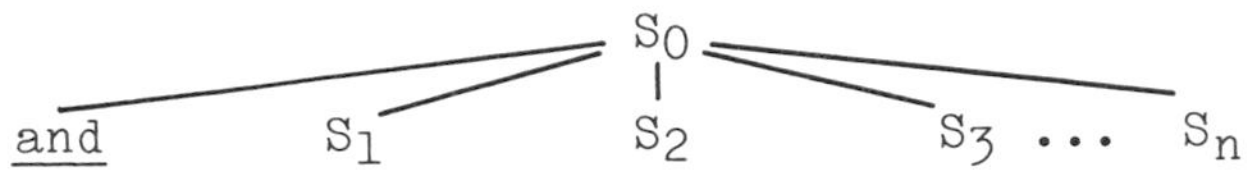

Conditional sentences, however, are essentially binary in nature: although coordination within protasis or apodosis is potentially unrestricted, and although one conditional sentence may be embedded within the protasis or apodosis of another, there do not appear to be conditional sentences of the following type:

(46)

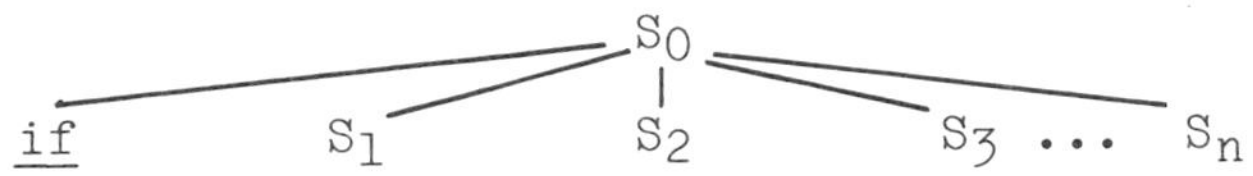

a surface string <u>S_1 if S_2 if S_3 if ... if S_n</u> being normally construable[3] only as:

(47)

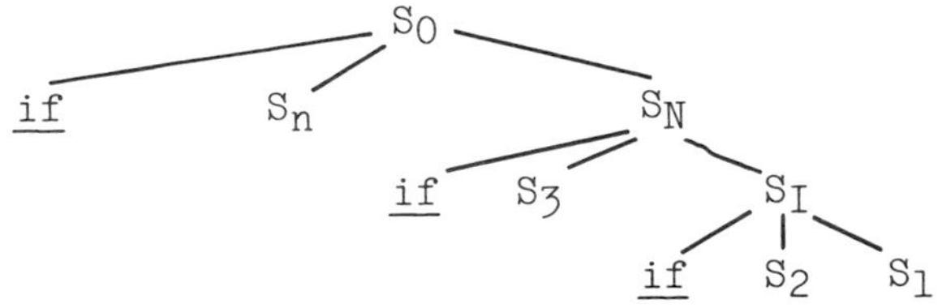

or as:

(48)

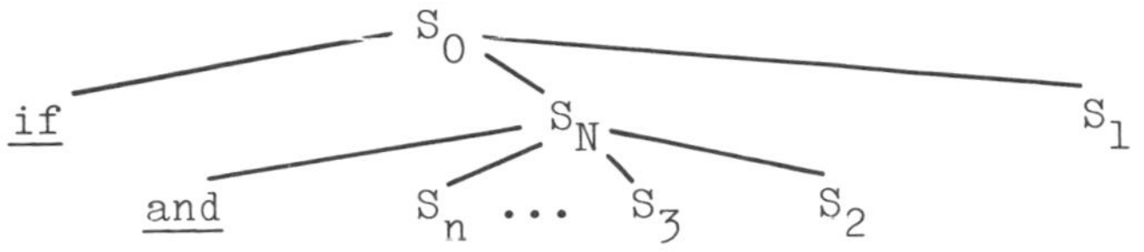

On the other hand, similar difficulties have been noted for the coordinating conjunctions but and or[4], with which if shares other properties, including, in English, some derived conjunction phenomena. Compare:

(49) a. Mary is attractive but Mary is stupid
==> Mary is attractive but stupid

and

b. The star is hot if the star is white
==> the star is hot if white (IMPLICATION)
c. Mary is attractive if Mary is stupid
==> Mary is attractive if stupid (CONCESSION, pseudo-conditional)
d. You are promoted if you are competent
==> You are promoted if competent (CONDITION or CONSEQUENCE)

Rivero (1972) proposed that protasis and apodosis are basically coordinate in nature and that MSp si is the surface realisation of a 'world-creating verb'[5]; that is, the surface sequence Si S_1, S_2 is underlain by the structure

(50)

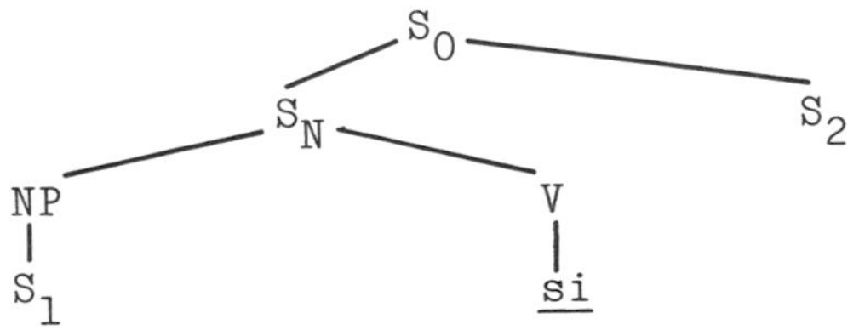

Her arguments for regarding si as a world-creating verb are based on the similarity of the properties of si and surface world-creating verbs like imaginar (que) and suponer (que). It is proposed that the sentences of (51), as well as standing in a paraphrase relation, shall be considered as syntactic parallels:

(51) a. Si hubiera contado la verdad...
b. Imagine que hubiera contado la verdad...
c. Suponga que hubiera contado la verdad...

The morphological parallel of these MSp examples is shared by cognate data in English and MIt:

(52) a. If he had told the truth...
Se avesse detto la verità...

b. Imagine/Suppose he had told the truth...
Immagini/Supponga che avesse detto la verità...

but not by that of MFr, where imaginer and supposer normally require a [+Subj] verb-form in a counterfactual complement, whereas Plup is the rule in a PAST COUNTERFACTUAL conditional sentence:

(53) a. Si vous m'aviez dit la vérité...
b. Imaginez/Supposez que vous m'eussiez (written)/ayez (spoken) dit la vérité...

Morphological parallelism should not necessarily, therefore, be taken as providing grounds for a relationship between the sentences of (51).

In support of the view that the constituent clauses of a conditional sentence are coordinate in nature, Rivero points to: (a) the interdependence of protasis and apodosis with regard to mood, (b) the coordinate nature of several types of construction which are semantically very close to conditionals, examples of which I have already considered in (2) and (3) above, (c) the time-reference pattern in conditional sentences, which is the same as for a conjunct of (i) a world-creating verb + complement and (ii) another clause:

(54) Si te escribió te alegrarás
= Imagina que te escribió y te alegrarás
(alegrar is posterior to escribir in both cases)

(d) a more complex phenomenon concerning 'negative-transportation' in CONCESSIVE conditionals, which I shall sketch here. Rivero proposes that

(55) a. No lo comprenderé incluso si me lo explicas
b. Ni siquiera si me lo explicas, lo comprenderé

are related by a rule of NEGATIVE-TRANSPORTATION by which the NEG element of the apodosis is transported to combine with incluso and yield ni siquiera; when the underlying structure is construed as (56), the necessary structural description for NEGATIVE-TRANS-

PORTATION is met:

(56)

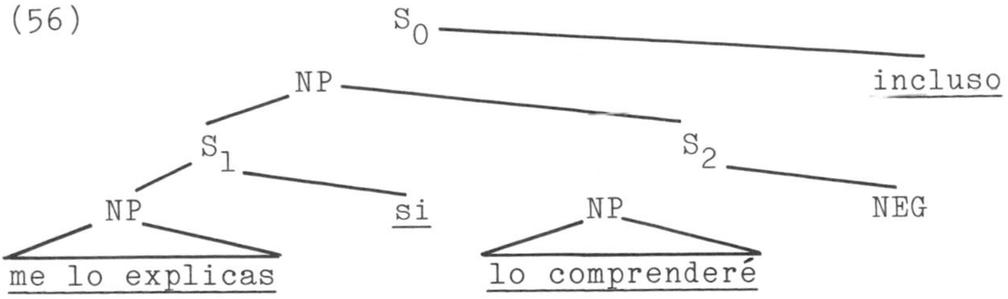

An underlying structure like (57), on the other hand, in which the protasis was subordinate to the apodosis, would not supply the necessary structural description for NEGATIVE-TRANSPORTATION:

(57)

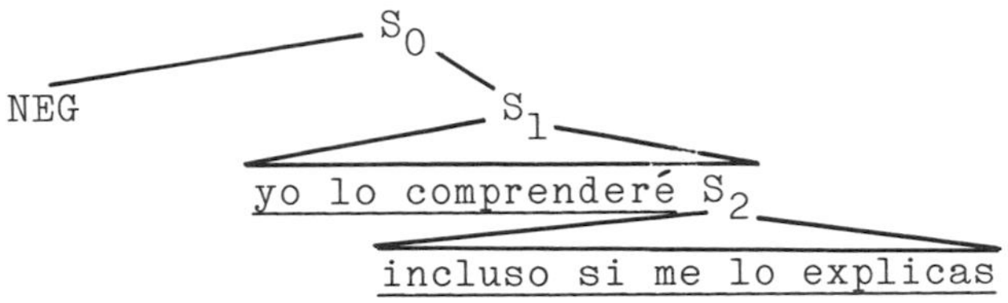

Unfortunately, Rivero's proposed analysis of conditional sentences is not without its problems. There are important syntactic and semantic differences between the behaviour of si and that of world-creating verbs like MSp imaginar and suponer.

A. The verb-form in the complement clause of the world-creating verb, like that of the si-clause, may be [+Subj] or [-Subj] according to whether the sentence is COUNTERFACTUAL or OPEN. The semantic difference between

(58) a. Si hubiera salido...
b. Si salió...

appears to be analogous to that between

(59) a. Suponga que hubiera salido...
b. Suponga que salió...

However, the choice between [+Subj] and [-Subj] forms is open to the complements of world-creating verbs where it is not open to si-clauses:

(60) a. Supón que haya salido a las cinco; pues antes de las ocho puede estar aquí (Moliner (1967:1237))

but

b. *Si haya salido a las cinco, puede estar aquí antes de las ocho

MSp si-clauses do not admit [-Past, +Subj] forms. This lack of parallelism removes even from MSp the possibility of using similarity of verb-form choice as a criterion for establishing a syntactic relation between the protases of conditional sentences and the complements of world-creating verbs.

B. The semantic parallel between si-clauses and the complements of world-creating verbs is unhappy for CONDITIONAL and CONSEQUENCE conditionals. Thus:

(61) a. Si me das el dinero te daré el libro
b. = (Te prometo que) te daré el libro a condición de que me des el dinero

but

c. ?Supón que me das el dinero, te daré el libro

d. Si te acercas más te mato
e. = (Te amenazo con) matar si te acercas más

but

f. ?Supón que te acercas más, te mato

Such phenomena receive a natural explanation when we delve further into the underlying structures associated with (61a-f). If supón is taken to be a genuine imperative, then (61c) and (61f) will represent different types of speech-act and will be different in nature from (61a-b and d-e); (61c), for instance, may be construed as having the following underlying structure:

(62)

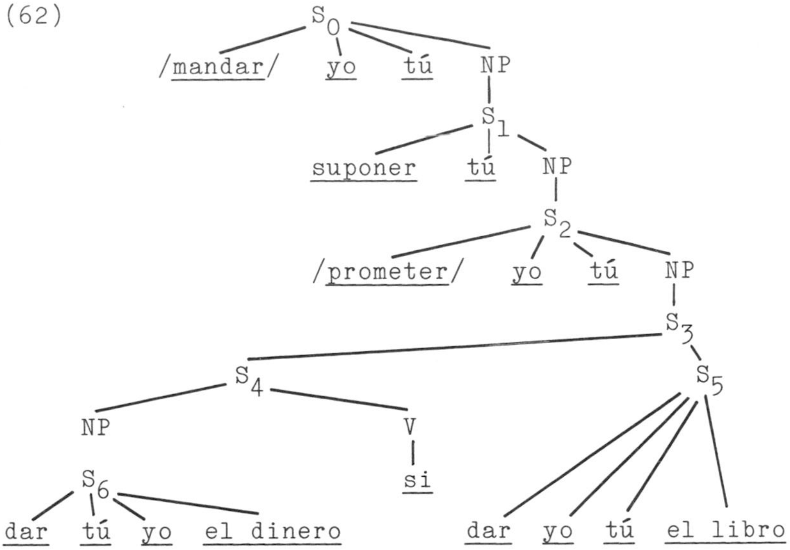

("Yo te mando que supongas tú que yo te prometo que si tú me das el dinero yo te daré el libro")

In (62), /prometer/ is not the verb of the highest clause, and hence does not function as a performative (speech-act) verb. However, even if we propose an underlying structure for (61c) in which /prometer/ does belong to the highest clause, thereby regaining the speech-act status it has in (61b), the resulting surface structure is still not in paraphrase relation with (61a and b):

(63)

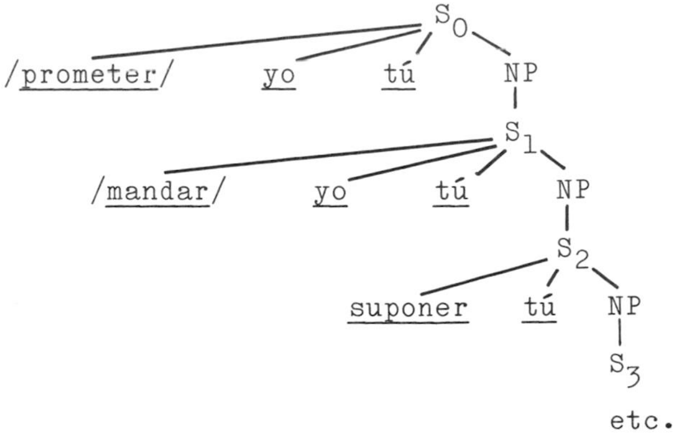

("Yo te prometo que yo te mandaré que tú supongas que si...")

A parallel argument may be elaborated for (61d-f). This state of affairs strongly suggests that conditional sentences which belong to the categories of CONDITION and CONSEQUENCE do not have a valid relation with sentences containing an overt world-creating verb.

C. We have seen that CONDITIONAL conditionals allow their protases to be qualified by English <u>only</u>, Fr <u>seulement</u>, Sp <u>sólo</u>, It <u>solamente</u>. The world-creating verb construction, however, does not happily admit similar qualification:

(64) a. Sólo si me das el dinero te daré el libro

but

b. ?Sólo supón que me des el dinero, te daré el libro

D. In pseudo-conditionals, the parallel breaks down altogether, as might be expected, since a pseudo-conditional does not involve any notion of a hypothetical world. While surface <u>si</u> is capable of introducing a proposition which may be presupposed to have a positive truth-value, a world-creating verb is not:

(65) Si dijimos eso, fue porque lo creíamos
≠ Supón que dijimos eso, fue porque lo creíamos

E. The 'dependent' nature of the protasis of a conditional sentence is not exactly paralleled by a world-creating verb and its complements, which more easily form an independent utterance:

(66) a. No entiendes lo que digo? Pues bien, {supón que / ?si} llegó a las siete

b. {Supón que / ?Si} hubiera llegado a las siete e imagínate si hubieras hecho eso

A more general objection to Rivero's account of <u>si</u> is that while her hypothesis that <u>si</u> is a world-creating verb gives an explanatory account of the use of ImpSubj and PlupSubj in the protases of MSp conditional sentences, she pays little attention to the equally interesting occurrences of Cond, Cond Perf (and in some styles ImpSubj and PlupSubj) in the apodosis.

It is clear that suponga que and si by no means coincide in syntactic properties; to save Rivero's hypothesis, it would be necessary to regard one or the other as an exceptional form of the class of world-creating verbs from the point of view of choice of complement verb-form. Alternatively, one or the other must be regarded as a sui generis class.

THE VERB-FORMS OF CONDITIONAL SENTENCES

In the preceding section, I have pointed out the difficulties both in viewing conditional sentences as matrix-and-subordinate structures and in equating si, etc., with an underlying 'world-creating verb'. Given these difficulties, it is not clear how the verb-forms of conditional sentences should be generated. If a matrix-and-subordinate structure had been appropriate, it would have been natural to construe the subordinate clause verb as dependent upon that of the matrix clause and to generate the latter first. If the 'world-creating verb' hypothesis had been accepted, the generation of the protasis verb-form and that of the complement of the 'world-creating verb' would be one and the same process, and the apodosis verb-form (about which, as we have seen, little is said by Rivero) would be the product of some other kind of rule.

Let us look for a moment at the surface pattern of the chief verb-form sequences[6] encountered in MFr, MSp and MIt (see also Tables 6.7-10):

(67) MFr:

	OPEN	COUNTERFACTUAL
FUTURE	Si Pres/Fut	Si Imp/Cond
PRESENT	Si Pres/Pres	Si Imp/Cond
PAST	Si Imp/... Pret/... (written) Perf/...	Si Plup/CondPerf

MSp:

	OPEN	COUNTERFACTUAL
FUTURE	Si Pres/Fut	Si ImpSubj/Cond
PRESENT	Si Pres/Pres	Si ImpSubj/Cond
PAST	Si Imp/... Pret/... Perf/...	Si PlupSubj/CondPerf

MIt:

	OPEN	COUNTERFACTUAL
FUTURE	Se Pres/Fut Se Fut/Fut	Se ImpSubj/Cond
PRESENT	Se Pres/Pres	Se ImpSubj/Cond
PAST	Se Imp/... Pret/... Perf/...	Se PlupSubj/CondPerf

While any major generalisation concerning the interrelation of these types is impossible, there is nevertheless discernible a certain structural unity. In the FUTURE and PRESENT categories, the COUNTERFACTUAL forms are [+Past] relative to the OPEN forms, and the protasis verb-form of the COUNTERFACTUALs is also [+Subj]. PAST COUNTERFACTUALs are [+Perf] relative to FUTURE and PRESENT COUNTERFACTUALs. None of the three languages seems to distinguish morphologically between PRESENT and FUTURE COUNTERFACTUALity, and the same is true of English:

(68) a. If it were raining {now / tomorrow}, I wouldn't go out

b. S'il pleuvait {maintenant / demain}, je ne sortirais pas

c. Si lloviera {ahora / mañana}, no saldría

d. Se piovesse {adesso / domani}, non uscirei

The ambivalent time-reference of the sequence-of-tense patterns in (68a-d) need present no difficulty, since it is in principle no different in nature from the time-referential ambivalence of a verb-form in isolation, many examples of which we have already noted (see Chapter 2). As a working hypothesis let us concede that conditional sentences may legitimately be viewed as a structural group. Appropriate combinations of verb-forms could be inserted in modular form according to the pattern of time-reference and truth-value presuppositions associated with the sentence (or, conversely, a particular reading will match individual modular combinations of verb-forms). Thus, for example, the adverbial specification PAST in underlying structure and an associated presupposition of COUNTERFACTUALity will require the Plup/CondPerf 'module' in MFr and the ImpSubj/CondPerf 'module' in MSp and MIt to be inserted in surface structure.

This approach to sequence of tense in conditional sentences has the syntactic advantages that neither protasis form nor apodosis form is in any sense 'prior' and that the necessary 'agreement' between protasis and apodosis form is achieved. Semantically, the modular approach allows the interpretation of the whole conditional structure to be dealt with in one operation without the necessity of separating protasis and apodosis. This is an important advantage, particularly with respect to truth-value presuppositions, since while protasis and apodosis may be 'mixed' with regard to time-reference, 'mixing' of truth-value presuppositions (except, as we have seen, in the case of CONCESSIVE conditionals) produces sentences of doubtful acceptability, e.g. from Fr:

(69) a. Si je savais la réponse, je te le dirais
(PRESENT/FUTURE COUNTERFACTUAL)

but

b. ?Si je savais la réponse, je te le dirai
(PRESENT/FUTURE; COUNTERFACTUAL/OPEN)

The important links between surface sequence-of-tense patterns and the semantic parameters of time-reference and truth-value presuppositions contrasts with the total lack of relation between sequence-of-tense and the semantic classes of conditional sentences (CONSEQUENCE, CONDITION, etc.) identified above, which have no effect on sequence-of-tense choice.

The verb-form sequences of pseudo-conditional sentences may be seen simply as not forming part of the genuine conditional system. The verb-forms of pseudo-conditionals are those that are associated with straightforward declarative sentences; if we consider the Romance equivalents of (9c) above, for instance:

(70) Fr: Si Thomas sera ici dans dix minutes, je m'en vais tout de suite
Sp: Si Tomás estará aquí en diez minutos, me voy ahora mismo
It: Se Tommaso sarà qui in dieci minuti, me ne vado subito

it can be seen that the constituent sentences are:

(71) Fr: Thomas sera ici dans dix minutes. Je m'en vais tout de suite
etc.

In English, as in MFr and MSp (but not MIt), there is in the FUTURE type a morphological marking which characterises the pseudo-conditional and sets it apart from the genuine conditional. Fut may appear in the 'protasis' of a pseudo-conditional whereas in a genuine conditional it is prohibited:

(72) a. If you {look / *will look[7]} out of the window, you will see her

b. Si vous {regardez / *regarderez} par la fenêtre, vous la verrez

c. Si {mira / *mirará} por la ventana, la verá

However, in the FUTURE of MIt, and in the PRESENT and PAST of English, MFr, MSp and MIt, there is an overlap between genuine and pseudo-conditionals, since the OPEN genuine conditionals here have verb-form sequences which are identical with declarative sentence usage. Accordingly, FACTUALity in PRESENT and PAST pseudo-conditional sentences is signalled by much more elusive factors. Often, only the context clarifies whether a pseudo-conditional or genuine conditional reading is involved:

(73) a. I don't know whether he's in the library or not, but if he is, he will see the book on the table (Genuine)

b. You saw him in the library, did you? Well, if he's in the library, he must be working (Pseudo)

I would suggest that it is this morphological overlap between pseudo-conditionals and OPEN genuine conditionals, coupled with the reliance on context for establishing the truth-value presupposition of the si, etc., clause as FACTUAL or OPEN, that is responsible for the "légère coloration hypothétique" that gives pseudo-conditionals a slight genuine conditional connotation. In other words, the full meaning of pseudo-conditionals can be understood only through the surface sequence-of-tense patterns they display, a sequence that corresponds to one of the genuine conditional possibilities being inevitably interpretable as such.

World-creating verbs revisited

I would like now to turn to the syntax of Sp suponer. In its imperative form, suponer admits at least three verb-forms in a PRESENT-referring que + S complement:

(74) Suponga que { a. está / b. esté / c. estuviera } aquí

It is difficult to gloss these accurately with English translation-equivalents. Spanish speakers normally explain the difference by saying that (74c) is definitely COUNTERFACTUAL and that (74a-b) are 'OPEN', with (74b) more 'unlikely' than (74a). There is a similar choice of verb-forms, with similar semantic readings, after aunque, and many conjunctions which are [Subj]-requiring allow a choice between PresSubj and ImpSubj, the choice being apparently determined by a truth-value presupposition of COUNTERFACTUALity or OPENness:

(75) { Aun cuando / Ni que / Suponiendo que / En el supuesto que / Siempre que / Con tal que / A condición de que / A menos que / . . . } { esté / estuviera } aquí...

The imperative form of suponer fits neatly into the same scheme, with the additional provision that its complement clause may also be [-Subj]. This latter possibility may well have to do with the fact that other forms of the verb normally take a [-Subj] form in their complement clauses - indeed, the non-imperative forms of the verb cannot of their nature have COUNTERFACTUAL complements:

(76) Supongo que { está / ?esté / *estuviera } aquí

There appears to be a fairly close semantic relationship between suponga que and the forms of (75), and it could be argued that the latter are all alternative surface forms of world-creating verbs. Yet the choice between PresSubj and ImpSubj is also available with the optative ojalá:

(77) ¡Ojalá {esté / estuviera} aquí!

where again ImpSubj is associated with COUNTERFACTUALity. Yet it is difficult to imagine ojalá also being an alternative surface form for suponga que.

I have so far stressed the dissimilarities between si, suponga que, the conjunctions in (75) and ojalá in order to show that any purely syntactic rule that seeks to express parallels among them must make several provisions for irregularities. But now let us consider the similarities. It is interesting, for example, that Cond appears as the main verb-form in sentences which act as 'companions' to most, if not all, of the structures so far discussed, when these are followed by ImpSubj:

(78) a. Suponga que estuviera aquí: podríamos hablarle.
b. Aunque estuviera aquí, podríamos hablarle.
c. Siempre que estuviera aquí, podríamos hablarle.
d. ¡Ojalá estuviera aquí! Podríamos hablarle.

ImpSubj/Cond is, of course, the sequence found with PRESENT COUNTERFACTUAL si. This data receives a more explanatory description, I believe, if the modular insertion principle outlined for conditional sentences is extended. If, for example, the sequence ImpSubj/Cond is associated with the semantic category of PRESENT COUNTERFACTUALity rather than with any one kind of syntactic construction instanced in (78), then all the data can receive a unified description. Similar matching of presupposition to verb-form will likewise offer a descriptive framework for the two-way choice between [-Past] and [+Past] forms in (75) and (77) and the three-way choice between these and [-Past, -Subj] in (74). The job has already been done for the choices available after si in (67). The link between these various phenomena may now be expressed as follows: among the different semantic and syntactic possibilities open to each kind of construction, all coincide in being associated with a semantically PRESENT COUNTERFACTUAL complement represented syntactically by the sequence ImpSubj/Cond. But this coincidence should not persuade us that deeper-seated syntactic parallels between conditional sentence and 'world-creating verbs' necessarily exist.

This solution goes beyond the bounds of any model of description which is based on the unit of the single sentence, since we are attempting to describe the sequence of verb-forms across sentence boundaries (in (78a) and (78d), for example). Yet the constituent sentences of (78a) and (78d), although separate, obviously stand in a general relation of CONSEQUENCE or CONDITION. It must be quite arbitrary to insist on the separability of such sentences. Many parallel phenomena concerning coordinate structures appear to involve similar issues: consider, for example, the semantic link between the coordinate sentence (79a) and the two sentences of (79b):

(79) a. It will be six soon and no one will have come
b. It will be six soon. No one will have come.

Indeed, in view of the difficulties surrounding the precise description of the structure of conditional sentences, it is more than tempting to entertain the conclusion that conditional sentences are an obligatorily collapsed pair of separate sentences, whose conjoining does not call for notions of coordination and subordination as such, but simply for the idea of a general semantic relation holding between the two sentences and the marking of this relation in the surface by a particular sequence of verb-forms.

The conditional sentence construction with si, etc., is therefore to be seen as one particular surface realisation of a pair of sentences between which there is a definable semantic relation of CONSEQUENCE, CONDITION, etc. The verb-forms of the constituent sentences are to be selected simultaneously according to the time-reference of each sentence, which may be distinct, and the truth-value presupposition, which except in the case of CONCESSIVE conditionals will be common to both sentences.

NOTES

1. Further examples are given in Lamérand (1970:28).

2. Protasis-apodosis is the 'natural' order in the medieval texts I examine in Chapter 6. Lorian

(1964:114ff.) finds that preposing of the protasis is roughly twice as common as postposing in a variety of Fr texts. See also Greenberg (1963:84), who proposes protasis-apodosis ordering as "the normal order in all languages".

3. Sentences of this kind are not frequent and usually sound contrived, e.g., I'll mow the lawn if it's fine and if you give me a pound.

4. See Stockwell et al. (1973:368-76) for an explicitly inconclusive discussion.

5. On the notion 'world-creating verb', see G. Lakoff (1968).

6. These are not exhaustive lists of possibilities, but may be taken to represent the 'standard' language. An account of additional stylistic and dialectal possibilities will be found in Chapter 6.

7. Will look may here have a 'polite' value (= "be willing to look"); compare If you will excuse me.... But it cannot be regarded as a simple FUTURE-referring Fut.

Chapter Five

THE VERB AS CONSTITUENT: WHEN-SENTENCES

From the semantic point of view, when-sentences divide into two major categories: (a) those which express only a temporal relation between matrix clause and when-clause; (b) those which, although they may still express a temporal relationship of sorts, carry an additional reading which is not temporal.

TEMPORAL WHEN-SENTENCES

The temporal relationship expressed in when-sentences of category (a) may be a **precedence-relation** of SIMULTANEITY (SIM), when the matrix clause event or state and the when-clause event or state are simultaneous, of ANTERIORITY (ANT), when the matrix clause event or state is anterior to the when-clause event or state, or of POSTERIORITY (POST), when the matrix clause event or state is posterior to the when-clause event or state. The ANT precedence-relation, for example, is illustrated in the sentence

(1) I had watered the garden when she arrived
(water is anterior to arrive)

In particular, there is a category of when-sentences which I shall label 'inverse-when' sentences, following their designation as 'cum inversum' by Latin grammarians[1], which characteristically exhibit the ANT relation, e.g.:

(2) He pushed the car to the edge of the cliff, when it fell to the rocks below
(push is anterior to fall)

Sentences may be ambiguous between POST and SIM readings. Of the sentences

(3) a. He left when she arrived
    b. He$_i$ banged the door when he$_i$ left

(3a) is ambiguous in a way that (3b) is not. In (3a), the events *leave* and *arrive* may be construed as being either simultaneous or non-simultaneous (in the latter case, *leave* is posterior to *arrive*). In (3b), however, *bang* and *leave* would most normally be simultaneous when the two occurrences of *he* are co-referential. The ambiguity of (3a) and the difference in nature between (3a) and (3b) may be revealed in at least two ways. First, the Simple Past in the *when*-clause of (3a) may be replaced by Plup when there is the possibility of a POST reading - a possible paraphrase for (3a) is

(4) He left when she had arrived

but there is no such paraphrase for (3b):

(5) !He$_i$ banged the door when he$_i$ had left

Secondly, in *when*-sentences which have POST readings, *when* is commutable with exclusively POST connectives like *after*, *once*, *immediately*, etc.:

(6) He left {after / once / immediately / when} she (had) arrived

but again, there is no such substitution possible for the *when* of (3b):

(7) !He$_i$ banged the door {after / once / immediately / when} he$_i$ (had) left

An additional category of *when*-sentences which should be mentioned at the outset is that to which I shall refer as UNIVERSAL. Such sentences express general rules and repeated occurrences of events and states which cannot be limited to any one time. In English, the *when* of such sentences is commutable with *whenever* (cf. MSp *cuandoquiera que*) and the sentence as a whole is paraphrasable by the overt statement of an adverbial involving the universal quantifier:

(8) I go out when/whenever she comes
=imp= On all occasions that she comes, I go out

UNIVERSAL when-sentences may also be PAST or FUTURE:

(9) a. I went out when (= whenever) she came
b. I will go out when (= whenever) she comes

They are also characterisable according to the precedence-relations between matrix- and when-clauses identified above:

(10) a. He slams the door when he goes out (UNIVERSAL SIM)
b. She wakes me up when I go to sleep (UNIVERSAL POST)
c. He's always finished when I get there (UNIVERSAL ANT)

In some when-sentences there appears to be no clearcut precedence-relation between the constituent clauses. Rather, the when-clause expresses a vague time-reference, e.g.:

(11) That happened when they blew up the bridge

where it is unclear precisely how happen and blow up are ordered chronologically; the when of this sentence can be paraphrased only by expressions like on the occasion that, round about the time that. The when-clause serves to pinpoint another event which pertains to the general period during which the event or state of the matrix-clause occurs. Since none of the precedence-relations I have so far identified is appropriate to the description of this type of when-sentence, I shall consider it in isolation and label it TIME.

NON-TEMPORAL READINGS FOR WHEN-SENTENCES

A full semantic interpretation of many when-sentences calls for more than the fairly straightforward scheme of temporal relations so far proposed. Additional semantic factors sometimes appear to be subordinate to the purely temporal reading, but often they are foregrounded to such an extent that they take over from the temporal reading as the primary interpretation of the sentence. Here are a few instances of such non-temporal readings:

A. A when-sentence may state an IMPLICATION:

(12) He lied when he said that
=imp= His saying that was a lie

There are examples of when-sentences which are ambiguous between IMPLICATION and a purely temporal reading, e.g.:

(13) She made a mistake when she finished speaking
=imp= Her finishing speaking was a mistake (IMPLICATION)
or
=imp= After she had finished speaking, she made a mistake (TEMPORAL POST)

B. Many when-sentences which have a POST precedence-relation carry also a reading of CONSEQUENCE, e.g.:

(14) He left when she started to cry

In (16), start to cry is not simply an event which helps to define the temporal position of leave; it is an event which can (and normally would) be construed as giving rise to the event leave. Compare the expanded contexts

(15) a. When did he leave?
He left when she started to cry (TEMPORAL)
b. Why did he leave?
I don't really know, but people think he left when she started to cry (CONSEQUENCE)

Note that the when-clause is not commutable with a true consequence clause; it could not, for example, stand in isolation as an answer to the question in (15b), but answers the question "Why?" only, as it were, elliptically. Most probably it is the very general semantic association of post hoc and propter hoc that accounts for the phenomenon.

C. Some when-sentences have an associated reading of CAUSALITY, e.g.:

(16) Don't say that when you know the answer
=imp= Since you know the answer, don't say that

In English there is the possibility of ambiguity between a CAUSAL reading for a sentence like (16), for which the time-reference of the when-clause is PRESENT, and a SIM TEMPORAL reading, for which the time-reference is FUTURE; in this latter reading, (18) is paraphrasable by

(17) When you get to know the answer, don't say that

This possibility does not exist in MFr, MSp and MIt, where a different verb-form is required in the when-clause according to the reading:

(18) CAUSAL:
Quand vous savez la réponse, ne la dites pas
Cuando sabes la respuesta, no la digas
Quando sa la risposta, non la dica
TEMPORAL:
Quand vous saurez la réponse, ne la dites pas
Cuando sepas la respuesta, no la digas
Quando saprà la risposta, non la dica

D. A reading of CONCESSION may be associated with the following when-sentences:

(19) a. When everything seems all right, there's still trouble somewhere
=imp= Even though everything seems to be all right, there's still trouble somewhere
b. He left me in the lurch, when I'd done him so many favours
=imp= Even though I'd done him so many favours, he left me in the lurch

Just what principles allow us to predict a non-temporal reading for a when-sentence it is difficult to say. The most fruitful way of viewing the question would seem to lie in an examination of the general semantic relationships between the constituent clauses of when-sentences. A necessary condition for the assigning of an IMPLICATION reading will no doubt be that the matrix-clause event or state can in some way predicate a property of the when-clause event or state; the assigning of a CONCESSION reading will require at the very least some notion of contrast between the matrix-clause proposition and that of the when-clause. A CAUSALITY reading is possible only with certain time-reference patterns. It will be remembered that similar observations were made with regard to pseudo-conditional readings for sentences containing if, etc., in the preceding Chapter. The impression that such constraints on semantic interpretation lie fairly deep in the grammar (if indeed they are properly part of the grammar at all) is confirmed when we notice that very similar ranges of readings are also available for sentences containing if:

(20) a. If he said that he was lying
=imp= His saying that was a lie (IMPLICATION)
b. If she starts to cry I'll go
=imp= The consequence of her starting to cry will be that I'll go (CONSEQUENCE)
c. If you know the answer, don't say that
=imp= Since you know the answer, don't say that (CAUSAL)
d. If everything seems all right, there's still trouble somewhere
=imp= Even though everything seems all right, there's still trouble somewhere (CONCESSIVE)

The same constituent clauses connected by and can also produce sentences whose readings go far beyond simple conjunction in semantic force:

(21) a. He said that and he was lying
b. She started to cry and left
c. He knows the answer and doesn't say that
d. Everything seems all right, and there's still trouble somewhere

THE SYNTACTIC STRUCTURE OF WHEN-SENTENCES

The relative adverb hypothesis

Superficially, there is a good deal of evidence to suggest that when/quand/cuando/quando is a relative adverb which participates in an adverbial clause. English when contains the wh- element shared with several other relatives; MFr quand, MSp cuando and MIt quando show the reflex of the CL qu- element which is similarly common in Romance relatives. 'Wh-' words in English and 'qu-' words in Romance are likewise similar in serving both as relatives and interrogatives, in which function they stand as leftmost constituents in their clauses; when/quand/cuando/quando shares these properties too[2].

It is well-known that relative clauses fall into two major classes, usually termed 'restrictive' and 'non-restrictive' (or 'appositive') respectively. These classes are exemplified in the sentences

(22) a. The student who liked music stayed (restrictive)
     b. The student, who liked music, stayed (non-restrictive)

Informally, we may say that the relative clause in (22b) simply adds information about the student whereas in (22a) the relative clause has a deictic value, 'restricting' (here, singling out a particular member of) the set of students according to a distinguishing characteristic. Some properties distinguishing restrictive and non-restrictive relative clauses are listed by Stockwell et al. (1973: 422):

> Appositives, but not restrictives, require comma intonation after the head NP.
> Restrictives, but not appositives, permit that as a relative pronoun.
> Appositives, but not restrictives, may modify proper nouns that have no determiners: *John that came early also left early.
> Restrictives, but not appositives, may modify an entire proposition (He said he would resign, which I thought was a good idea).
> The constraints which determine what can be fronted along with the shared NP in the relative clause are not the same in the two types: cf. The crimes, over which his anguish was intense, were less serious than he thought, but not *The crimes over which his anguish was intense were less serious than he thought.

There are problems with proposing underlying structures for both types of relative clause. Non-restrictive relative clauses have been held to originate from conjoined sentences in underlying structure; restrictive relatives seem to require underlying structures which are quite dissimilar from their surface forms (see Stockwell et al. (1973:441-2)). These problems are not our concern here, however. If when-sentences are in fact relative in nature, it may be expected that they will raise analogous problems, and that when apropriate underlying structures and derivational histories are proposed for other relatives, these will also be appropriate for when-sentences. Our immediate task is to see how well when-sentences do in fact compare with other relative structures.

If when-sentences are relative structures, it is to be expected that, just as the underlying structures of (22) will in some way involve the propositions The student stayed and The student liked music and will have as a necessary condition for relativisation coreference between the two occurrences of student, so also a when-sentence will consist in its underlying structure of two propositions which each contain an adverbial of time, and that coreferentiality between the adverbials will be a necessary condition for the generation of a when-sentence. When-sentences differ significantly from other relative structures, however, in that there may or may not be a surface antecedent in the matrix-clause:

(23) a. I was free on Sunday, when you were busy
b. I was free when you were busy

If consistency with a relative analysis is to be preserved, a sentence like (23b) will need to have in its underlying matrix-clause an abstract adverbial which is not lexicalised in surface structure, and with which a presumably abstract adverbial in the subordinate clause (which when replaces in surface structure) can be considered coreferential.

For when-sentences which exhibit a surface antecedent, there are clearly possibilities for restrictive and non-restrictive readings:

(24) a. I was free on Sundays, when you were busy (non-restrictive)
b. I was free on Sundays when you were busy (restrictive)

Here, when may be construed as an alternative surface form for on which. Pairs like (24a) and (24b) exhibit nearly all the differentiating properties listed above by Stockwell et al.: (a) 'comma intonation' for (24a) but not for (24b); (b) (24b) may have that as a surface alternative to when, but (24a) may not; (c) if in (24a) and (24b) Sunday is substituted for Sundays (i.e. by a proper noun without a determiner), (24a) remains acceptable, but (24b) does not; (d) if in (24a) and (24b) Sundays is replaced by any Sunday, (24a) is unacceptable but (24b) is not. In several respects, then, when-sentences containing an antecedent appear to correspond well enough to the pattern established for other relative clauses.

I now turn to when-sentences without a surface antecedent. The assumed abstract adverb in the matrix-clause of the underlying structure of sentences like

(25) a. I left when he arrived (read as SIM)
b. I was free when you were busy

may have a surface realisation, (24a) and (24b) being paraphrased by

(26) a. I left at the time at which he arrived
b. I was free at the times at which you were busy

It is clear that the sentences of (26) must be considered restrictive relative structures, since (a) 'comma intonation' is impossible:

(27) a. *I left at the time, at which he arrived
b. *I was free at the times, at which you were busy

(b) the relative pronoun may be lexicalised as that:

(28) a. I left at the time that he arrived
b. I was free at the times that you were busy

(c) the matrix NP in (27b) (but not (27a) where it is a singular concept) may include the quantifier any:

(29) I was free at any times at which you were busy

It seems, then, that there are good grounds for considering when-sentences without a surface antecedent as restrictive relatives. They present analogous problems, too, from the semantic point of view. Compare

(30) a. All the students who liked music stayed
b. I was free (at all the times) when you were busy

The truth of (30a) does not entail the truth of its apparent matrix-clause all the students stayed; likewise the truth of (33b) does not entail the truth of I was free at all times (whatever the reference of the times might be taken to be). Appropriate paraphrases in logical form for (30a) and (30b) are again analogous, and are of a conditional type:

(31) a. (For (30a)) If s is a student, then if s liked music, s stayed.
b. (For (30b)) If t is a time, then if I was free at t, you were busy at t.

There are also when-sentences without an antecedent which do take 'comma intonation', notably the inverse-when class and paraphrase equivalents:

(32) a. When we rounded the bend, we saw the sea
b. We rounded the bend, when we saw the sea (inverse-when)

The comma intonation suggests that (32a) and (32b) are non-restrictive relatives. As in the case of (25a) and (25b), it is possible to lexicalise the abstract adverbial which must be assumed to be in the underlying structure for these sentences and to derive

(33) a. We saw the sea at a certain time, at which time we rounded the bend
b. We rounded the bend at a certain time, at which time we saw the sea

(33a) and (33b) satisfy such criteria as may be applicable to qualify as non-restrictive relatives. They may also be paraphrased by conjoined structures, which, as was noted at the outset of this discussion, is a typical property of non-restrictive relatives: hence (32a) and (33a) may be compared with

(34) We rounded the bend at a certain $time_t$ and we saw the sea at a certain $time_t$

The non-restrictive relative structure

(35) The boy, whom I met at the station, was wearing a grey suit

may be considered to be underlain by the conjoined structure

(36) I met the boy_b at the station and the boy_b was wearing a grey suit

which may be converted into a surface relative structure in two different ways; either occurrence of the boy may become the antecedent in the matrix-clause, and the second occurrence of the boy will then become the relativised element in the subordinate clause. An alternative surface realisation of (36) is therefore

(37) I met the boy, who was wearing a grey suit, at the station

In exactly the same way, therefore, (32a) and (32b) may be construed as alternative surface realisations of (34).

The principal challenge to the relative adverb hypothesis is of a semantic nature. When does not always have the reading "at the time at which" (SIM), but may also have the reading "after the time at which" (POST). A POST precedence-relation is the most normal reading for (38), for instance:

(38) He visited the castle when he arrived

which may be understood as

(39) He visited the castle Adv_{temp_s} after he arrived Adv_{temp_t}

Adv_{temp_s} cannot be exactly coreferential with Adv_{temp_t}. Since the condition for relativisation is coreferentiality between antecedent and its corresponding element in the subordinate clause, and since there is no such coreferentiality in (38), relativisation ought not, strictly, to take place. There are in principle three ways of circumventing this difficulty: (a) when-sentences are not after all relative structures, but are so construed that a more revealing account can be given of sentences like (38); (b) sentences like (33) have special exemption from the coreference rule (perhaps they exhibit some form of vague coreference, the importance of which I have already drawn attention to in the establishment of the TIME category of when-sentences); (c) sentences like (38) have some alternative structure that makes them compatible with their being construed as relatives. Recourse (b) would be a weak solution and a last resort. Before looking at the possibilities of (c), I shall review alternative hypotheses that have been proposed for the description of when-sentences.

The comparative hypothesis

The description of when-sentences as comparative structures derives from Geis's (1970) work on the temporal connectives before and after. The sentence

(40) I will leave before he leaves

may be construed in underlying structure as follows[3]:

(41)

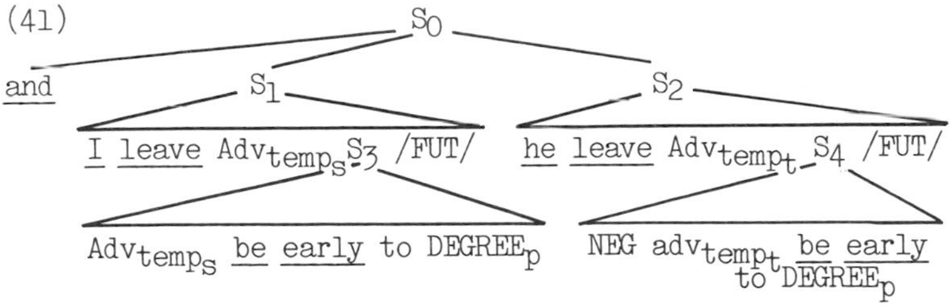

By relativisation and comparative-formation rules the string

(42) I leave /FUT/ Adv_{temp_s} REL be early + -er than Adv_{temp_t} REL he leave /FUT/

"I will leave at a time which is earlier than the time at which he will leave"

is formed. Simplification of the relative clauses produces

(43) I will leave earlier than Adv_{temp} REL he will leave

and subsequent deletion of the unspecified Adv_{temp} REL structure yields the surface form *I will leave earlier than he will leave*. *Before* may be regarded as an alternative lexicalisation of *earlier than*. Similarly, and as the result of a parallel derivation, *after* may be construed as an alternative lexicalisation for *later than*. Geis's arguments for the parallel between (40) and the structure in (37) rest on the observation that sentences containing the elements *before* and *after* undergo optional rules of substitution and deletion in just the same way as comparative structures, e.g.:

(44) Comparatives:

a. Mary washed more frequently than John washed
==> Mary washed more frequently than John did (DO-SUBSTITUTION)
==> Mary washed more frequently than John (IDENTICAL VP-DELETION)

Before/after structures:

b. I left [before / after] he left

==> I left [before / after] he did (DO-SUBSTITUTION)

==> I left [before / after] him (IDENTICAL VP-DELETION)

The kind of hypothesis that might now be advanced for when-sentences would be that when-sentences with POST TEMPORAL readings are alternative surface realisations of sentences containing the connectives later than or after, and that when-sentences with SIM TEMPORAL readings are alternative surface realisations of sentences containing comparative structures like at the same time as. Thus there would be two underlying structures for

(45) I left when he left

as follows:

(46) a.

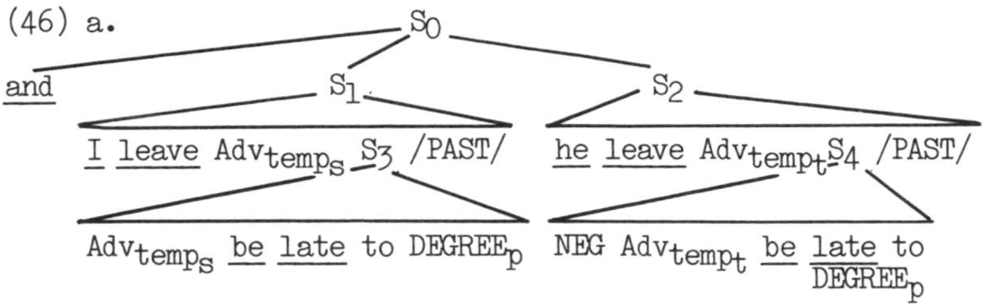

"I left at a time which was later than that at which he left"

b.

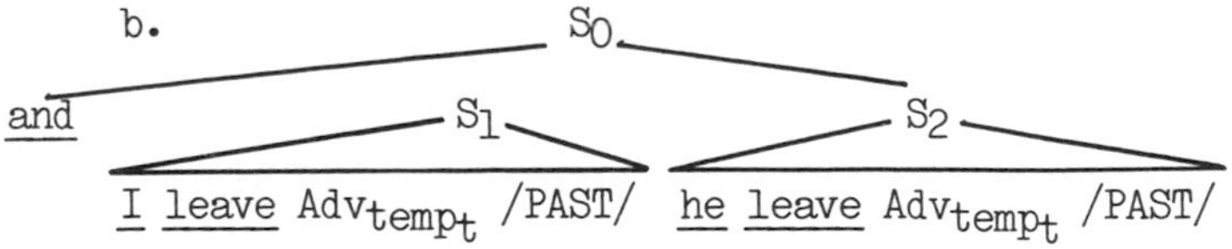

"I left at the time at which he left"

Unfortunately, the behaviour of before and after is markedly different from that of when, despite the tempting semantic parallels. Firstly, when-sentences, in both their SIM and POST TEMPORAL readings, do not allow IDENTICAL VP-DELETION as exemplified in (44):

(47) I left when he left
  ==> I left when he did
  but
  =≠> *I left when him

This may of course be linked to the fact (secondly) that when, unlike before and after, has no prepositional function in English:

(48) {Before / After / *When} the meeting...

There is, moreover, a major difficulty even with the analysis of before and after as comparatives. While the parallels outlined above work well so long as the verb in the two constituent clauses of such structures is the same, the picture is complicated severely when they are different. Whereas in

(49) He arrived later than I arrived

later is commutable with at a time later than, a sentence like

(50) He arrived later than I left

carries the implications he arrived late and I left late, which are not carried by

(51) a. He arrived after I left
  or
  b. He arrived when I left

Before leaving the comparative hypothesis, we should note that parallel data in the Romance languages does not favour the hypothesis to the same degree. The rules which were crucial to the proposed parallel between comparative structures and sentences containing the temporal connectives before and after, namely, DO-SUBSTITUTION and IDENTICAL VP-DELETION, do not work in exactly the same way in MFr, MSp and MIt. The equivalent of DO-SUBSTITUTION in not so easily permitted with intransitive verbs and verbs which represent a state rather than an event or action:

(52) MFr:
  *Il connaît plus de gens que je ne le fais
  *Il est parti avant que je l'aie fait

MSp:
*Él conoce a más personas que yo lo hago
*Salió él antes de que yo lo hiciese

MIt:
*Egli conosce più di persone che io lo faccio
*È partito prima che io lo facessi

The equivalent of IDENTICAL VP-DELETION exists in Romance, but the subordinating temporal conjunctions are sometimes slightly different in form when they appear in the surface context of a following NP (if, indeed, in this context they can be considered conjunctions at all - they are more appropriately described as prepositions). Thus

(53) MFr:
Avant qu'il soit parti...
but
Avant lui

Après qu'il est/soit parti...
but
Après lui

MSp

Antes que saliese...
but
Antes que/de él

Después (de) que salió...
but
Después que/de él

MIt:

Prima che partisse...
but
Prima di lui

Dopo che è partito
but
Dopo di lui

The Romance data might still nevertheless be described in the same way as the English, since DO-SUBSTITUTION will simply not be available in as many circumstances, and surface adjustments can be made to the conjunction-prepositions. But it is not possible to use the Romance data in support of the comparative hypothesis.

The conjoined sentence hypothesis

The possibility of a SIM/POST ambiguity for *when*-sentences like (3a) above is paralleled by the same kind of ambiguity for sentences conjoined by *and*. *And* may be either 'symmetric' (in which case the sentences it conjoins can be switched without undue change to thc meaning of the sentence as a whole) or 'asymmetric' (in which case the sentences it connects are in a fixed precedence-relation); examples are, respectively:

(54) a. John did the accounts and I read the paper
= I read the paper and John did the accounts

b. I boarded the yacht and sailed away
≠ I sailed away and boarded the yacht

(Discussion of this phenomenon can be followed in R. Lakoff (1971).) It is not difficult to construct a sentence with *and* which has both symmetric and asymmetric readings:

(55) I shall see his car outside and I shall know the reason
= ... and (all the time) I shall be aware of the reason
or
= ... and then I shall become aware of the reason

The corresponding *when*-sentence exhibits exactly the same ambiguity:

(56) When I see his car outside, I shall know the reason

There are also parallels between *when*-sentences with ANT TEMPORAL readings and sentences conjoined by *and*:

(57) When I got there he had got up
= I got there and he had got up

The hypothesis would accordingly run that *when*-sentences are derived from an underlying structure of the form

(58)

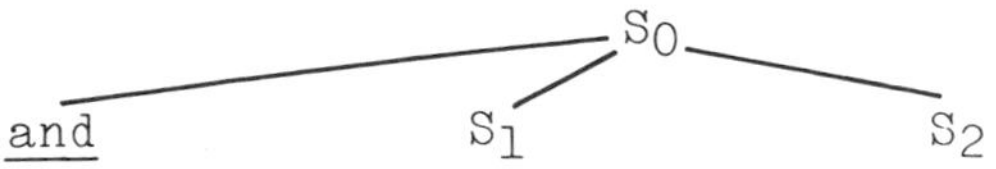

We come up here against a parallel difficulty to that encountered over the hypothesis considered in the previous Chapter, that is, that conditional sentences are coordinate in nature: while an infinite number of clauses may potentially be conjoined by and (in either its symmetric or asymmetric reading), it is possible to link only two basic clauses with when. Compare

(59) a. I boarded the yacht, cast off, lit my pipe and sailed away
b. *When I (had) boarded the yacht, when I (had) cast off, when I (had) lit my pipe, I sailed away.

Conjoining may of course take place within the matrix-clause or the when-clause:

(60) a. When I had boarded the yacht, cast off and lit my pipe, I sailed away
b. When I had boarded the yacht, I cast off, lit my pipe and sailed away
etc.

This constraint is easily expressible under the relative adverb hypothesis, since it can be specified that only one when-clause per matrix-clause is permissible.

Saving the relative adverb hypothesis

Since alternative hypotheses for the structure of when-sentences do not seem to yield satisfactory results, I will return to the possibility of modifying the relative adverb hypothesis.

The chief objection to the relative adverb hypothesis was the difficulty of giving adequate representation to non-SIM precedence-relationships, due to the postulation of an underlying adverbial at the time as the source of surface when. Let us assume, however, that when can be underlain not only by at the time but also by after the time and before the time. Such a device would have the immediate advantage of providing an explanation of the ambiguity noted in (3a), since when would have the necessary distinct underlying sources. Underlying structures could accordingly be proposed as follows:

(61) I had watered the garden when she arrived (1)
==> [I water the garden AT THE TIME$_t$ [she arrive AT THE TIME$_t$ /PAST/] /PAST/]

(62) He left when she arrived (3a)
==> [He leave AT THE TIME$_t$ [she arrive AT THE TIME$_t$ /PAST/] /PAST/]
or
==> [He leave AFTER THE TIME$_t$ [she arrive AT THE TIME$_t$ /PAST/] /PAST/]

Conversion of the underlying structure of (61) into surface structure must include the requirement that if _when_ is chosen as the relative adverbial, the matrix-clause verb-form is obligatorily [+Perf], a specification which is optional (from a purely syntactic point of view, at any rate) with _before_:

(63) I {watered / had watered} the garden before she arrived

In the conversion of the POST underlying structure of (62) into surface structure, the _when_-clause verb-form is optionally [+Perf], as also when _after_ is used:

(64) He left {when / after} she {arrived / had arrived}

By continuing in this way, a whole system of constraints on verb-form usage in _when_-sentences can be established. Indeed, such a system must be established if the revised relative adverb hypothesis is not to be too powerful a device, for the relation between precedence-relation and verb-form sequence is an extremely close one, as will be seen by the description of various Romance systems in Chapter 7.

THE VERB-FORMS OF _WHEN_-SENTENCES

Semantic constraints

Time-referential. The choice of verb-forms in matrix-clause and _when_-clause in Romance and English is subject to constraints that are unknown in other kinds of sentence containg a relative clause, but which follow naturally from the construing of _when_, etc., as a realtive adverb. A very general constraint is that matrix-clause and _when_-clause in TEMPORAL _when_-sentences must share the same area of time-reference (PAST, PRESENT, FUTURE, UNIVERSAL): thus in MFr:

(65) a. Quand il viendra (FUTURE) je le verrai (FUTURE)

but

b. *Quand il est venu (PAST) je le verrai (FUTURE)

c. *Quand il viendra (FUTURE) je l'ai vu (PAST)

etc.

I shall refer to sentences such as (65a) in which there is identity of time-reference between matrix-clause and when-clause as having a **joint axis** of time-reference. Lack of identity of time-reference between matrix-clause and when-clause (a **disjoint axis**) is generally the sign of a non-temporal reading:

(66) Il va me planter là (FUTURE), quand je lui ai fait tant de faveurs (PAST) (CONCESSION)

=imp= ... quoique je lui aie fait tant de faveurs

The only apparent exception to this general rule is in when-sentences with UNIVERSAL reference, in which a POST precedence-relation may be expressed by using a [+Perf] form in the when-clause; in such cases, the time-reference pattern may appear to be disjoint:

(67) Quand on a fait la visite de la cathédrale (PAST) on doit aller au chateau (PRESENT-FUTURE)

But if UNIVERSAL reference is not available as a reading, such an interpretation is not available:

(68) Quand j'ai fait la visite de la cathédrale je dois aller au château

can be interpreted only as having a non-temporal CAUSAL reading ("Since/Now that I've visited the cathedral, I should go to the castle").

Exactly the same constraints would hold for the lexicalised relative adverb construction: compare (65a-c), (67) and (68) with the (rather artificial)

(69) a. I will see him at the time at which he will come

⇐== [I see him AT THE TIME$_t$ [he come AT THE TIME$_t$ /FUTURE/] /FUTURE/]

but

b. *I will see him {after / at} the time at which he came
⇐== [I see him AT/AFTER THE TIME$_t$ [he come AT THE TIME$_t$ /PAST/] /FUTURE/]

c. *I saw him {after / at / before} the time at which he will come
⇐== [I see him AT/AFTER/BEFORE THE TIME$_t$ [he come AT THE TIME$_t$ /FUTURE/] /PAST/]

d. One should go to the castle after any time at which one has visited the cathedral
⇐== [One should go to the castle AFTER ANY TIME$_{t_{1...n}}$ [one visit the cathedral AT ANY TIME$_{t_{1...n}}$ /UNIV/] /UNIV/]

but

e. I should go to the castle after the time at which I have visited the cathedral[4]
⇐≠= [I should go to the castle AFTER THE TIME [I visit the cathedral AT THE TIME$_t$ /PAST/] /FUTURE/]

The selection of verb-forms in temporal when-sentences must then be consonant with an overall temporal axis, which must be represented by the appearance of the same abstract temporal adverbial in the underlying structure of both constituent clauses.

Aspectual. I have already discussed the close interrelation between lexical aspect, morphological aspect and surface adverbials of time in simple sentences. Now I turn to an observation of how these elements also play their part in when-sentences.

I will first consider the case of a when-sentence in which the verb-forms of both matrix clause and when-clause are unmarked for morphological aspect. Four basic lexical aspectual configurations are available: PUNCTUAL/PUNCTUAL, PUNCTUAL/DURATIVE, DURATIVE/PUNCTUAL and DURATIVE/DURATIVE (the first element in these pairs refers to the matrix clause verb-stem, the second to the when-clause verb-stem). When there is no additional overt adverbial modification, the precedence-relation between matrix clause and when-clause will be SIM in the last three cases; thus:

(70) a. He will arrive (PUNCTUAL) when she is asleep (DURATIVE)
(arrive simultaneous with be asleep)
b. He will be asleep (DURATIVE) when she arrives (PUNCTUAL)
(be asleep simultaneous with arrive)
c. He will be asleep (DURATIVE) when she is at home (DURATIVE)
(be asleep simultaneous with be at home)

It is the PUNCTUAL/PUNCTUAL configuration that produces examples like (3a) which may have either a SIM or a POST reading. This same pattern - a SIM reading for any aspectual configuration which has DURATIVE as one of its terms, and a reading potentially ambiguous between SIM and POST for a PUNCTUAL/PUNCTUAL aspectual configuration - can clearly be observed when morphological aspectual phenomena are involved, as in MSp[5]. An Imp inflection in combination with either a PUNCTUAL or a DURATIVE aspectual lexical stem yields a derived DURATIVE aspectual reading, and for any configuration of verb-forms in which Imp is one of the terms, a SIM precedence-relation is normally the rule. Similarly, there is an inevitable problem with a PUNCTUAL/PUNCTUAL morphological configuration (Pret/Pret). A verb-stem which is lexically DURATIVE combines with a PUNCTUAL inflection to yield either a derived DURATIVE value (susceptible of combination with a DURATIVE 'fixed term' adverbial as in (71a) or a derived PUNCTUAL value which represents the 'initiative phase' of the event or state (susceptible of combination with a PUNCTUAL adverbial as in (71b):

(71) a. Estuvo (stem DURATIVE, inflection PUNCTUAL) una hora (DURATIVE) en el bar
b. Poco después de medianoche (PUNCTUAL) estuvo (stem DURATIVE, inflection PUNCTUAL) en el bar

The possible combinations in when-sentences, together with acceptable and unacceptable readings, are given in (72):

(72) a. Se fue ella cuando llegó él (lexical PUNCTUAL/PUNCTUAL)
AFTER llegó (PUNCTUAL) él, se fue (PUNCTUAL) ella
AT THE SAME TIME AS llegó (PUNCTUAL) él, se fue (PUNCTUAL) ella

b. Trabajó ella cuando se fue él (lexical DURATIVE/PUNCTUAL)

AFTER se fue (PUNCTUAL) él, trabajó (PUNCTUAL inceptive phase) ella

AFTER se fue (PUNCTUAL) él, trabajó (DURATIVE fixed time) ella

?AT THE SAME TIME AS se fue (PUNCTUAL) él, trabajó (PUNCTUAL inceptive phase) ella

?AT THE SAME TIME AS se fue (PUNCTUAL) él, trabajó (DURATIVE fixed time) ella

c. Se fue él cuando trabajó ella (lexical PUNCTUAL/DURATIVE)

AFTER trabajó (PUNCTUAL inceptive phase) ella, se fue (PUNCTUAL) él

*AFTER trabajó (DURATIVE fixed time) ella, se fue (PUNCTUAL) él

?AT THE SAME TIME AS trabajó (PUNCTUAL inceptive phase) ella, se fue (PUNCTUAL) él

?AT THE SAME TIME AS trabajó (DURATIVE fixed time) ella, se fue (PUNCTUAL) él

d. Trabajó él cuando se quedó ella allí (lexical DURATIVE/DURATIVE)

AFTER se quedó (PUNCTUAL inceptive phase) ella allí, trabajó (PUNCTUAL inceptive phase) él

*AFTER se quedó (DURATIVE fixed time) ella allí, trabajó (PUNCTUAL inceptive phase) él

*AFTER se quedó (DURATIVE fixed time) ella allí, trabajó (DURATIVE fixed time) él

AFTER se quedó (PUNCTUAL inceptive phase) ella allí, trabajó (DURATIVE fixed time) él

?AT THE SAME TIME AS se quedó (PUNCTUAL inceptive phase) ella allí, trabajó (PUNCTUAL inceptive phase) él

?AT THE SAME TIME AS se quedó (PUNCTUAL inceptive phase) ella allí, trabajó (DURATIVE fixed time) él

?AT THE SAME TIME AS se quedó (DURATIVE fixed time) ella allí, trabajó (PUNCTUAL inceptive phase) él

AT THE SAME TIME AS se quedó (DURATIVE fixed time) ella allí, trabajó (DURATIVE fixed time) él

POST precedence-relation readings are possible for a Pret/Pret sequence, then, when the when-clause verb has derived PUNCTUAL value. A SIM precedence-relation reading is possible either when both matrix- and when-clause verbs have PUNCTUAL value for both stem and inflection, or when both matrix- and when-clause verbs have derived DURATIVE value. Derived PUNCTUAL/DURATIVE sequences may therefore yield POST readings; it can be seen that in such examples, lexical aspectual properties override morphological aspectual properties.

Syntactic constraints

In many cases, the verb-forms of the constituent clauses of when-sentences are those that would be found in the corresponding simple sentences in isolation:

(73) When he arrived, I saw him
     corresponds to
     He arrived. I saw him.

However, in FUTURE-referring when-clauses, there is considerable variation in usage from language to language. MFr apparently has at first sight no special requirement:

(74) Quand il arrivera, je le verrai
     corresponds to
     Il arrivera. Je le verrai.

However, in MFr, the expression of FUTURE is restricted to verb-forms which are morphologically [+Fut]; although, as we have seen in Chapter 2, Pres can have FUTURE reference in a simple sentence (il arrive demain), Fr does not allow

(75) *Quand il arrive, je le verrai

MSp requires PresSubj in these clauses:

(76) Cuando llegue, lo veré

and MIt requires either Fut or PresSubj:

(77) Quando {arriverà / arrivi} lo vedrai

In English, by contrast, the verb cannot be Fut:

(78) When he {comes / *will come} I will see him

The use of verb-forms with FUTURE-referring when-clauses hence depends exclusively on the FUTURE time-reference of the clause; the verb-form of the matrix-clause is unaffected.

Another area in which there is not necessarily a correspondence between when-sentence usage and simple sentence usage is the use of [+Perf] forms. As we saw in Chapter 2, the [+Perf] forms imply a time-reference of ANTERIORITY to another reference-point, which in the case of when-sentences is supplied by the when-clause for a [+Perf] form in the matrix-clause and vice versa. The use of a [+Perf] form in a simple sentence in isolation, is, as we saw, often strange. In all the languages with which we are concerned, however, the [+Perf] forms are used in when-sentences to mark precedence-relations: [+Perf] forms in the when-clause are optionally used to mark a POST precedence-relation:

(79) Fr: Quand il {était arrivé / est arrivé} il a diné
Sp: Cuando {hubo llegado / llegó} cenó
It: Quando {era arrivato / è arrivato} cenò

and obligatorily in the matrix-clause to mark an ANT precedence-relation:

(80) Fr: Quand il est arrivé, nous étions partis
Sp: Cuando llegó, habíamos salido
It: Quando è arrivato, eravamo partiti

The insertion of [+Perf] forms into the constituent clauses of when-sentences can therefore depend crucially on the precedence-relation contracted between when-clause and matrix-clause. In the case of a [+Perf] form in the matrix-clause this need not create a special problem, since the [+Perf] form simply marks ANTERIORITY to an adverbial, which is represented by a when-clause: such a precedence-relation between verb-form and adverbial will have to be catered for in the generation of a [+Perf] form in simple sentences, therefore. But in the case of a [+Perf] form in a when-clause, the precedence-relation between when-clause and matrix-clause seems the only factor on which it can depend.

The factors which led me in Chapter 4 to propose the modular insertion of sequences of tense in conditional sentences do not seem to apply to when-sentences, despite the close relation between matrix-clause verb-form and when-clause verb-form. There is no restriction on the verb-forms that may appear in the matrix-clause of a when-sentence, as there is on the apodosis form of a conditional sentence, and the matrix-clause of a when-sentence is not so exceptional in isolation, either semantically or morphologically, that it has to be understood as part of a whole when-sentence structure. The matrix-clause of a sentence like When we had finished, we left, for instance, has in isolation exactly the same semantic properties as it has in the complex sentence: it has the same time-reference (PAST) and the same truth-value (positive), and it is the same speech-act type (declarative). There appears to be no reason, therefore, why the verb-form of the matrix-clause of a when-sentence cannot be inserted first and the verb-form of the when-clause be considered as 'dependent' upon it, to be selected in accordance with the time-referential and precedence-relation properties of the sentence as a whole according to the constraints I have noted in this Chapter.

NOTES

1. Cf. Gildersleeve and Lodge (1895:§581). An 'inverse-when' sentence of the form "X, when Y" corresponds semantically to the 'ordinary' when-sentence "When X, Y", when having the value "and then", thus (2) is the equivalent of When he (had) pushed the car to the edge of the cliff, it fell to the rocks below or He pushed the car to the edge of the cliff and then it fell to the rocks below.

2. The hypothesis that MSp cuando may be treated as a relative adverbial is put forward by Cressey (1969). Whilst I am in agreement with his conclusions, I find his account of the data over-simplistic: in particular, he does not mention the question of precedence-relation in when-sentences and rather summarily dismisses the problem of the appearance of [+Subj] forms in FUTURE-referring Sp when-sentences.

3. This underlying structure follows, in an abbreviated fashion, Seuren's (1969:128-30) account of the comparative.

4. Have visited can of course have FUTURE reference in English, in which case the sentence is acceptable.

5. The examples could be paralleled in English, where the Continuous forms have much in common with [-Punc] in Romance.

Chapter Six

CONDITIONAL SENTENCES FROM CLASSICAL LATIN TO MODERN ROMANCE

In this Chapter and the following Chapter, a number of abbreviatory descriptive conventions will be used. Sequences of verb-forms are represented in the form SI/SE or QUAND/QUANDO/CUANDO VF_1/VF_2, where VF_1 is the protasis or when-clause verb and VF_2 is the apodosis or matrix clause verb. A double broken line beneath a form (e.g., ImpSubj) indicates that the form is syntactically determined by factors which are unconnected with the conditional or when-sentence in question. A straight unbroken line beneath a verb-form (e.g., Imp) indicates that the form is a modal auxiliary. Ø indicates that there is no finite surface verb-form present.

CONDITIONAL SENTENCES IN CLASSICAL LATIN

Conditional sentences in CL may be classified, according to the parameters identified in Chapter 4, as in Table 6.1. It may be seen that there is in CL a clear match between form and function in the system of conditional sentences. COUNTERFACTUAL sequences use exclusively [+Subj] forms; OPEN sequences exclusively [-Subj] forms. In the majority of sequences there is symmetry between protasis and apodosis in the sense that the same verb-form is used in each clause; the only exception to this being in the FUTURE OPEN category where there is an apparent ban on Fut in the protasis and SI Pres/Fut is the pattern encountered. We should notice, however, that FutPerf, the [+Perf] counterpart of Fut, may appear in the protasis, and in fact is normally required when the protasis event or state is ANTERIOR to the apodosis event or state. There are nevertheless several attested variants of these patterns in CL. A number of COUNTERFACTUAL examples with a [+Subj] form in the protasis and a [-Subj] form in the apodosis are attested: in several of these it seems that the 'protasis' has been added as an afterthought, in parentheses, so to speak, e.g.:

(1) Eum contumeliis onerasti quem patris loco, si ulla in te pietas esset, colere debebas. (Cic., Ph., 2.99, in Woodcock (1959:156))
"You loaded with insults him whom you should have reverenced as a father, (had there been any natural feeling in you)."

and in OPEN conditionals, a [+Subj] form in the apodosis may express UNIVERSAL reference, e.g.:

(2) Si quis collegam appellasset, ab eo ad quem venerat ita discedebat ut paeniteret non prioris decreto stetisse. (Livy 3.38.3, in Woodcock (152))
"If anyone appealed to another member of the board, he used to come away from the one regretting that he had not abided by the decree of the former."

Within the CL period we may detect a shift in the COUNTERFACTUAL system prior to the establishment of the pattern shown in Table 6.1. Examples from early CL are found in which the SI PresSubj/PresSubj sequence is used with PRESENT reference, e.g.:

(3) Nam si curent, bene bonis sit, male malis, quod nunc abest (Ennius, Tr. 271, in Woodcock (1959:153))
"For if they cared, it would go well with the good and ill with the bad, which is not now the case[1]."

It may be too that the sequence SI ImpSubj/ImpSubj was used with PAST reference, though opinions are not unanimous[2]. Nutting (1925:150-63) discusses a number of examples of SI ImpSubj/PlupSubj in which ImpSubj appears to have PAST and PRESENT reference, e.g. (150):

(4) Hoc si Romae fieri posset, certe aliqua ratione expugnasset iste... (Cic., Verr., 2.2.130)
"If this were/had been possible in Rome, certainly he would somehow have pushed [it] through..."

(5) Nolite existumare maiores nostros armis rem publicam ex parva magnam fecisse. Si ita esset, multo pulcherrimam eam nos haberemus... (Sallust, Bell. Cat., 52.19)

"... For if it had been so, we would consider it very fine..."

If we suppose that SI ImpSubj/ImpSubj was used with PAST reference at some stage in the history of CL, we could visualise the following structural change in the COUNTERFACTUAL system:

FUTURE	SI PresSubj/PresSubj		SI PresSubj/PresSubj
PRESENT		>	SI ImpSubj/ImpSubj
PAST	SI ImpSubj/ImpSubj		SI PlupSubj/PlupSubj

This shift may be described as the addition of a degree of morphological 'pastness' to verb-form sequences: thus [-Past] sequences become [+Past] and [+Past] sequences become [+Past, +Perf].

CONDITIONAL SENTENCES IN EARLY ROMANCE

Protases with FUTURE reference

In OFr and OIt, conditional sentences with FUTURE-referring protases fall into two easily recognisable categories. The first is that of FUTURE OPEN condition, and is expressed in both languages most commonly by a sequence of [-Past, -Subj] forms:

(6) Se je me lais caïr, je briserai le col... (Auc, 16.12-13)

"If I fall, I will break my neck..."

(7) ... ma se io non ne vado, io sarò tutta sera aspettato a cena, e farò villania. (Dec, 110)

"... but if I do not go, they will wait dinner for me all evening, and I shall be a nuisance."

The second category is that of ANTICIPATED COUNTERFACTUAL condition, which in OFr is most frequently expressed by a SE Imp/Cond sequence:

(8) - Sire, fait ele, se vos cou faissiés, je l'iroie querre, por vos et por li que je molt aim. (Auc, 40.20-1)

"'Sire,' she said, 'if you did that, I would go and seek her, for your sake and for the sake of her that I love dearly.'"

and in OIt by a SE ImpSubj/Cond sequence:

(9) - Forza mi potrebbe fare il re, ma di mio consentimento mai da me, se non quanto onesto fosse, aver non potrebbe. (Dec, 154)

"The king could take me by force, but unless his intentions were honourable, he could never have his way with my consent."

The existence of two different sequence-of-tense patterns cannot in itself be taken as evidence of the existence of two different presuppositional categories of FUTURE condition in OFr and OIt. The danger of applying such a criterion will become apparent when we look at the rather different OSp situation below. Of course, we may consider it reasonable to hypothesise immediately that since the distinction between what we have called OPEN and ANTICIPATED COUNTERFACTUAL conditions shows up with similar sequence-of-tense patterns in MFr and MIt, there existed a parallel distinction in the medieval languages. But close scrutiny of the texts for information concerning the semantic value of examples gives us a more trustworthy justification for our descriptive categories. If in OFr we consider the 13 examples of SE Imp/Cond with FUTURE reference that appear in Erec (the texts in which these are most numerous, and therefore the texts from which we may expect to draw the most general conclusions), it is remarkable how all may be matched with 'marked' speech-act types or pragmatic contexts. They may be roughly categorised as follows:

A. A strong implication that the protasis is going to have a negative truth-value, e.g.:

(10) Mançonge sanbleroit trop granz,
Se je disoie que cinc çanz
Tables fussent mises a tire
An un palés, ja nel quier dire... (6925-8)

"It would seem too great a lie if I said that five hundred tables were set in rows in a palace, [so I will not say it...]"

B. Strong pleas for mercy, e.g.:

(11) Merci! Ne m'ocirre tu pas.[!]
Des que tu m'as outré et pris;
Ja n'an avroies los ne pris.
Se tu des or mes me tochoies,
Trop grant vilenie feroies. (994-8)

"Mercy! Do not kill me, now that you have overcome me and taken me; you would have neither praise nor glory if you touched me any more; you would be doing too great a villainy."

C. Deferential invitation, e.g.:

(12) Se vos preniiez mon conroi,
Vos me feriiez grant enor... (1264-5)

"If you would accept my hospitality you would do me great honour."

D. Threats, e.g.:

(13) Mes tart vandroiz au repantir,
Se voir ne me reconoissiez. (2538-9)

"But you would come to regret it later if you did not reveal the truth to me."

E. Fear, e.g.:

(14) Mes se mes sire estoit or morz,
De moi seroit nus reconforz;
Morte seroie et maubaillie. (2971-3)

"But if my lord were killed, I would have no comfort: I should be killed and ill used."

F. Concern, e.g.:

(15) Mes se vos veoie antrepris
Ou de vostre cors anpirié,
J'an avroie le cuer irié. (5624-6)

"But if I saw you captured or your body injured, I should be distressed in my heart."

G. Irony, e.g.:

(16) Se la reïne le veoit,
Je cuit qu'ele le conoistroit. (1109-10)

"If the queen were to see him I think she would know him [because the approaching knight was the cause of affront to her and her maid]."

In OIt, the text with the most frequent occurrence of the SE ImpSubj/Cond sequence is Dec. There does not appear to be the same range of pragmatic context here as in OFr Erec; all the examples seem to fall into the first category described above, and carry the presupposition that the protasis is highly unlikely or unexpected, e.g.:

(17) Egli non mi si lascia credere che i dolori de' suoi sventurati accidenti l'abbian tanto lasciata viva; ma, se pur fosse, sommamente mi saria caro... (125)

"I cannot believe that the pains of her unfortunate troubles have left her alive; but, if it turned out that she were alive, I should be very glad..."

(18) ... gran villania sarebbe la mia se io ogni cosa che a grado ti fosse non m'ingegnassi di fare... (93)

"... I would be most impolite if I did not set about doing everything that was your pleasure..."

In OSp, we find three types of FUTURE-referring conditional, the protasis verb being Pres, FutSubj or ImpSubj^{se}. Those with ImpSubj^{se} in the protasis seem to exhibit clear ANTICIPATED COUNTERFACTUAL value, e.g.:

(19) Mas dim agora sis acaeciesse, lo que por ventura non sera, que tormenta se leuantasse en la mar, por que tu uiesses la muert a oio, ¿que uoluntad te semeia que auries estonce...? (PCG, 41.12L)

"But tell me, if it happened (which happily it may not) that a storm arose at sea, and you came face to face with death, what do you think your desire would be then?"

Conditional sentences with FutSubj in the protasis seem to incline more towards OPEN conditional value than towards ANTICIPATED COUNTERFACTUAL value, although some cases are far from clear. Representative examples are:

(20) sy muy sorda non fuere, oyra nuestro apellido. (LBA, 1196d)

"Unless she is very deaf, she will hear our cry."
[The expectation is almost FACTUAL]

(21) 'Si lo fizieredes, Çid, lo quc avedes fablado,
tanto quanto yo biva sere dent maravillado.'
(Cid, 1037-8)

"'If you do what you have said, Cid, as long as I live I will marvel at it.'"
[Closer to ANTICIPATED COUNTERFACTUAL: the Count may not believe the Cid, but the latter has issued a promise.]

As can be seen from Table 6.3, both FutSubj and Pres in the protasis of conditional sentences in OSp normally combine with Fut in the apodosis. In Cid and Mil, FutSubj is more favoured than Pres, and in LBA, numbers are approximately equal. ImpSubj^{se} in the protasis, on the other hand, like ImpSubj in OFr and OIt, normally combines with Cond in the apodosis. This suggests that even from a purely morphological point of view, the values of Pres and Fut Subj in the protasis are comparable in OSp.

Variants

In OIt, the protasis verb-form of the FUTURE OPEN conditional may be either Pres or Fut. The texts vary in their preferences; in Inf Fut is used infrequently, whereas in Nov and Dec it is substantially attested, examples with Fut being approximately half as numerous as examples with Pres. It is difficult to perceive any appreciable semantic difference between the two types, as this example from Nov shows:

(22) Quale di queste due è il meglio? Se tu dirai: Quella, che voll'essere consolata, dirai il vero. Dunque, perchè piangi? Se mi di': Piango il figliuolo mio, perchè la sua bontà mi facea onorare, dico che non piangi [lui, ma piangi] il danno tuo. (139)

"Which of these two is better? If you say, 'The one who was willing to be consoled', you will be right. So, why weep? If you say, 'I am weeping for my son, because his goodness honoured me', I say that you are not weeping for him, but rather for your own loss."

However, it seems that sometimes Fut in the protasis is motivated by a 'balancing' with the apodosis verb-form: as will be seen from the frequency tables, Fut in the protasis combines most readily with another Fut in the apodosis, whereas Pres in the protasis will combine with Fut, Imper and Pres Subj in the apodosis; furthermore, in four of the ten examples of SE Fut/Fut in Nov the lexical verb-stem is identical in protasis and apodosis, as it is in (22). Another possible motivation for the use of Fut in the protasis is the ATTENUATION modality associated with Fut (see above, p.64), e.g.:

(23) ... se tu ti vorrai bene ricordare, tu vedrai ben che io sono il tuo Ricciardo di Chinzica. (Dec, 173)

"... if you will remember well, you will see that I am your Ricciardo di Chinzica." [Compare the use of Fut in my English gloss.]

Indeed, there is one example from Dec involving a protasis Fut which strictly must have PRESENT reference:

(24) ... di che voi, se savie sarete, ottimamente vi guarderete. (81)

"... and if you are wise, you will take great care."

Fut is not found in the protases of FUTURE OPEN conditionals in OSp. In the OFr texts examined, there is one apparent example:

(25) Si ceo avi[e]nt cum jeo vus di,
[E] nus serum issi trahi,
Ne m'en puis mie departir,
Que mei nen estuce murir. (Marie, Y, 207-10)

"If it happens as I tell you, [and] we are so betrayed, I shall not be able to leave here for I shall have to die."

But there are problems with this example. Ewert (179) suggests that serum could be read as seium, under which reading it would be the verb-form of a second conjoined protasis, which would be regularly [+Subj]; compare:

(26) S'ele refuse ma prïere
E tant seit orgoilluse e fiere,
Dunc m'estuet [il] a doel murir
E de cest mal tuz jurs languir.
(Marie, G, 403-6)

"If she refuses my plea and is so proud and haughty, then I will have to die of grief and suffer always from this wound."

(Of course, the conjectural [e] in line 208 of (25) could regularise the example, nus serum issi trahi then being construable as an apodosis; but this would lead to a shortfall of one syllable in the line.) It is doubtful in fact whether Fut is acceptable as a protasis verb-form at all in OFr. Anglade (1965:210) cites the following SI Fut/Fut example:

(27) Si je monterai el ciel, tu iluec iés;
si je descendrai en enfer, tu iés.
(Oxford Psalter, 138.7)

"If I go up into heaven thou art there; if I go down into hell, thou art there also."

with the comment that the pattern scarcely exists outside translations from Latin, and that even there it is rare. (Compare the Vulgate Si ascendero in caelum, tu illic es; si descendero in infernum, ades (SI FutPerf/Pres).) Even Gamillscheg (1957:718), who would no doubt have preferred there to be convincing examples of protasis Fut in order to substantiate his theory of the CL FutPerf's replacement by the Romance Fut, has to admit that there are no examples of genuine conditionals with Fut in the protasis, although he quotes several which have a RATIONAL reading.

In ANTICIPATED COUNTERFACTUAL sequence-of-tense patterns, we have already seen how OFr, in preferring an exclusively [-Subj] sequence, differs from OSp and OIt, which both have ImpSubj as the protasis verb-form. ImpSubj in the protasis is attested in OFr, however, although there is considerable variation in frequency from text to text. In Rol the one and only example of an ANTICIPATED COUNTERFACTUAL conditional has the sequence SE ImpSubj/Cond; in Erec there is one example of SE ImpSubj/Ø as against sixteen of SE Imp/Cond or other form; SE Imp/Cond similarly dominates in Auc; in Marie, however, SE ImpSubj/Cond seems to be the favoured sequence. Sometimes it is difficult to say whether examples are FUTURE- or PRESENT-referring, e.g.:

(28) Aprés parlat et dist: 'De quei
Sui en estrif e en effrei?
Uncor ne sai ne n'ai seü

S'ele fereit de mei son dru;
Mes jeo savrai hastivement.
S'ele sentist ceo ke jeo sent,
Jeo perdrei[e] ceste dolur. (Marie, Eq, 91-7)

"Then he spoke and said, 'Why am I in distress and fear? I do not yet know nor do I already know whether she will take me as her lover; but I will quickly find out. If she feels/should turn out to feel what I feel, I would lose this pain."

but there are clear cases where FUTURE reference is the only feasible interpretation:

(29) 'Se veïssum Rollant, einz qu'il fust mort,
Ensembl'od lui i durriums granz colps.'
(Rol, 1804-5)

"'If we saw Roland before he were dead, we would give great blows there beside him.'"

In all three languages, both the 'regular' and the 'variant' sequence-of-tense patterns are [-Past] for FUTURE OPEN conditionals and [+Past] for ANTICIPATED COUNTERFACTUAL conditionals. We also find, however, 'mixed' forms, which can be interpreted as starting out as one semantic type and then changing to the other in mid-stream. The following examples all show the sequence SE Pres/Cond, and hence appear to have OPEN protases but ANTICIPATED COUNTERFACTUAL apodoses:

(30) ... dites li qu'il a une beste en ceste foret, ... et s'il l'i puet prendre, il n'en donroit mie un menbre por cent mars d'or, non por cinc cens ne por nul avoir. (Auc, 18.18-21)

"... tell him that there is a wild animal in this forest,... and that if he can catch it, he would not give away a limb of it for a hundred gold marks, nor for five hundred, nor for anything."

(31) "E si encubre del todo su ferida e su dolor,
"si ayuda non demanda por auer śalut mjjor,
"por ventura me vernja otro peligro peor,
"morria de todo en todo: nunca vy cuyta mayor."
(LBA, 593)

"'And if all its wound and pain is covered; if it does not seek help in order to have better health; perhaps another greater danger will come upon me, I will completely die: never has greater sorrow been seen.'"

(32) ... se io li le cheggio, darèbbemelo egli? (Nov, 72)

"... if I ask him, would he give it to me?"

This 'mixing' appears to be much more common in the OFr texts than in either OSp or OIt texts, and may reflect the greater ease with which OFr uses the [-Past] tenses with the reference of their [+Past] counterparts (e.g., Pres with the function of either Imp or Pret, as a 'historic' Present).

Another reason for the breaking of [-Past] or [+Past] sequence is ellipsis. Superficially, the following example has the sequence SE Pres/Pret:

(33) Se vus estes pruz e curteis,
Emperere ne quens ne reis
N'ot unkes tant joie ne bien...
(Marie, L, 113-5)

"If you are prudent and courteous, no emperor, count or king ever had such joy or wealth..."

The full meaning of the sentence may be taken, however, as, "No emperor, count or king ever had such joy or wealth [as you will have] if you are prudent and courteous...", and hence the sentence represents a potentially SE Pres/Fut sequence.

Protases with TRANSPOSED FUTURE reference

OFr has a large number of possible patterns in this category, due to the apparently optional nature of [Past]-AGREEMENT. [+Past] forms are sometimes found in both protasis and apodosis, e.g.:

(34) Enne m'eüstes vos en covent que quant je pris les armes et j'alai a l'estor, que se Dix me ramenoit sain et sauf, que vos me lairiés Nicolete ma douce amie tant veïr que j'arois parlé a li deus paroles ou trois, et que je l'aroie une fois baisie m'eüstes vos en covent... (Auc, 10.48-52)

"Did you not give me your word that when I took up arms and went to combat, that if God brought me back safe and sound, that you would let me see Nicolette my sweet love long enough for me to say two or three words to her, and for me to kiss her once - did you not give me your word...?"

or to neither, e.g.:

(35) Bien jure Diu et son non,
Ja ne prendera baron,
S'ele n'a son ameor,
Que tant desire. (Auc, 39.33-6)

"And swore by God and his name, that she would never take a man if she did not have the love of him that she so much desired."

or to one but not the other, e.g.:

(36) Par sun message li manda
Que, si li plest, el l'amera.
(Marie, M, 27-8)

"By her message she sent him [word] that, if it pleased him, she would love him."

It is interesting to observe the choice of [+Past] forms in the embedded conditional. In addition to SE Imp/Cond, as in (34), SE ImpSubj/Cond and SE ImpSubj/ImpSubj are also encountered:

(37) La dame l'en ad mercié
E dit que mut li sot bon gre,
E si de ceo l'aseürast
Que pur autre ne la lessast,
Hastivement purchacereit
A sun seignur que mort sereit;
Legier sereit a purchacier,
Pur ceo k'il li vousist aidier.
(Marie, Eq, 229-36)

"The lady thanked him for this and said that she was very grateful to him, and if he would assure her that he would not leave her for another she would quickly arrange for her lord's despatch; it would be very easy to bring about provided he would help her."

(38) An cuer et an panser li vint,
Que il ira la dame querre,
....
Se li cuens ne li vossist randre
Volantiers le cors et la dame,
Tot meïst a feu et a flame.
(Erec, 4956-7; 4962-4)

"It came into his heart and mind that he would go and seek the lady... [and that] if the count should not wish to give him freely the body and the lady he would put everything to fire and flame."

SE Imp/Cond would seem to be the expected [+Past] equivalent of the FUTURE OPEN SE Pres/Fut. SE Imp Subj/Cond is identical with the FUTURE ANTICIPATED COUNTERFACTUAL sequence, and has undergone no modification as a result of [Past]-AGREEMENT. SE Imp Subj/ImpSubj is associated with PRESENT COUNTERFACTUAL conditions, however, and is not the [+Past] equivalent of any FUTURE-referring conditional sequence in OFr. We may conjecture that the SE Imp Subj/ImpSubj pattern is attracted to TRANSPOSED FUTURE conditions because of its [+Past] sequence, and possibly also because of its close relation to SE ImpSubj/Cond, which is also a PRESENT COUNTERFACTUAL sequence.

In OSp and OIt, [Past]-AGREEMENT invariably applies, and in both languages the preferred form is SI/SE ImpSubj(se)/Cond. In the OSp texts, there is only one example of a TRANSPOSED FUTURE condition which does not have ImpSubj in the protasis: SE Cond/Cond in PCG, where it is likely that the unusual [+Fut] form in the protasis expresses an ATTENUATION modality:

(39) Ella respuso les que aurie su acuerdo si lo podrie fazer... (PCG, 35.11L)

"She replied to them that she would agree if she could..."

Similarly, in the OIt texts there is only one such example, a SE Imp/Imp sequence from Dec:

(40) ...ma disse lui aver potuto da alcuno de' fanti della casa sapere la qualità della camera e in simil manera avere avute le cose; per che, se altro non dicea, non gli parea che questo bastasse a dovere aver vinto. (Dec, 163-4)

"... but he said that he could have got to know about the room from one of the servants of the house and got hold of the things in the same way; so that if he did not say anything else, he did not think that was enough for him to have won [the bet]."

Examples of TRANSPOSED FUTURE conditionals are sufficiently numerous in OSp PCG and OIt Dec for us to assert that the [+Subj] form was favoured, if not used exclusively, in the protasis of these conditional types, and that hence the sequence-of-tense pattern in TRANSPOSED FUTURE OPEN conditionals and ANTICIPATED COUNTERFACTUAL conditionals was the same; furthermore, that the distinction between OPEN and ANTICIPATED COUNTERFACTUAL is practically neutralised in the TRANSPOSED structure. And although, as we have seen, OFr shows more variation in sequence-of-tense type, it is similarly very difficult to show that a distinction between OPEN and ANTICIPATED COUNTERFACTUAL condition existed in the TRANSPOSED category.

Protases with PRESENT reference

PRESENT OPEN conditions need not detain us, since, as the Tables show, Pres is invariably the protasis verb-form. In COUNTERFACTUAL conditionals, the most frequent pattern in OSp and OIt is SE ImpSubj(se)/Cond, e.g.:

(41) "sy non fuese tan mj vešina non seria tan penado." (LBA, 602d)

"'If she were not my neighbour I would not be so grieved.'"

(42) se fosse amico il re de l'universo,
noi pregheremmo lui de la tua pace...
(Inf, 5.91-2)

"If the King of the universe were our friend,
we would pray him for your peace..."

OFr does not have such a regular pattern, however. Except in Rol, which has no examples of PRESENT COUNTERFACTUAL conditionals[3], the most frequently encountered pattern is SE Imp/Cond, e.g.:

(43) Se j'estoie fix a roi,
S'afferriés vos bien a moi,
Suer, douce amie! (Auc, 25.12-14)

"If I were the son of a king, you would suit me well, sister, sweet love!"

but SE ImpSubj/ImpSubj is substantially attested (along with SE Imp/Cond) in Erec and Marie, e.g.:

(44) "Sire! mal ne dolor n'eüsse,
Se an grant dotance ne fusse
De mon seignor..." (Erec, 4177-9)

"'Sire, I should have no trouble or grief if I were not in great distress for my lord...'"

and there is one example of SE ImpSubj/Cond in Marie:

(45) Cest' amur sereit convenable
Si vus amdui feussez estable.
(Marie, G, 451-2)

"This love would be fitting if you were both constant."

OFr therefore differs from OSp and OIt on two counts: first, because of the variety of sequence-of-tense patterns available to express PRESENT COUNTERFACTUALity, and second, because one of these sequences (SE ImpSubj/ImpSubj) is not also capable of expressing FUTURE ANTICIPATED COUNTERFACTUALity.

TRANSPOSED PRESENT conditionals are rare in the texts examined. On the other hand, OSp PCG has two examples which contrast as respectively OPEN and COUNTERFACTUAL. The sequences concerned are SE Imp/Imp, which may be taken as the [+Past] equivalent of SI Pres/Pres:

(46) La reyna Dido... repuso les assi: que si aquella uida que ella e los suyos fazien no les semeiaua buena... quel plazie, e que bien consintrie que casassen. (PCG, 37.34R)

"Queen Dido replied to them thus: that if the life which her people were leading did not seem good to them... it did not matter to her, and she would consent to her people marrying [others]."

and SI ImpSubj^{se}/Cond, which is identical to the normal PRESENT COUNTERFACTUAL sequence:

(47) Los sabios antiguos... touieron que menguarien en sos fechos et en su lealtad si tan bien no lo quisiessen pora los que auien de uenir como pora si mismos... (PCG, 3.3L)

"The ancient philosophers... held that they would be lacking in their work and their loyalty if they did not wish [knowledge] for those who were to come as well as for themselves."

Protases with PAST reference

Any PAST-referring tense is admissible in the protases of PAST OPEN conditionals; for OFr this includes Pres, but OSp and OIt appear not to have this possibility. PAST COUNTERFACTUAL conditionals offer a considerable number of sequence-of-tense types in all three languages, though the most regular picture of usage emerges from OIt. Here, PlupSubj is the commonest protasis form, and SE PlupSubj/CondPerf is the most frequent combination in all three texts, e.g.:

(48) S'i' fossi stato dal foco coperto,
gittato mi sarei tra lor di sotto,
e credo che 'l dottor l'avria sofferto...
(Inf, 16.46-8)

"If I had been sheltered from the fire, I would have thrown myself among them below, and I think the Teacher would have permitted it."

Examples from OIt with ImpSubj in the protasis of PAST COUNTERFACTUAL conditionals appear to be always of a special kind which involve the phrase se non fosse or equivalent, where essere acts as an existential or a 'clefting' verb, e.g.:

(49) Alza questa spada, e fedito l'avrebbe, se non fosse uno, che lo tenne per lo braccio. (Nov, 183)

"He draws [= drew] out the sword, and would have killed him, if there had not been someone who held him by the arm [= if someone had not held him by the arm]."

In OSp we are confronted with a bewildering array of PAST COUNTERFACTUAL sequences with little indication as to which might be said to be the preferred form at any one stage; though in Mil 12 examples of SI ImpSubj^{se}/Cond predominate, e.g.:

(50) Si tú no li dissiesses qe Sanctïago eras,
tú no li demostrasses sennal de mis veneras,
non dannarié su cuerpo con sus mismas tiseras,
nin yazdrié como yaze fuera por las carreras.
(Mil, 203)

"If you had not told him that you were Santiago, if you had not shown him a sign of my shells [pilgrims' shells, carried as an emblem of St. James], he would not have harmed himself with his own scissors, nor would he be lying as he is out here on the road."

and in LBA the sequence -ra/-ra is in the majority, e.g.:

(51) ssy dios, quando formo el om̃e, entendiera
que era mala cosa la muger, nonla diera
al om̃e por conpañera njn del nonla feziera...
(LBA, 109a-c)

"If God, when he made man, had thought that woman was a bad thing, he would not have given her as a companion to man nor made her from him..."

The sequence PlupSubj^{se}/CondPerf is found only in Mil, in one example:

(52) Si non fuesse Sïagrio   tan adelante ido,
si oviesse su lengua   un poco retenido,
non seriĒ enna ira   del Crïador caído,
ond dubdamos qe es   ¡mal peccado! perdido.
(Mil, 70)

"If Siagrio had not gone so far, if he had held his tongue a little, he would not have fallen into the wrath of the Creator, where we doubt not but that, evil sinner, he is lost."

ImpSubj^{se} appears in the protasis with a wide range of [+Past] apodosis forms besides Cond, all of which appear to have genuine PAST reference; thus we find SI ImpSubj^{se}/Imp:

(53) ... que yuan ya uençudos si por el non fuesse. (PCG, 47.10R)

"... they would have been conquered had it not been for him."

SI ImpSubj^{se}/-ra:

(54) Si yo non uvias   el moro te jugara mal...
(Cid, 3319)

"If I had not helped, the Moor would have used you ill..."

SI ImpSubj^{se}/PlupSubj^{ra}:

(55) si ante lo sopiessen   lo qe depués sopieron,
no li ovieran fecho   esso qe li fizieron.
(Mil, 148c-d)

"If they had known beforehand what they knew afterwards, they would not have done to him what they did do to him."

A similar range of apodosis possibilities is available with the less frequent protasis form Plup Subj^{se}.

In OFr, SE ImpSubj/ImpSubj is in every text the most frequent pattern, e.g.:

(56) 'S'altre le desist, ja semblast grant
mençunge.' (Rol, 1760)
"'If another had said this, it would have seemed a great lie.'"

SE PlupSubj/PlupSubj has a substantial attestation in Erec, and also occurs in Marie, e.g.:

(57) Si cele ne l'eüst tenue,
Ele fust a tere chaüe. (Marie, G, 767-8)
"If [the damsel] had not held her, she would have fallen to the ground."

PlupSubj does not appear in the protasis in Rol, and Brunot (1913:255) and Brunot and Bruneau (1949: §845.2) observe that the sequence SE PlupSubj/Plup Subj is rare before the 12th. Century. However, SE ImpSubj/PlupSubj[4] is attested in Rol:

(58) Se·m creïsez, venuz i fust mi sire...
(Rol, 1728)
"If you had paid me heed, my lord would have come..."

I identified only one example of a [-Subj] form in the protasis of a PAST COUNTERFACTUAL conditional: the sequence SE Plup/Cond:

(59) Se juré l'avoie et plevi,
Ne vos conteroie je mie
Sa biauté tote ne demie. (Erec, 3228-30)
"[Even] if I had sworn and pledged, I would not be able to tell you half how handsome he was."

But it is not absolutely clear that (59) does have PAST reference; it could be construed as FUTURE, as indeed must the three other examples of SE Plup/Cond in Erec.

No examples of TRANSPOSED PAST COUNTERFACTUAL conditonals were found in the OIt texts. In OFr, Marie yields one example of a SE ImpSubj/ImpSubj sequence, and Auc has an elliptical example with Plup in the protasis which can be read as PAST or FUTURE:

(60) Jure Diu de Maïsté,
Qu'il li poise plus assés
De Nicholete au vis cler,
Que de tot sen parenté,
S'il estoit a fin alés. (Auc, 35.5-9)

"He swore by Almighty God, that it grieved him much more about the fair-faced Nicolette than [it would have done] about all his kin, if they had come to an end."

Both OFr examples are COUNTERFACTUAL. In OSp, Mil offers one example of SI ImpSubj^{se}/Cond and LBA one of SI -ra/-ra; again, both are COUNTERFACTUAL. It appears that no morphological modification is made in either OFr or OSp as a result of [Past]-AGREEMENT.

Protases with UNIVERSAL reference

Conditional sentences with UNIVERSAL reference may be OPEN:

(61) Qu'autrement n'est fame esposee,
Se par son droit non n'est nomee.
(Erec, 2027-8)

"For otherwise a woman is not married, unless she is called by her proper name."

or what may be described as COUNTERFACTUAL or ANTICIPATED COUNTERFACTUAL (i.e., the protasis represents an impossible or unlikely condition), e.g.:

(62) - Veramente, se per ogni volta che elle a queste così fatte novelle attendono, nascesse loro un corno nella fronte, il quale desse testimonianza di ciò che fatto avessero, io mi credo che poche sarebber quelle che v'attendessero... (Dec, 161)

"Truly, if every time they were unfaithful a horn were to spring from their foreheads which would testify to what they had done, I believe there would be few who were unfaithful..."

The sequence-of-tense types encountered are essentially those of the PRESENT OPEN and PRESENT COUNTERFACTUAL categories we have already examined.

UNIVERSAL PAST conditionals usually have the sequence SI/SE Imp/Imp for OPEN conditions and the sequence corresponding to PAST COUNTERFACTUAL for COUNTERFACTUAL conditions; there is an interesting example from OIt Nov, however, in which there is variation between Imp and ImpSubj in a series of conditional sentences which presumably must have the same presuppositional structure:

(63) E convenia che, s'elli si volea affibbiar da mano, ch'elli mettesse lo filo nella cruna dell'ago; e se alle tre volte avvisasse che non lo vi mettesse, si li toglieano le donne tutto suo arnese e non li rendeano neente. E se mettea il filo alle tre volte, nell'ago, sì li rendeano l'arnese suo e donavanli di belli gioielli. (Nov, 118-9)

"And if he wanted to fasten his cuff (?), he had to put the thread through the eye of the needle; and if at the third attempt it turned out that he could not thread it, the ladies took all his possessions and gave him back nothing. And if he did put the thread into the needle at the third attempt, they gave him back his possessions and gave him beautiful jewels."

It is likely that the writer's mind here oscillates between OPEN and COUNTERFACTUAL presuppositions.

Pseudo-conditionals

FUTURE- and PRESENT-referring pseudo-conditionals utilise the same verb-form as genuine OPEN conditionals, and proliferation of examples therefore seems unnecessary. PAST-referring pseudo-conditionals, however, exhibit slightly different sequences, particularly striking being the appearance of Pret in the 'protasis', e.g.:

(64) e s'i' fui, dianzi, a la risposta muto,
fate i saper che 'l fei perché pensava
già ne l'error che m'avete soluto.
(Inf, 10.112-4)

"And if I was dumb at the reply before, tell him that it was because I was thinking in the erroneous way which you have resolved for me."

We may note incidentally that in OSp the -ra form is found in the 'protases' of pseudo-conditional sentences in texts where it is absent from the protases of genuine conditionals, e.g.:

(65) Si ante fora bueno, fo desende mejor...
(Mil, 493a)

"If he had been good before, he was better from then onwards..."

Polite Formulae

Several conditional sentences appear to have extremely weak conditional force whilst not being classifiable as pseudo-conditionals; they are conventional expressions of politeness (cf. MFr s'il vous plaît). The protasis form is usually Pres:

(66) Car je m'an irai avuec vos,
Et si manrai ansanble o nos
Conpeignons, s'a pleisir vos vient.
(Erec, 5285-7)

"For I shall go with you and shall take companions with us, if it meets your pleasure."

or the form found in the protasis of ANTICIPATED COUNTERFACTUAL conditionals, e.g., ImpSubj in OIt:

(67) Se a voi piacesse di mandargliele sotto la mia guardia, questo sarebbe grande onor di voi, e di me gran bene... (Dec, 143)

"If it should please you to send her back under my protection, it would be a great honour to you and a great advantage to me..."

Although such polite formulae are not at variance in their sequence-of-tense types with the genuine conditionals described above, I have nevertheless not included them among the genuine conditionals in the frequency tables for each text.

FROM MEDIEVAL TO MODERN ROMANCE

French

A profile of verb-form usage in MFr conditional sentences is given in Table 6.7. Apart from the appearance of new verb-forms like Fut < VL amare habet and Perf VL habet amatum, OFr and MFr exhibit little change from the CL state of affairs as regards OPEN conditionals. Forms participate in protasis and apodosis with their residual time-reference values; the only special restriction pertaining to conditional sentences is that, as in CL, there is a ban on Fut in the protases of genuine conditionals, and in Fr this ban extends to all the [+Fut] forms.

The COUNTERFACTUAL system offers more complications. FUTURE ANTICIPATED COUNTERFACTUAL conditionals are expressed in Rol (one example only) by SE ImpSubj/Cond, a sequence which is still dominant in Marie, although Auc and Erec show a preference for

SE Imp/Cond. Neither of these is the direct descendant of a CL sequence: Cond has its origin in the VL paraphrase amare + habebat, i.e., what would have been the [+Past] counterpart of the periphrastic Fut amare + habet[5], and Fr ImpSubj is the direct descendant of CL PlupSubj (amavisset). CL PlupSubj was used in the protasis of PAST COUNTERFACTUAL conditionals; and from Merovingian Latin we have an example of Imp being used in the protasis of a FUTURE ANTICIPATED COUNTERFACTUAL conditional which foreshadows the Fr usage:

(68) Si iubebas, accederemus ad prilium
(Fredegarius, 80,11)
"If you so ordered, we would go to battle."[6]

OFr possessed the means for distinguishing, as did CL, between FUTURE ANTICIPATED and PRESENT COUNTERFACTUAL: in Marie, SE ImpSubj/ImpSubj and SE Imp/Cond are found for PRESENT COUNTERFACTUAL in apparent contrast with the preferred SE ImpSubj/Cond for FUTURE ANTICIPATED COUNTERFACTUALs, and in Erec, SE ImpSubj/ImpSubj expresses PRESENT but not FUTURE ANTICIPATED COUNTERFACTUALity. But a movement towards the obliteration of a formal distinction between PRESENT and FUTURE ANTICIPATED COUNTERFACTUALity can be clearly discerned: in Erec and Auc SE Imp/Cond is the favoured form for both categories. (Against Wagner's insistence (536) that the pattern SE ImpSubj/ImpSubj "n'était pas francais" I submit the Tables for the texts I examined, and suggest that the 'competition' between SE ImpSubj/ImpSubj and other sequences within the same semantic category in OFr is typical of the medieval Romance languages.) The MFr COUNTERFACTUAL system may be seen as a continuation and extension of some of the tendencies observed in OFr: in the FUTURE ANTICIPATED COUNTERFACTUAL category, SI Imp/Cond has become the dominant form, ousting the [+Subj] sequence, and FUTURE ANTICIPATED and PRESENT COUNTERFACTUAL categories are clearly merged.

PAST COUNTERFACTUALs in OFr almost without exception retain [+Subj] sequences. SE ImpSubj/Imp Subj, the direct etymological descendant of CL SI PlupSubj/PlupSubj, is the favoured form evidenced in all texts, though SE PlupSubj/PlupSubj (Fr PlupSubj eüst aimé < VL periphrastic habuisset amatum) is to be found to an appreciable extent in Erec. The development of the MFr sequence SI Plup/CondPerf does not take place until the 16th. Century, according to Wagner, and is even then rare. In OFr, ImpSubj could be used as a protasis form in FUTURE ANTICIPATED, PRESENT and PAST COUNTERFACTUAL conditionals, and the sequence SE ImpSubj/ImpSubj could be used with both PRESENT and PAST reference. The emergence of SE PlupSubj/PlupSubj as the dominant form for the expression of PAST COUNTERFACTUALity in OFr, which antedates the development of the [-Subj] sequence SE Plup/CondPerf, can be seen as a resolution of the temporal ambiguity of sequences involving ImpSubj.

So it is that Fr has eventually developed a conditional system in which COUNTERFACTUALity is represented by [+Past] rather than [+Subj]; we shall see that the other Romance languages have not evolved so far in this respect.

Spanish

Table 6.5 is extracted from Mendeloff's (1960:34-7) study of COUNTERFACTUAL conditionals in OSp, and indicates the frequency of each sequence encountered on a century-by-century basis. The figures obtained by Keniston (1937a) for 16th-Century Sp are given in Table 6.6 and a statement of modern usage in Table 6.8. There are still many variants in the MSp COUNTERFACTUAL system: a frequency study of forms encountered in three modern texts appears in Table 6.9.

As in Fr, there is a ban on Fut in the protasis of a conditional sentence in Sp. But in OSp the sequence SI FutSubj/Fut, the direct descendant of CL SI FutPerf/Fut, is found, declining in popularity only in the course of the 16th. Century. An interesting consequence of this survival is that there is in OSp the possibility of a distinction between PRESENT and FUTURE OPEN conditionals, the SI Fut Subj/Fut sequence being used only for the latter; in MSp the distinction is not made morphologically. The strict CL rule for SI FutPerf/Fut was that Fut Perf was used in the protasis when the protasis event or state was ANTERIOR to the apodosis event or state. An erosion of this rule which had the effect of making FutPerf a straight alternative to Fut can already be perceived in VL texts, e.g.:

(69) Si omnes scandalizati fuerint in te, ego numquam scandalizabor (Vulgate, Matt. 26.33, in Nunn (1958:§172))
"If all men shall be offended in thee, yet will I not be offended."

Väänänen (1963:§380) mentions that the SI FutPerf/

Fut pattern is frequent from the time of Vitruvius and Columellus, gains in popularity over other FUTURE-referring sequences, and is well attested in such legal VL texts as the Lex Salica, the Lex Ribuaria and the Edictus Rothari.

In OSp, the regular form of FUTURE ANTICIPATED COUNTERFACTUAL conditionals appears to have been SI ImpSubj^{se}/Cond, which is cognate with OFr and OIt SE ImpSubj/Cond. In contrast with OFr, there is no suggestion in OSp of a totally [-Subj] sequence emerging in this category.

There is insufficient evidence to show whether there was a morphological distinction between FUTURE ANTICIPATED COUNTERFACTUAL and PRESENT COUNTERFACTUAL conditionals in Cid and PCG; but Mil and LBA quite clearly show SI ImpSubj^{se}/Cond being used for both categories, as indeed it is also used for the expression of PAST COUNTERFACTUALity. Mendeloff (1960:6-7) quotes Gamillscheg's view (1913) that SI ImpSubj^{se}/Cond represented merely 'unreality' (i.e., COUNTERFACTUALity) and was neither PAST nor PRESENT in time-reference, the ambivalence of the sequence being a stylistic advantage to writers. I have already suggested how Fr resolved a similar ambiguity; in OSp too the great virtuosity displayed by, for example, Mil in finding alternative sequences for the expression of PAST COUNTERFACTUALity seems to betoken a need for a distinction based on time-reference in the COUNTERFACTUAL system. By the time of the development of the -ra/-ra sequence in LBA as the most favoured exponent of PAST COUNTERFACTUALity, systematic distinction in the COUNTERFACTUAL system between PRESENT and FUTURE on the one hand and PAST on the other has been achieved. Some of the forms employed in the alternative PAST COUNTERFACTUAL sequences of Mil are new Romance creations which have no direct ancestor in CL (e.g. SI Plup Subj^{se}/CondPerf, the components of which derive from VL habere habebat amatum (CondPerf) and habuisset amatum (PlupSubj^{se})); the -ra form, on the other hand, is the direct descendant of CL Plup (OSp amara < CL amaverat), which participated in PAST COUNTERFACTUAL sequences exceptionally in CL. OSp SI Imp Subj^{se}/-ra could therefore be viewed as a continuation of CL SI PlupSubj/Plup, and we could suppose that it was an older form which the ubiquitous SI ImpSubj^{se}/Cond came to dominate. The advent (or survival) of -ra in the PAST COUNTERFACTUAL category is remarkable, since it is not unequivocally a [+Subj] form; in some respects, consequently, it is analogous to Cond and may be viewed as a [+Perf] (though also [-Fut]) equivalent of Cond. Although Wright (1933) refers to the -ra form in the protasis and the apodosis of PAST COUNTERFACTUAL conditionals as a 'subjunctive', its appearance in a conditional structure is no good reason for its being so labelled. The -ra form may only be unequivocally considered [+Subj] on syntactic grounds when it is the [+Past] equivalent of PresSubj; but, as Wright points out, this is the last stage of the -ra form's shift in function. Its use in conditional structures is a part of the Plup > ImpSubj continuum, an interesting and not precisely qualifiable twilight stage. It is interesting to note how the -ra form also appears in OIt in COUNTERFACTUAL conditionals, e.g.:

(70) Qual dolor fora, se de li spedali
di Valdichiana tra 'l luglio e 'l settembre
e di Maremma e di Sardigna i mali
fossero in una fossa 'nsembre...
(Inf, 29.46-9)

"Such pain as there would be if the diseases of the hospitals of Valdichiana, between July and September, and Maremma and Sardinia, were all together in one ditch..."

We may guess that stabilisation of the COUNTERFACTUAL system of Sp has still not taken place. In the modern 'standard' language, the commonest patterns are SI ImpSubj^{ra}~ImpSubj^{se}/Cond (PRESENT and FUTURE) and SI PlupSubj^{ra}~PlupSubj^{se}/CondPerf (PAST), with a marked preference for the -ra form in the protasis, especially in educated speech. But in colloquial Sp, the pattern SI ImpSubj/Imp is perceptibly emerging for the expression of PRESENT and FUTURE ANTICIPATED COUNTERFACTUALity (see Table 6.8). Keniston finds examples of the sequence, though with PAST COUNTERFACTUAL reference, in Golden Age Sp, and Gessner (1890:54-5) has examples of Imp in the apodosis from Cervantes:

(71) Si al cabo de tanto tiempo volviera sin blanca y sin jumento a mi casa, negra ventura me esperaba.

"If I had returned home after so long without a copper and without my ass, ill fortune would have awaited me."

In South American Sp and in some parts of the Peninsula, the pattern SI Cond/Cond is similarly attested for FUTURE ANTICIPATED and PRESENT COUNTERFACTUAL conditionals (Kany (1951:159-60)).

We may conclude, then, that Sp holds on to [+Subj] forms in COUNTERFACTUAL protases, though the development of the SI -ra/-ra sequence in OSp and the SI Cond/Cond sequence in MSp are interesting departures from the general pattern.

Italian

Sequence-of-tense patterns in It conditional sentences have not undergone any very great change between the medieval period and the present day, as may be seen in Table 6.10. The most striking departure from CL sequences observed in OIt was the availability of Fut in the protases of FUTURE OPEN conditionals; this remains a possibility in the modern language, and Herczeg (1976:398) also quotes an example of FutPerf:

(72) Ma, se questo lavoratore... avrà pagato per intero l'imposta calcolata sul reddito di lavoro, dovrà attendersi poi la restituzione delle somme pagate.

The COUNTERFACTUAL system shows greater variation, although the most frequent OIt patterns of SE Imp Subj/Cond for PRESENT and FUTURE and SE PlupSubj/CondPerf for PAST have been preserved with the same degree of favour. Wędkiewicz (1911:64-5) notes that for the expression of PAST COUNTERFACTUALity SE PlupSubj/Imp achieves some success in Dante (see also my Table 6.4) and that [-Subj] sequences (SE Imp/CondPerf and SE Imp/Imp) are frequently attested in Ariosto. The movement towards the creation of [-Subj] sequences continues in MIt: the sequence SE Imp/Imp is very common in spoken MIt as a PAST COUNTERFACTUAL sequence and is indeed well enough established to be mentioned in many grammars of 'standard' It. MIt thus is comparable to MSp in preserving a [+Subj] protasis form for COUNTERFACTUAL sequences in the standard language but having a popular (and much better established) movement towards the symmetrical [-Subj] sequence.

The availability of [+Fut] protasis forms in OPEN conditionals in MIt does not extend to the COUNTERFACTUAL system. Cond and CondPerf appear to be used in 'protases' in MIt only when the sentence has a CONCESSIVE value:

(73) Anche se me lo dicesse/direbbe lui, gli direi di no (Leone (1974:114))

when Cond is otherwise motivated:

(74) Se avrebbe fatto questo, non lo voglio più vedere
[=imp= Se ha fatto questo, come dicono...; Cond is the Cond of supposition. (Ibid., 115)]

or when the protasis is understood as embedded in another (unexpressed) conditional structure:

(75) Perchè occorreva agitarsi se non si sarebbe ottenuto nulla? [se si fosse agitato davvero] (Lepschy (1977:235))

PresSubj and PerfSubj forms are found in MIt in conditionals which are apparently OPEN; they are limited to elevated registers such as legal codes, where the usage may be an imitation of the similar CL UNIVERSAL usage of [+Subj] forms after cum (see Schmitt Jensen (1970) and Herzceg (1974)).

The conspectus of COUNTERFACTUAL conditional patterns in the Italo-Romance dialects given by Rohlfs (1954:§§743-9) shows many routes of development, the sequences attested being as follows:

PRESENT and FUTURE ANTICIPATED COUNTERFACTUAL: symmetrical sequences:

SE Cond (< VL amare habebat)/Cond (< VL amare habebat):

Bevarío se saría aqua (Istrian)

SE Cond (< VL amare habuit)/Cond (< VL amare habuit):

Se lo cercaresti, lo trovaresti (Siena)

SE Imp/Imp:

Si putívunu, cumprávunu ḍḍa vacca (S. Calabrian)

SE -ra (< CL amaverat)/-ra:

Vivèra, si cce fòra l'acqua (Mangone)

SE ImpSubj (< CL amavisset)/ImpSubj:

Vivissi, si ci fussi acqua (Sicily)

SE ImpSubj (< CL amaret)/ImpSubj:

S'essère bbène cottu, nde dia manducare (Sardinian)

Asymmetrical sequences:

SE Imp/Cond (< VL amare habebat):

Si jo sapía, jo andaría (Bastia[7])

SE Imp/Cond (< VL amare habuit):

Se me vevi i to bẹsi, vuravi comprà purisiè roba (Istrian[8])

SE ImpSubj (< CL amavisset)/Cond (< VL amare habebat):

Bevaria se ghe fose aqua (Venetian)
Vẹvarría sẹ ccẹ stessẹ l'acqua (Neapolitan)

SE ImpSubj (< CL amavisset)/-ra (< CL amaverat):

Mangèrra, si ti facissi fami (Calabrian)

PAST COUNTERFACTUAL: symmetrical sequences:

SE Imp/Imp:

Se tu mi amavi come mi dicevi, all'isola dell' Elba non andavi (Popular Tuscan)

SE CondPerf (< VL habere habuit amatum)/CondPerf:

Se non saresti venuta da me, non avreste camminato più (Tuscan)

The General Pattern

A probable sequence of events in the development of Romance conditionals is as follows. The fall of CL ImpSubj would lead naturally to a reorganisation of the conditional system, since the sequence SI Imp Subj/ImpSubj was the principal exponent of PRESENT COUNTERFACTUALity in CL. Only in Logudorese do we find a descendant of the CL SI ImpSubj/ImpSubj sequence. One way in which reorganisation of the system took place was for the CL SI PlupSubj/PlupSubj sequence to be 'brought forward' from the expression of PAST COUNTERFACTUALity to cover PRESENT COUNTERFACTUALity as well, the consequence being that there was for a time (and that time, as we have seen, extended some way into the early Romance period) no formal distinction between PRESENT and PAST COUNTERFACTUALity. Such a 'forward movement' might be seen as the most highly expected therapeutic recourse for the Romance languages. Nutting (1925:124), discussing the similar 'forward movement' within CL of SI ImpSubj/ImpSubj from PAST to PRESENT reference, observes that

> Taking the whole field into account, it seems manifest that, as various Indo-European languages reached a well-developed stage, some

> general peculiarity inherent in contrary to fact thinking naturally led them severally to the upward shift of a past tense to convey the present contrary to fact idea...

Indeed, were it not for the general demise of CL Imp Subj, we might well suggest that such a 'drift' in the history of Indo-European was capable in itself of having brought about change within the Romance conditional systems.

A second factor which we must consider in the reorganisation of the conditional system is the fall of the CL sequence SI PresSubj/PresSubj, which expressed FUTURE ANTICIPATED COUNTERFACTUALity. The reason for the fall of this form is more difficult to construe, since the verb-form involved survives directly over a wide area of Romance. The fact remains, however, that in no Romance language, to my knowledge, is a descendant of the SI PresSubj/Pres Subj sequence in use. PresSubj does occur after SI, but usually in a clear volitive or hortative sense which denies a purely conditional reading, e.g.:

(76) "Deh, se riposi mai vostra semenza", prega' io lui, "solvetemi quel nodo..."
(Inf, 10.94-5)

"'Ah! May your seed sometime have rest,' I asked him, 'solve me the knot...'"

or, in OFr, when the protasis is the second of two conjoined protases (see example (26) above)[9]. What could be the reason for the disappearance of the SI PresSubj/PresSubj sequence? The fall of SI ImpSubj/ ImpSubj must have had a disturbing effect on the COUNTERFACTUAL system and destroyed the equations of PresSubj = FUTURE, ImpSubj = PRESENT, PlupSubj = PAST. But the SI [+Subj]/ [+Subj] pattern was still strongly enshrined in the SI PlupSubj/PlupSubj sequence. We now need to look at a second kind of reorganisation of the conditional system which must have taken place in the VL and early Romance period, namely, the development of new sequences to represent COUNTERFACTUALity.

These new sequences typically involve the Romance verb-form Cond as the apodosis tense. Cond is in OFr the [+Past] equivalent of the Romance Fut; the same is true of OSp and OIt Cond, although in Tuscan the [+Past] inflections are those of Pret, not of Imp, as in Fr and Sp. The creation of the new sequences is therefore once again in line with the principle of 'drift' enunciated by Nutting: the desire to express COUNTERFACTUALity by a 'past' tense has in this case led to the use of (even creation of[10]) a verb-form which was not previously used in the conditional system.

Two converging tendencies are therefore at work in the development of an alternative expression of PRESENT COUNTERFACTUALity: (a) the increased exploitation of COUNTERFACTUAL sequences that were already in use, and (b) the creation of new COUNTERFACTUAL sequences. Both processes might equally have independent motivation in that they both represent movements towards a 'more Past' sequence of tenses. I would propose that the shape of the various Romance conditional systems can basically be understood in terms of these two tendencies. In Fr, the second process has had more success, in that an exclusively [-Subj] sequence has been evolved for the expression of PRESENT and FUTURE ANTICIPATED COUNTERFACTUAL conditions; in Sp and It, the two processes have more thoroughly converged, in that the SI/SE ImpSubj(se)/Cond sequence draws the protasis verb-form from the CL PlupSubj, which is capable not only of PRESENT but of FUTURE reference, and the Cond form from the newly created [+Past] equivalent of Fut, which is able to participate not only in FUTURE conditions, but also in PRESENT. In the course of this convergence, the distinction between PRESENT and FUTURE presumably became dispensable, and SI PresSubj/PresSubj disappeared. In any case, the strength of the challenge posed by sequences involving Cond in the apodosis, which was the [+Past] counterpart of a [+Fut] form, would have tended towards the ousting of the FUTURE-referring SI PresSubj/PresSubj sequence.

The next, and typically Romance, stage in the evolution of Romance conditionals is the recovery of the distinction between PAST COUNTERFACTUAL conditionals on the one hand and PRESENT and FUTURE on the other. In Fr, Sp and It the recourse is the same: PASTness is expressed by the [+Perf] counterparts of the PRESENT- and FUTURE-referring sequences. It can easily be seen that there is no other device available, since the [+Past] forms themselves are already utilised; the association of [+Perf] with ANTERIORITY and hence with PASTness provides a satisfactory alternative, however, and is a further stage in the 'drift' which has already been acknowledged as a factor of prime importance in the development of conditional sequences. In Fr, the first development is to SE PlupSubj/PlupSubj, the [+Perf] counterpart of SE ImpSubj/ImpSubj; with the demise of SE ImpSubj/ImpSubj and its replacement in the expression of PRESENT COUNTERFACTUALity by SE Imp/Cond, SI Plup/CondPerf, equally [+Perf], becomes the PAST COUNTERFACTUAL sequence. In It, SE Plup Subj/CondPerf is the [+Perf] equivalent of SE Imp Subj/Cond. The great variety of forms in Sp can now be seen as crucially dependent upon the status of the -*ra* form. This is particularly complex, since not only was the -*ra* form a Plup in OSp, but it also functioned from early times as an alternative to Cond[11]. It was natural therefore that the -*ra* form should appear in the apodoses of COUNTERFACTUAL conditionals as a substitute for Cond. However, -*ra* itself has no corresponding [+Perf] form; but perhaps because it could also be construed as [+Perf] in its own right, it achieved great popularity as an apodosis form in OSp. For other reasons, which I shall discuss shortly, it also came to be used in the protasis of PAST COUNTERFACTUAL conditionals. In MSp, though, the relation between PRESENT and PAST COUNTERFACTUAL conditionals is comparable with that which obtains in Fr and It: the PAST sequence SI PlupSubj$^{ra\ se}$/CondPerf being the [+Perf] equivalent of the FUTURE and PRESENT sequence SI ImpSubj$^{ra\ se}$/Cond.

It seems clear that a major factor in the evolution of conditional sentences in Romance is **analogy**. The appearance of Cond in the new COUNTERFACTUAL sequences of Romance has its most logical explanation in the description of Cond as the [+Past] equivalent of the new Romance Fut; the creation in the medieval period of new PAST COUNTERFACTUAL sequences can similarly be explained as an analogical process, the new sequences being the [+Perf] equivalents of the FUTURE and PRESENT sequences.

Another factor which appears to be of some importance in an understanding of the development of conditional patterns in Romance is that of **symmetry**. While the COUNTERFACTUAL system of CL shows symmetry between protasis and apodosis verb-form (except in cases where the time-reference of protasis and apodosis is different), that of many Romance languages does not. I would suggest that the reason for the lack of symmetry in Romance is that the new sequence for FUTURE ANTICIPATED and PRESENT COUNTERFACTUAL conditions (Fr SE Imp/Cond, Sp and It SI/SE Imp Subj$^{(se)}$/Cond) was the result of partial or total analogy with the one assymetric form of the CL system, namely, the FUTURE OPEN SI Pres/Fut. The new FUTURE ANTICIPATED and PRESENT COUNTERFACTUAL sequence also provided the model for the PAST COUNTERFACTUAL [+Perf] sequences in due course, and so the assymetry extended to the whole of the COUNTERFACTUAL system. And yet at several stages in the history of the Romance languages we can observe attempts at the restoration of symmetrical patterns. We should perhaps first remember that many Romance languages have preserved or developed symmetrical patterns (see the It dialect data presented above, and compare the Rum patterns DACĂ Cond/Cond (FUTURE ANTICIPATED and PRESENT COUNTERFACTUAL) and DACĂ CondPerf/CondPerf[12] sequences:

(77) a. Aş eşi, dacă aş avea timp
"I would go out, if I had time"

b. Desigur, aş merge la teatru dacă aş găsi bilet
"I would certainly go to the theatre if I had a ticket"

c. Ar fi încăput totul, dacă ar fi ştiut să-l aranjeze
"He would have finished it all, if he had known how to do it"

(Examples from Rauta (1947:224-6)

DACA Imp/Imp (and indeed any combination of Imp and CondPerf sequences in Rum) can also be used for the expression of PAST COUNTERFACTUALity: thus

(78) Încăpea/Ar fi încăput totul, dacă ştia/ar fi ştiut să-l aranjeze

are alternatives to (76c). There are two notable 'spontaneous' creations of symmetrical sequences in the languages we have examined. One is the development of the pattern SE Fut/Fut in It for the expression of FUTURE OPEN conditions; this pattern has no antecedent in CL and is not paralleled in Fr or Sp, where the use of Fut after SI is always the sign of a pseudo-conditional:

(79) Qui donc attendons-nous, s'ils ne reviendront pas? (Sten (1952:67))

[The truth of <u>ils reviendront</u> is expected]

The other is the pattern SI <u>-ra</u>/<u>-ra</u>, which first appears with PAST COUNTERFACTUAL value in OSp, and later with PRESENT COUNTERFACTUAL value. I have already suggested reasons for the appearance of <u>-ra</u> in the apodosis of these conditionals. The use of -ra in the protasis is at first sight extraordinary, since its original value in OSp is [-Subj]; it is the only [-Subj] form to be used in the protasis of a COUNTERFACTUAL conditional in the whole history of Sp, in fact, apart from the SI Imp/Imp sequence which is increasingly attested in modern times. Admittedly, the -ra form already possessed some kind of 'modal' value in OSp, as we have seen, but it was far from being a genuine subjunctive, even in Golden Age Sp. Furthermore, it is likely that its [+Subj] value developed specifically from its use as a conditional protasis form, i.e., in what was felt as a 'subjunctive' context (cf. Keniston 1937a:§32.8), rather than the other way round. The oddity of the use of -ra in the protasis of PAST and PRESENT COUNTERFACTUAL conditionals in OSp may therefore be most conveniently explained as an instance of symmetrical copying of the apodosis -ra form.

Finally, we should consider the case of the SE Imp/Imp sequence, which is found in MIt. It is possible to see the apodosis Imp as having developed as the [+Past] equivalent of Pres, which is a common, and perhaps increasingly common, FUTURE OPEN apodosis form. It is unlikely, given the aversion of It to [-Subj] forms in the protases of COUNTERFACTUAL conditionals, to visualise the sequence SE Imp/ Imp as a straight [+Past] equivalent of the SE Pres/Pres FUTURE and PRESENT OPEN sequence, on a par with the development of Fr SI Imp/Cond as the [+Past] equivalent of SI Pres/Fut. All in all, the first stage in the evolution of the SE Imp/Imp form is likely to have been the use of Imp in the apodosis, and we may therefore suspect that symmetry may have had a role to play in the 'copying' of this form in the protasis.

NOTES

1. In the translations of CL examples, I have generally kept the glosses supplied by the commentators from whose work the example is quoted, modifying the gloss only when it seemed not to bring out a relevant point sufficiently.

2. Compare Gildersleeve and Lodge (1895:§597 Rem. 1) and Woodcock (1959:§199).

3. Anglade (1965:211) is of the opinion that SE Imp/Cond is scarcely encountered until the 12th. Century.

4. Gamillscheg (1957:724) discerns a tendency for the [+Perf] form to appear in only one of the constituent sentences of a conditional structure, and for a preference for [-Perf] forms in the protasis.

5. See Väänänen (1963:§303), and the accounts of the analogical creation of Romance Cond given by Grandgent (1907:§130) and Harris (1971:28).

6. See Bourciez (1946:§257b) and Väänänen (1963:§381).

7. Rohlfs suggests the possibility of French influence for this Corsican example.

8. Rohlfs comments that this is an extremely rare type. In fact, this example is not convincing, since vuravi (= It vorrei) is a modal auxiliary the tense of which may represent an attenuation modality.

9. There is a controversial example of Pres Subj as a protasis form in Rol:

> S'en ma mercit ne se colzt a mes piéz,
> Et ne guerpisset la lei de chrestiiens,
> Jo li toldrai la corone del chief. (2682-4)
>
> "If he does not prostrate himself at my mercy at my feet and abandon the law of the Christians, I will take the crown from his head."

Gamillscheg (1957:718-9) has an important discussion on PresSubj as a protasis form. He refers to the apparent frequency of examples in Anglo-Norman texts, but feels that instances may be explained as transfers of PresSubj from a second conjoined protasis sentence to the first. Discussing the above example from Rol specifically, Gamillscheg points to Bédier's (1922) translation: "S'il n'implore pas ma merci, couché à mes pieds...", and suggests that coucher may be felt as belonging to a second conjoined protasis.

10. See M. Harris (1971:31): "... it was at this point in the language [the admission of the -ra form to conditional complexes] that the -ra form was originally conceived of as a subjunctive."

11. See Wright (1932: Table facing 160) and my Table 6.3; use of the -ra form in a conditional apodosis is attested as early as Cid and the Apolonio.

12. Cond and CondPerf are really designations of convenience for the Rum forms; they are not cognate with Cond and Cond Perf in French, Italian and Spanish. For a brief discussion of the origins of these forms (respectively, ar cînta and ar fi cîntat), see Elcock (1960:108 n.1).

Table 6.1: Conditional sentences in CL

	OPEN	COUNTERFACTUAL
FUT	SI Pres/Fut SI FutPerf/Fut	SI PresSubj/PresSubj
PRES	SI Pres/Pres	SI ImpSubj/ImpSubj
PAST	SI Imp/Imp SI $Perf_{1-2}$/$Perf_{1-2}$	SI PlupSubj/PlupSubj
UNIV	SI Pres/Pres	
PAST UNIV	SI Imp/Imp	

Table 6.2: Conditional sentences in OFr

	OPEN	COUNTERFACTUAL
FUT	SE Pres/Fut: Rol 24, Erec 33, M 20, Auc 24 SE Pres/Other: Rol 15, Erec 22, M 22, Auc 11 SE Pres/Ø: Erec 7, Auc 1 SE Perf/Fut: Auc 1 (SE PresSubj/Fut: Rol 1) SE PresSubj/various: M 3 Other: Erec 1	SE Imp/Cond: Erec 13, M 1, Auc 8 SE Imp/Other: Erec 3, Auc 2 SE Plup/Cond: Erec 3, M 1, Auc 1 SE Plup/CondPerf: M 1 SE ImpSubj/Fut: M 1 SE ImpSubj/Cond: Rol 1, M 5 SE ImpSubj/Ø: Erec 1 SE ImpSubj/Cond: Auc 1 SE PlupSubj/Cond: M 1
	TRANSPOSED: SE Pres/Fut: Rol 3, M 4, Auc 2; SE Pres/Pres: Erec 2; SE Pres/Other: Erec 4, M 4 SE Imp/Cond: Erec 3, M 3, Auc 1; SE Imp/Imp: Erec 1, M 1; SE Imp/Fut: M 1; SE Imp/ImpSubj: Auc 3 SE ImpSubj/Cond: Erec 3, M 4; SE ImpSubj/ImpSubj: Erec 3, M 4; SE ImpSubj/Ø: M 3; SE ImpSubj/Other: Erec 1, M 2	
PRES	SE Pres/Pres: Rol 1, Erec 1, M 1 SE Pres/Other: Erec 5, M 3	SE Imp/Cond: Erec 6, M 2, Auc 4 SE Imp/ImpSubj: Auc 1 SE ImpSubj/Cond: M 1 SE ImpSubj/ImpSubj: Erec 3 M 4 SE ImpSubj/Other: Erec 1
	TRANSPOSED: SE Imp/ImpSubj: M 1 SE ImpSubj/Fut: M 1	

Table 6.2 (cont'd)

	OPEN	COUNTERFACTUAL
PAST	SE Pres/Fut: Rol 4 SE Pres/Pres: Rol 1, M 4 SE Pres/Ø: Erec 1 SE Pres/Other: Erec 2 SE Perf/Pret: Erec 1 SE Perf/Other: Erec 4 Other: Erec 1	(SE Plup/Cond: Erec 1) SE ImpSubj/Pres: Rol 1 SE ImpSubj/ImpSubj: Rol 6, Erec 13, M 5, Auc 1 SE ImpSubj/PlupSubj: Rol 2 Erec 2 SE ImpSubj/Ø: Rol 1 SE PlupSubj/Imp: M 1 SE PlupSubj/ImpSubj: Erec 1 SE PlupSubj/PlupSubj: Erec 7, M 1
	TRANSPOSED: SE Plup/Ø: Auc 1 SE ImpSubj/ImpSubj: M 1	
UNIV	SE Pres/Pres: Erec 2, M 6 SE Pres/Other: M 4	
PAST UNIV	SE Pres/Pres: Rol 2, M 1 SE ImpSubj/Pret: Rol 1 SE Imp/Imp: Erec 1 SE Imp/ImpSubj: M 1, Auc 1	SE ImpSubj/ImpSubj: M 2 SE ImpSubj/Other: M 5

Table 6.3: Conditional sentences in OSp

	OPEN	COUNTERFACTUAL
FUT	SI Pres/Fut: Cid 11, PCG 3 Mil 8, LBA 16 SI Pres/Other: Cid 5, PCG 2, Mil 7, LBA 19 SI Pres/Ø: Cid 1, Mil 1 SI FutSubj/Fut: Cid 22, PCG 4, Mil 16, LBA 16 SI FutSubj/Other: Cid 5, Mil 10, LBA 16 SI FutSubj/Ø: Cid 3	SI ImpSubj^{se}/Cond: Cid 5, PCG 3, Mil 6, LBA 11 SI ImpSubj^{se}/Imp: Cid 1, PCG 1, Mil 2 SI ImpSubj^{se}/Other: Mil 1, LBA 2 SI ImpSubj^{se}/Ø: Mil 1, LBA 1
	TRANSPOSED: SI ImpSubj^{se}/Cond: Cid 5, PCG 20, Mil 2; SI ImpSubj^{se}/Imp: PCG 2, LBA 1; SI ImpSubj^{se}/ImpSubj^{se}: Cid 4, Mil 1; SI ImpSubj^{se}/PlupSubj^{se}: PCG 2; SI ImpSubj^{se} /-ra: PCG 1; SI ImpSubj^{se}/PresSubj: LBA 1; SI ImpSubj^{se}/Ø: PCG 2, Mil 1	
PRES	SI Pres/Pres: Cid 1, PCG 1 LBA 4 SI Pres/Fut: Cid 1, LBA 3 SI Pres/Other: PCG 3, LBA 7	SI ImpSubj^{se}/Cond: LBA 7 SI ImpSubj^{se}/Imp: PCG 1 SI ImpSubj^{se}/Ø: Cid 1
	TRANSPOSED: SI Imp/Imp: PCG 1 SI ImpSubj^{se}/Cond: PCG 1	

Table 6.3 (cont'd)

	OPEN	COUNTERFACTUAL
PAST	SI Imp/Pres: Mil 1 SI Pret/PresSubj: Mil 1	SI ImpSubj^{se}/Cond: Mil 12, LBA 1 SI ImpSubj^{se}/Imp: LBA 1 SI ImpSubj^{se}/-ra: Cid 2, PCG 2, Mil 1 SI ImpSubj^{se}/PlupSubj^{ra}: Mil 2 SI ImpSubj^{se}/Other: Cid 1, PCG 1 SI PlupSubj^{se}/Cond: Mil 2 SI PlupSubj^{se}/CondPerf: Mil 1 SI PlupSubj^{se}/Imp: Mil 1 SI PlupSubj^{se}/-ra: Mil 1 SI -ra/-ra: LBA 6 SI -ra/Cond: LBA 1
	TRANSPOSED: SI ImpSubj^{se}/Cond: Mil 1 SI -ra/-ra: LBA 1	
UNIV	SI Pres/Pres: LBA 32 SI Pres/Fut: LBA 6 SI Pres/Other: LBA 4 SI Pres/Ø: LBA 1 SI FutSubj/Fut: LBA 5 SI FutSubj/Pres: LBA / SI FutSubj/Other: LBA 3	SI ImpSubj^{se}/Cond: PCG 1, Mil 2
PAST UNIV	SI Imp/Imp: PCG 1, Mil 1, LBA 3 SI Pret/Pret: Mil 1 SI ImpSubj^{se}/Pres: PCG 1	

Table 6.4: Conditional sentences in OIt

	OPEN	COUNTERFACTUAL
FUT	SE Fut/Fut: Nov 10, Inf 1, Dec 8 SE Fut/Other: Nov 1, Inf 1, Dec 3 SE Pres/Fut: Nov 9, Inf 15 Dec 11 SE Pres/Other: Nov 10, Inf 29, Dec 16 Other: Nov 1, Inf 1	SE ImpSubj/Cond: Nov 1, Inf 3, Dec 14 SE ImpSubj/Other: Nov 2, Inf 1, Dec 4 SE PlupSubj/Cond: Dec 1 SE PlupSubj/Other: Nov 1
	TRANSPOSED: SE Imp/Imp: Dec 1 SE ImpSubj/Cond: Dec 5; SE ImpSubj/Other: Dec 12; SE ImpSubj/Ø: Dec 1	
PRES	SE Pres/Pres: Nov 1, Inf 18, Dec 17 SE Pres/Other: Nov 4, Inf 19, Dec 10	SE ImpSubj/Cond: Nov 3, Inf 9, Dec 6 SE ImpSubj/Imp: Nov 1, Inf 1 SE ImpSubj/Other: Nov 2, Inf 2, Dec 1
	TRANSPOSED: SE Pret/ImpSubj: Dec 1 SE ImpSubj/Cond: Dec 1; SE ImpSubj/Other: Dec 4 SE PlupSubj/CondPerf: Dec 1	
PAST	SE Pret/Other: Nov 1, Inf 3, Dec 4 SE Imp/Other: Inf 1, Dec 3 SE Perf/Other: Inf 3, Dec 2	SE ImpSubj/Cond: Inf 1 SE ImpSubj/CondPerf: Nov 1 Inf 1, Dec 2 SE ImpSubj/Other: Inf 2 SE Plup Subj/Cond: Nov 1. Inf 1, Dec 3 SE PlupSubj/Imp: Inf 2 SE PlupSubj/CondPerf: Nov 4, Inf 6, Dec 11 SE PlupSubj/Other: Dec 6

Table 6.4 (cont'd)

	OPEN	COUNTERFACTUAL
UNIV	SE Pres/Pres: Nov 2, Inf 3 Dec 4 SE Fut/Pres: Dec 1 SE Pres/Other: Dec 1	SE ImpSubj/Cond: Dec 5 SE ImpSubj/Other: Dec2
PAST UNIV	SE Imp/Imp: Nov 1, Dec 1 SE Imp/Other: Nov 1 SE Perf/PresSubj: Dec 1	SE ImpSubj/Imp: Nov 2 SE ImpSubj/Pret: Dec 1

Table 6.5: PAST and PRESENT COUNTERFACTUAL conditional sentences in OSp (from Mendeloff (1960))

	PAST		PRESENT	
12th and 13th Cent	SI ImpSubj^{se}/Cond	63	SI ImpSubj^{se}/Cond	41
	SI ImpSubj^{se}/-ra	31		
	SI PlupSubj^{se}/-ra	14		
	SI -ra/-ra	11		
	SI PlupSubj^{se}/Cond	9		
	SI ImpSubj^{se}/PlupSubj^{ra}	6		
	SI ImpSubj^{se}/Imp	6		
	SI ImpSubj^{se}/CondPerf	4		
	SI PlupSubj^{se}/CondPerf	4		
	SI PlupSubj^{se}/PlupSubj^{ra}	4		
	SI PlupSubj^{ra}/-ra	2		
14th Cent	SI -ra/-ra	41	SI ImpSubj^{se}/Cond	68
	SI ImpSubj^{se}/Imp	4	SI ImpSubj^{se}/-ra	4
	SI PlupSubj^{ra}/-ra	2	SI -ra/-ra	4
15th Cent	SI -ra/-ra	33	SI ImpSubj^{se}/Cond	47
	SI -ra/Imp	2	SI -ra/-ra	7
	SI -ra/Cond	2	SI ImpSubj^{se}/-ra	6

Table 6.6: Conditional sentences in 16th.-Century Spanish (from Keniston (1937a))

	OPEN	COUNTERFACTUAL
FUT	SI Pres/Various forms Si FutSubj/Various forms (75/219 in first half of century dropping to 22/120)	SI ImpSubj^{se}/Cond (24/72) SI ImpSubj^{se}/ImpSubj^{se} (5/6) SI ImpSubj^{se}/Imp (1/1) SI ImpSubj^{se}/CondPerf SI ImpSubj^{se}/ImpSubj^{ra} SI ImpSubj^{ra}/Cond SI ImpSubj^{ra}/ImpSubj^{ra} SI PlupSubj^{se}/Cond
PRES		SI ImpSubj^{se}/Cond (15/54) SI ImpSubj^{se}/Imp SI ImpSubj^{se}/ImpSubj^{ra} SI ImpSubj^{ra}/ImpSubj^{ra} SI ImpSubj^{ra}/Cond SI Imp/Cond
PAST	Any combination of PAST-referring forms	SI ImpSubj^{ra}/ImpSubj^{ra} (30/141) SI ImpSubj^{ra}/Imp (7/11) SI ImpSubj^{ra}/Cond SI ImpSubj^{ra}/Plup SI ImpSubj^{ra}/PlupSubj^{ra} SI PlupSubj^{ra}/ImpSubj^{ra} (12/12) SI PlupSubj^{ra}/PlupSubj^{ra} SI PlupSubj^{ra}/Imp SI PlupSubj^{ra}/Cond SI Imp/Imp SI PlupSubj^{se}/Cond
UNIV	SI Pres/Pres	

Table 6.7: Conditional sentences in MFr

	OPEN	COUNTERFACTUAL
FUT	SI Pres/Fut	SI Imp/Cond
PRES	SI Pres/Pres	Si Imp/Cond
PAST	SI Perf/Perf SI Imp/Imp etc.	SI Plup/CondPerf (SI Plup/Imp[a]) (SI PlupSubj/CondPerf[b])
UNIV	SI Pres/Pres	
PAST UNIV	SI Imp/Imp	

a Si vous n'étiez pas venu, je vous faisais appeler (A. France, in Gobert (1966:467); cf. also Damourette and Pichon (1936:§1740))

b C'est une fille qui, en d'autres circonstances et si elle eût été de mon monde, j'aurais eu plaisir à chasser le renard (Anouilh)

Table 6.8: Conditional sentences in MSp

	OPEN	COUNTERFACTUAL
FUT	SI Pres/Fut	SI ImpSubj^{ra}/Cond SI ImpSubj^{se}/Cond (SI ImpSubj^{ra}/Imp[a]) (SI ImpSubj^{se}/Imp[b])
PRES	SI Pres/Pres	SI ImpSubj^{ra}/Cond SI ImpSubj^{se}/Cond (SI ImpSubj^{se}/ImpSubj^{ra}[c])
PAST	SI Pret/Pret SI Imp/Imp	SI PlupSubj^{ra}/CondPerf SI PlupSubj^{se}/CondPerf (SI PlupSubj^{se}/PlupSubj^{ra}[d]) (SI ImpSubj^{se}/PlupSubj^{ra}[e])
UNIV	SI Pres/Pres	
PAST UNIV	SI Imp/Imp	

a Si tuviera dinero, compraba un coche (Atlas lingüístico-etnográfico de Andalucía, map 1853: the commonest pattern in Andalusian Spanish)

b Si ahora viniese un amor, os quedábais perdidas (Linares Rivas, in Keniston (1937b:§31))

c ¿Piensa usted que estuviera yo viva, si esa esperanza no me animase? (Baroja, in Harmer and Norton (1935:§240))

d Si hubiese sido hombre, el sentido de su libertad hubiera sido más amplio (Gómez de la Serna, in Keniston (§31))

e La cosa hubiera sido interminable, si la Corregidora... no dijese por último a D. Eugenio... (Alarcón, in Harmer and Norton (§240))

Table 6.9: COUNTERFACTUAL conditional sentences in three MSP texts*

FUT	SI ImpSubj^{ra}/Cond: *Jar* 4, *Zanc* 1, *T* 1
	SI ImpSubj^{ra}/Ø: *Jar* 4, *Zanc* 1
	SI ImpSubj^{se}/Cond: *Jar* 1, *T* 1
	SI ImpSubj^{se}/Ø: *Zanc* 3
	SI Imp/Imp: *Jar* 2
PRES	SI ImpSubj^{ra}/Cond: *Jar* 3, *Zanc* 1, *T* 4
	SI ImpSubj^{ra}/Imp: *Jar* 2
	SI ImpSubj^{ra}/Ø: *Jar* 4
	SI ImpSubj^{se}/Cond: *Jar* 1, *Zanc* 3, *T* 5
	SI ImpSubj^{ra}/ImpSubj^{ra}: *T* 1
PAST	SI PlupSubj^{ra}/CondPerf: *Jar* 1, *Zanc* 3, *T* 1
	SI PlupSubj^{ra}/Ø: *Jar* 1
	SI PlupSubj^{se}/CondPerf: *Jar* 1, *Zanc* 8, *T* 2
	SI PlupSubj^{se}/Imp: *Jar* 1
	SI PlupSubj^{se}/Ø: *Jar* 1
	SI PlupSubj^{se}/PlupSubj^{se}: *Zanc* 2, *T* 1

* *Jar*: R. Sánchez Ferlosio, *El Jarama*, Barcelona, 1946
Zanc: V. Soto, *La Zancada*, Barcelona, 1967
T: *Triunfo* (26 September 1970, no. 434)

Table 6.10: Conditional sentences in MIt

	OPEN	COUNTERFACTUAL
FUT	SE Fut/Fut SE Pres/Fut	SE ImpSubj/Cond
PRES	SE Pres/Pres	SE ImpSubj/Cond
PAST	SE Perf/Perf SE Imp/Imp SE Pret/Pret etc.	SE PlupSubj/CondPerf (SE Imp/Imp[a]) (SE Imp/CondPerf[b])

a Se morivo, non soffrivo tanto (Battaglia and Pernicone (1968:562))

b Se riuscivo sarei stato felice (<u>ib.</u>)

Chapter Seven

WHEN-SENTENCES FROM CLASSICAL LATIN TO MODERN ROMANCE

Quando in CL is used as (a) an interrogative adverbial of time and (b) as the corresponding indirect question relativiser, e.g.:

(1) Quando exivit?
Rogavi quando exiverit

but it is attested as a temporal connective too already in the Classical period: Gildersleeve and Lodge (1895:§580 n.3) observe over 70 examples in Plautus, mainly with FUTURE- and UNIVERSAL-referring sentences. Quando is also found with a CAUSAL value in CL texts; Lewis and Short (1879:1505) cite three examples from Cicero in which quando combines with igitur to give a reading of "since then" or "because then", e.g.:

(2) Quando igitur virtus est adfectio animi constans (Cic. Tusc., 4.15.34)
"Since therefore virtue is a constant state of mind..."

Quando with the value of quoniam is, according to Lewis and Short, found frequently in Livy, and is also attested in poetic style and in post-Augustan Latin. In all the major Romance languages, the descendant of CL quando comes to assume a wide range of functions entirely comparable to those discharged by the polyvalent CL cum, which in the written language was by far the most common temporal connective. These functions are: (a) participation in sentences in which there is a POST, SIM or ANT precedence-relationship between matrix sentence and when-sentence, (b) the special function I labelled 'inverse when' in Chapter 5, and (c) as a CAUSAL or CONCESSIVE connective. CL and the Romance languages also coincide in possessing alternative temporal connectives to cum and Fr quand Sp cuando It quando which are more limited in function. In CL, a POST precedence-relationship could be expressed by postquam, ubi, ut or simulac (cf. MFr après que, aussitot que, etc., MSp después que, luego que, etc., MIt dopo che, tosto che, etc.), a SIM precedence-relation by dum or quoad (cf. MFr comme, à mesure que, etc., MSp mientras, a medida que, etc., MIt mentre, allorchè, etc.).

I give a summary of the pattern of verb-forms available with CL cum in Table 7.1. Woodcock (1959: 187ff.) draws an important parallel between cum-clauses in CL and relative clauses, a connection which, incidentally, lends support to the relative adverb hypothesis for when, etc., proposed in Chapter 5. He distinguishes among (a) "determinative" (= "restrictive") relative clauses which take [-Subj] forms, (b) "descriptive" or "generic" relative clauses (usually involving a negative or quantified antecedent) which take [+Subj] forms, (c) "generalising" (UNIVERSAL-referring) relative clauses which take [-Subj] forms, and (d) causal or concessive relative clauses which take [+Subj] forms. In early CL, much the same kinds of parameter can be adduced to characterise the use of cum: "determinative" cum (with [-Subj] forms) has the reading "at the time at which" and contrasts with a "descriptive" cum (with [+Subj] forms) which has the reading "at a time at which". "Generalising" cum (with [-Subj] forms) has the reading "at any time at which", and cum clauses with a reading of CAUSALITY take [+Subj] forms. By the time of Cicero, however, [+Subj] forms are regularly used in a cum-clause in a PAST narrative, and by the time of Livy, [+Subj] forms are employed in PAST UNIVERSAL cum-clauses.

Cum-clauses are traditionally viewed as a phenomenon in their own right in descriptions of CL syntax. This is no doubt because of the dual function of cum as a temporal and causal connective and because of the use of [+Subj] forms in certain kinds of cum-clause. Other temporal connectives associated with POST and SIM precedence-relationships take [-Subj] forms only, although when their time-reference is UNIVERSAL, [+Subj] forms come to be the rule in later CL authors, notably the historians (see Gildersleeve and Lodge (1895:364 note)) - this may be a spread from the 'ideal second person' use of the [+Subj] forms which is closely associated with the notion of UNIVERSAL time-reference. Table 7.2 summarises these patterns. It will be noted that verb-form sequences with temporal connectives which express an ANT precedence-relationship must make use of an additional parameter, namely, the negative-polarity of the matrix sentence, and that there is a tendency for ImpSubj to appear in the embedded sentence of PAST-referring examples. Ignoring these ANT types, it may be seen that the chief area of discrepancy between verb-form sequences associated with cum and those associated with other temporal connectives is that of PAST- and PAST UNIVERSAL-referring patterns.

As far as verb-form usage with quando is concerned, the main verb of a simple sentence containing interrogative quando in CL follows the normal pattern for direct questions (see Woodcock (1959: 129ff.)), both [-Subj] and [+Subj] forms being encountered, the latter with "deliberative" value. In oratio obliqua the corresponding [+Subj] forms are used, Fut and FutPerf being paralleled by forms which may be labelled Future Subjunctive (amaturus sit) and Future Perfect Subjunctive (amaturus esset). The relatively few examples to hand in which quando may be viewed as a temporal connective do not show any departure from this scheme.

WHEN-SENTENCES IN EARLY ROMANCE

FUTURE-referring Joint Axes

In OFr and OIt, a [+Fut] form is obligatory in the when-sentence. In POST examples, FutPerf is an alternative to Fut:

(3) Al matin, quant jeo erc levez
E vus avrez les hus fermez,
Fetes semblant de fors eissir,
Si la lessez sule gisir... (Marie, Y, 245-8)

"In the morning, when I have risen and you have closed the doors, pretend to go out and leave her to lie alone..."

(4) Costui, quando tu gli sarai rincresciuta, con gran vitupero di te medesima ti caccerà via... (Dec, 175)

"When you have become tedious to this man, he will throw you out with great insults..."

In OSp, the when-sentence form is [+Fut, +Subj], e.g.:

(5) e quando las toviere partir se a la cort...
(Cid, 3168)

"And when he has them the court will break up..."

The texts reveal a number of interesting exceptions to this pattern, however. Examples (6), (7) and (8) exhibit, respectively, PresSubj, Pres and Fut in the when-sentence:

(6) "śeñora, que me prometadeś, de lo que de amor queremoś,
"que sy oujere lugar e tienpo, quando en vno estemoś,
"segund quelo yo deseo voś e yo noś abraçemoś...
(LBA, 684a-c)

"'Lady, [it is] that you promise me, for love's sake, that if there is time and place, when we are alone, you and I may embrace as I wish...'"

(7) "Sed cras ome, non vos tengan por tenjco;
"fablad, mas Recabdat quando y yo no fynco.
(LBA, 869c-d)

"'Be a man tomorrow, do not be taken for a mute; speak, but possess her when I am not there.'"

(8) Sed membrados commo lo devedes far;
a la mañana quando los gallos cantaran
non vos tardedes, mandedes ensellar...
(Cid, 315-7)

"Be mindful how you are to act; in the morning when the cocks crow, do not delay, give the order to saddle up..."

The verb-forms in question in all these examples occur line-finally and so may be a deliberate breaking of the normal rule to suit the demands of the rhyme-scheme. Additionally, the estemoś of (6) might be construed as falling under the scope of prometadeś; and cantaran in (8) could be construed as the verb of an adverbial clause in apposition with the adverbial a la mañana ("... in the morning, when the cocks will be crowing...").

It will be noted that a [+Perf] form is not obligatory in any of the three languages in the when-sentence of POST constructions, in contrast with CL cum-clauses. This means, as we shall see, that the distinction between POST and SIM is no longer necessarily morphologically marked.

TRANSPOSED FUTURE when-sentences in OFr undergo [Past]-AGREEMENT only optionally, but the sequences encountered are identical with, or the strict [+Past] equivalents of, the primary sequences. In OSp, [Past]-AGREEMENT appears to be obligatory. Since there is no verb-form specifiable as [+Past, +Fut, +Subj], ImpSubj^{se}, which satisfies the specification in all but [+Fut], is used:

(9) ... por que tenie que quandos ella fuesse, que leuarie tod aquel auer consigo que fuera del obispo, y el que lo tomarie... (PCG, 33.44R)

"... because he thought that when she went, she would take with her all the wealth which had been the bishop's, and that he would take it [from her]..."

(There is, incidentally, no example of the -ra form being used as an alternative to ImpSubj^{se}, a fact which indicates that the -ra form is not reckoned as a [+Subj] form at the time of the texts.) There is one example of Imp in the when-clause: the case is analogous to (8) above, and also from Cid:

(10) Las palabras son puestas que otro dia
manana quando salie el sol
ques tornasse cada uno don salidos son.
(Cid, 2111-2)[1]

"It was pledged that the next day in the morning when the sun was rising each should return from whence he came."

Examples of TRANSPOSED FUTURE when-sentences in OIt surprisingly have ImpSubj or PlupSubj in the when-clause, e.g.:

(11) ... ciascuno... pregava il padre... che quando a morte venisse a lui quello anello lasciasse. (Dec, 62)

"Each... asked his father... to leave the ring to him when he died."

However, all the examples concerned have ImpSubj in the matrix clause, and it may be under the influence of this that the form occurs in the when-clause too.

Quando in OIt has quite a substantial use as a conditional conjunction, and there are several examples in the texts of FUTURE-referring when-sentences with this value. Both PresSubj and ImpSubj are found as the "when"-clause form:

(12) Messere, quando di venir vi piaccia, ella v'attende in casa sua. (Dec, 107)
"Sir, if you would like to come, she is waiting for you in your house."

(13) Non che un di loro, che gentili uomini sono, ma un ribaldo, quando a voi piacesse, mi piacerebbe. (Dec, 125)
"I would be pleased not only with one of them, who are gentlemen, but [even] a ragamuffin, if it should please you."

PRESENT-referring Joint Axes

In OFr there are no purely temporal types of when-sentence in this category. The majority of examples have a reading of CAUSALITY, in which quant may be glossed as "since", e.g.:

(14) 'Sire,' dist Guenes, 'dunez mei le cungié;
Quant aler dei, n'i ai plus que targer.'
(Rol, 337-8)
"'Sire,' said Guenes, 'give me leave to depart; since I must go, I have no reason to delay longer.'"

Sometimes the when-clause appears to act as a factive complement[2], e.g.:

(15) "Haï!", fet il, "come il me poise,
Quant vos alez a tel viltance!
Grant duel en ai et grant pesance..."
(Erec, 3316-8)
"'Alas,' said he, 'how it grieves me that you are in such a lowly state! I am very sorry and grieved...'"

CAUSALITY is equally the usual reading for PRESENT-referring when-sentences in OSp and, when the when-sentence form is [-Subj], in OIt:

(16) 'Quando a vos plaze otorgo lo yo, señor.'
(Cid, 3415)
"'Since it pleases you, I grant it, my lord.'"

(17) ... "Malizioso son io troppo,
quand' io procuro a' mia maggior trestizia".
(Inf, 22.110-1)
"'I am too malicious, since I contrive greater sadness for my friends.'"

There is just one example in OSp which seems to be interpretable as a TEMPORAL PRESENT-referring when-sentence:

(18) "... quando bien me lo cato,
"como estaua solo, sy vjnjera el gato,
"ally me alcançara e me diera mal rrato."

"'When [= now that] I consider the matter, [I realise that] as I was alone, if the cat had come, he would have caught me there and given me a bad time.'"

OIt offers a similar example:

(19) ... ma fiorentino
mi sembri veramente quand' io t'odo.
(Inf, 33.12)

"... but when [= now that] I hear you, truly you seem to me a Florentine."

In OIt, as in FUTURE-referring when-sentences, a [+Subj] form in the "when"-clause signals a CONDITIONAL reading:

(20) Per che, quando tu vogli, io sono disposto...
ch'ella onestamente tua moglie divenga...
(Dec, 123)

"Therefore I am prepared, if you wish, that she should become your legitimate wife..."

PAST-referring Joint Axes

In OFr, [-Past] forms are used freely in PAST-referring when-sentences; there seem to be no constraints on their appearing in sequence with either [-Past] or [+Past] forms. The use of Pres in this way is particularly interesting: there are, as we have seen, no examples of its use in a genuine temporal when-sentence with PRESENT reference; but there are many examples of its 'historic' present usage with PAST reference, e.g.:

(21) Au matinet, quant il s'esvoillent,
Sont es chevaux mises les seles. (Erec, 5294-5)

"Early in the morning, when they awoke, the saddles were placed upon the horses."

The when-clause of POST when-sentences in OFr contains both [-Perf] forms like Pres and Pret and [+Perf] forms like Perf, Plup and PAnt. Imp is extremely rare in the when-clause[3] and relatively uncommon in the matrix clause of POST when-sentences; one example of the latter is found as the verb-form of a second conjoined clause:

(22) Quant Aucassins le perçut, si s'aresta tot a un fais, et li rais de le lune feroit ens. (Auc, 24.76-7)

"When Aucassin noticed it, he stopped all at once, and the shaft of moonlight struck within."[4]

and there is another example of Imp with a DURATIVE verb-stem representing a consequent state:

(23) Quant tut li ad dit e mustré
E il l'aveit bien escuté,
De l'aventure esteit dolenz...
(Marie, Lc, 145-7)

"When he had told and shown him everything, and he had listened, he was grieved about the incident..."

In OSp, the only text which shows anything of the freedom of OFr in the selection of PAST-referring verb-forms is Cid, where Pres, Imp and Pret appear wellnigh indiscriminately in when-sentences. Furthermore, in this text the aspectual distinction between Imp and Pret appears to be weak in the matrix clause, there being several examples of Imp used (albeit with PUNCTUAL verb-stems) in the matrix clause of a POST when-sentence, e.g.:

(24) Quando son pagados a todo so sabor
hya mandavan cargar iffantes de Carrion.
(Cid, 2586-7)

"When they were fully satisfied, the infantes of Carrión gave the order to load up."

PAnt and its [-Past] equivalent, Perf, are restricted to the when-clauses of POST when-sentences. Perf is never used in a matrix clause as a simple form with PAST reference, and so does not show any sign of functioning as a simple past verb-form. In other OSp texts, Pret and PAnt are the forms chiefly encountered in the when-clause of POST when-sentences, combining with all lexical aspectual types; Imp may occur in the matrix clause unusually when an event with a resultant state is represented by the matrix clause verb:

(25) Quando fo en su tierra, la carrera complida,
e udieron la cosa qe avié contecida,
tenién grandes clamores, era la gent movida
por veer esti Lázaro dado de muert a vida.
(Mil, 216)

"When he was back in his own land, his journey ended, and they heard what had happened, there was a great clamour, the people were moved to see this Lazarus raised from the dead to life."

Imp also appears rarely in the when-clause of a PAST POST when-sentence:

(26) Quando ál non podién las gentes con ardura,
" Valas / sancta María!" dizién a grand
pressura...[5] (Mil, 439a-b)

"When they could do no other, the people said quickly in their affliction, 'Help, Saint Mary!'"

In the OIt texts, Inf offers one example of a [-Past] sequence used with PAST reference:

(27) E quando noi a lei venuti semo,
poco più oltre veggio in su la rena
gente seder propinqua al loco scemo.
(Inf, 17.34-6)

"And when we came to him, I saw a little further on, on the sand, people sitting near the empty space."

The POST when-sentences encountered in the OIt texts have sequences limited to Pret in the matrix clause with either Pret or PAnt in the when-clause.

PAST SIM when-sentences generally exhibit a sequence in which at least one of the verb-forms has an overall non-punctual aspectual value. Typically they involve Imp in either matrix- or when-clause, e.g.:

(28) OFr QUANT Imp/Pret:

Quant il ierent en cel esfrei,
Deus puceles de gent cunrei
....
Virent venir la rue aval.
(Marie, L, 509-10, 513)

"When they were in this tumult, they saw two richly attired damsels coming down the road."

(29) OSp QUANDO Pret/Imp:

... e quando este llego a Espanna, tenie Uiriato cercado un castiello... (PCG, 28.36R)

"... and when he arrived in Spain, Viriathus was holding a castle under siege..."

(30) OIt QUANDO Imp/Imp:

... "Quando tu andavi
al fuoco, non l'avei tu così presto..."
(Inf, 30.109-10)

"...'When you were going to the fire you did not have it [your arm] so ready...'"

A Pret/Pret sequence will yield a SIM reading, however, provided that the events or states represented by the verbs are exactly contemporaneous, e.g., from OFr:

(31) Quant en lur païs s'en alerent,
La Coudre lur fille menerent...
(Marie, F, 511-2)

"When they returned to their country they took Coudre their daughter [with them]."

or when they contract relations of implication or hyponymy, e.g., from OSp:

(32) ... e quando passo por el sennorio de Francia tomo dessas gentes las que pudo auer. (PCG, 23.42L)

"... and when he went through the French domain he took those people he could." (Taking the people is part of the activity of the campaign.)

ANT examples are characterised by a [+Perf] form in the matrix-clause and the corresponding [-Perf] form in the when-clause, e.g., from OIt:

(33) Già era il sole inchinato al vespro, e in gran parte il caldo diminuito, quando le novelle delle giovani donne e de' tre giovani si trovarono esser finite. (Dec, 81)

"The sun had already dipped towards the west and the heat had decreased to a large extent, when the stories of the young ladies and the three young men came to an end."

The Pret/Pret sequence can however receive an ANT

interpretation, as can be seen from this OFr example:

(34) Ne demura ke une loëe,
Quant sa cumpaine i acurrut,
Si vit la place u ele jut...
(Marie, El, 1038-40)

"He [the weasel] had only been there a short time when his companion ran to him and saw the place where he [musteile, 'weasel', is feminine] lay..."

Sequences of tense in TIME examples do not differ from those encountered in POST and SIM types.

The non-temporal types in OFr and OSp (there appear to be none with PAST reference in the OIt texts) all have CAUSAL readings; the majority of examples in both languages involve [-Past] sequences, e.g.:

(35) Ne leisserai mon oste anuit,
Qui mout m'a grant enor portee,
Quant il sa fille m'a donee. (Erec, 1270-1)

"I will not leave my host tonight who has done me a very great honour since he has given me his daughter."

(36) ¡ved qual ondra creçe al que en buen ora naçio
quando señoras son sus fijas de Navarra e de Aragón! (Cid, 3722-3)

"See what honour redounded to him who was born in a lucky hour since his daughters were ladies of Navarre and Aragon!"

although OSp offers one example with a [+Past] sequence:

(37) parece que el riego todo d'ella manava
quando a menos d'ella nada non se guiava.
(Mil, 22c-d)

"It seems that the water all sprang from her since except through her nothing was guided."

TRANSPOSED PAST-referring when-sentences in OFr offer no distinct sequence from non-TRANSPOSED types, [Past]-AGREEMENT not applying in the available examples, e.g.:

(38) Dist cum[ent] est avenu:
S'onur e sun bien ad perdu,
Quant de tel fet s'est entremise...
(Marie, M, 58-9)

"She told him how it had happened: [that] she had lost her honour and her wellbeing when she became involved in such an affair."

In OSp, the -ra form is involved in all the TRANSPOSED PAST when-sentences, sometimes in both clauses:

(39) ... dixo que quando so padre muriera en Cezilia que prometiera de fazer grandes onras en su sepultura... (PCG, 39.49L)

"... he said that when his father had died in Sicily, he had promised to do great honours for his tomb..."

We may assume that the operation of [Past]-AGREEMENT in OSp, as in MSp, converts a verb-form that is already [+Past] into a corresponding [+Perf] form.

UNIVERSAL-referring when-sentences generally have Pres/Pres sequence in OFr, OSp and OIt, although the marking of a POST relation is possible through the use of a [+Perf] form in the when-clause, e.g., in OFr:

(40) D'euls deus fu il [tut] autresi
Cume del chevrefoil esteit
Ki a la codre se perneit:
Quant il s'i est laciez e pris
E tut entur le fust s'est mis,
Ensemble poënt bien durer...
(Marie, Che, 68-73)

"[That] with them it was just like the honeysuckle which took to the hazel: when it has twined around and clung to it and is completely round the trunk, they can live well together..."

One or two of the OIt examples have a [+Subj] form in the when-sentence, e.g.:

(41) Mostrato n'ha Panfilo nel suo novellare la benignità di Dio non guardare a' nostri errori, quando da cosa che per noi veder non si possa procedano...
(Dec, 57)

"Panfilo has shown us in his story that the loving kindness of God does not take notice of our errors, when they proceed from something which cannot be seen by us..."

FUTURE UNIVERSAL-referring when-sentences follow the pattern already established for FUTURF-referring types; LBA in OSp again has an example of PresSubj in the when-clause:

(42) "quando mejor te sepan, por diośs, de tilas tira. (LBA, 1167d)

"'When they taste best to you, for goodness sake cast them from you.'"

PAST UNIVERSAL-referring when-sentences generally have an Imp/Imp sequence (though once again OFr uses a [-Past] sequence extensively); in OSp there is an interesting example of the Compound Pluperfect (Plup) being used in the when-clause of a basically POST example:

(43) ... de guisa que quando las unas tierras auien apaziguadas, leuantauan se las otras... (PCG, 28.38L)

"... so that when they had pacified some lands others rose up..."

It seems possible that the motivation for the use of the compound form here rather than the -ra form is the preservation of the characteristic Imp inflection in both clauses. OIt has examples with [+Past, +Subj] forms in the when-clause, in parallel with the UNIVERSAL sequences we have observed, e.g.:

(44) ... quando elli vi passasse alcuno gentiluomo con molti arnesi, ed elle il faceano invitare e facèanli grandissimo onore. (Nov, 118)

"... that when there passed by a gentleman with many possessions, they invited him in and did him very great honour."

TRANSPOSED UNIVERSAL, FUTURE UNIVERSAL and PAST UNIVERSAL examples are no different from the corresponding non-UNIVERSAL types as far as OFr and OSp are concerned; however, OIt once again regularly employs a [+Subj] form in the when-clause, e.g.:

(45) ... ser Ciappelletto rispuose di sì, e molte volte; perciò che... con quello diletto e con quello appetito l'acqua bevuta avea, e spezialmente quando avesse alcuna fatica durata o

adorando o andando in pellegrinaggio, che fanno i gran bevitori il vino... (Dec, 51)

"... Ser Ciappelletto replied that he had, and many times; since... he had drunk water with the same pleasure and appetite, and especially when he had undergone some tiring activity like praying or going on a pilgrimage, as hardened drinkers do wine..."

Amongst the PAST-referring when-sentences in these texts there are a number of 'inverse when' examples; formally, the sequences involved are not distinct from the SIM and ANT sequences already noted, e.g.:

(46) La fu abatuz Sagremors,
Uns chevaliers de mout grant pris.
Toz estoit retenuz et pris,
Quant Erec point a la rescosse...
(Erec, 2238-41)

"There Sagremor, a knight of very great worth, was thrown down; he was about to be detained and taken, when Erec rushed to the rescue..."

(47) Già era in loco onde s'udia 'l rimbombo
de l'acqua che cadea ne l'altro giro,
simile a quel che l'arnie fanno rombo,
quando tre ombre insieme si partiro...
(Inf, 1-4)

"I was already in a place where there could be heard the resounding of the water which was falling into the other circle, like the humming of a beehive, when three shades came out together..."

Disjoint Axes

In OFr and OSp there are no examples of disjoint axis when-sentences with a temporal reading. A CAUSAL reading seems to be the rule in OFr, e.g.:

(48) QUANT Perf/Fut, PAST/FUTURE:
'Sire, quant parduné l'avez,
Jel vus dirai; si m'escutez!'
(Marie, F, 465-6)

"'Sire, since you have pardoned it, I will tell you; now listen to me!'"

and there are similar examples in OSp; additionally

in OSp, we find one example with a CONCESSIVE reading:

(49) e ruego a San Peydro que me ayude a rogar
por mio Çid el Campeador que Dios le curie de mal,
quando oy nos partimos en vida nos faz juntar!'
(Cid, 363-5)

"... and I pray to Saint Peter that he may help me to pray for my Cid the Campeador that God may keep him from harm; though today we part, may we meet again in life!"

In the OIt texts, where, it will be remembered, CAUSAL readings for when-sentences are not as common as in OFr and OSp, there is only one example of a disjoint axis, and this preserves a temporal reading, the sequence being QUANDO Perf/Pres and the value of quando being similar to ora che:

(50) In la palude va c'ha nome Stige
questo triste ruscel, quand' è disceso
al piè de le maligne piagge grige.
(Inf, 106-8)

"This sad stream goes into the marsh which is called the Styx when it has come down to the foot of the grey malignant shores."

FROM MEDIEVAL TO MODERN ROMANCE

French

The four medieval texts studied show a remarkable degree of uniformity. [+Subj] forms, unless independently motivated, are completely absent from when-sentences: FUTURE when-sentences have a [+Fut] form in their when-clauses, and PAST when-sentences have a wide range of PAST-referring forms in both when- and matrix-clause. When-sentences involving PRESENT reference and disjoint axes are never found with purely temporal readings. Marking of precedence-relation is often carried out by the choice of verb-form sequence. ANT is usually expressed by a [+Perf] marking in the verb-form of the matrix-clause; POST is optionally expressed by the use of a [+Perf] form in the when-clause, and SIM in PAST referring when-sentences may be expressed by a [-Punc] marking in the verb-form of either clause. Yet in many cases, the precedence-relation may be deduced only from the general context in which the when-sentence stands.

This general pattern of usage continues into MFr, although in the spoken language Plup has replaced PAnt and $Perf_2$ has replaced Pret. The 'supercompound' forms are also used for the marked expression of POST precedence-relations, e.g.:

(51) Quand j'ai eu terminé de relever les cotes, j'ai rempli une fiche rose (Cornu (1953: 147))[6]

Spanish

The most striking feature of the syntax of when-sentences in OSp is the use of a [+Subj] form, FutSubj, in the when-clause of FUTURE-referring when-sentences. In historical terms, this is readily comprehensible when it is remembered that OSp FutSubj is the direct descendant of CL FutPerf, which, as we have seen, was usual in the temporal subordinate clauses of CL, whether introduced by cum or by other temporal connectives, when there was a POST precedence-relation. The use of FutSubj may also have been reinforced by the strong survival of the form in the protases of FUTURE conditional sentences, as observed in the preceding Chapter.

Examination of the PAST-referring when-sentences of OSp allows us to begin to make sense of the plethora of [+Past, +Perf] forms encountered during this period. Setting aside the switching between [-Past] and [+Past] sequence which is typical of, but limited to, Cid, we find the following pattern. In PAST POST when-sentences, only PAnt or Pret appear in the when-clause, and the rule seems to be that a [+Punc] sequence is maintained. Plup (Compound Pluperfect) never appears, and the -ra form only appears when there is also a -ra form in the matrix-clause. On the other hand, when-sentences with TRANSPOSED PAST reference more regularly exhibit a QUANDO -ra/-ra sequence, and Plup is used in the when-sentence of a PAST UNIVERSAL when-sentence, where the matrix-clause would normally contain Imp, thus maintaining a [-Punc] sequence. The preservation of morphological sequence seems to be the crucial factor in determining the choice among PAnt, Plup and -ra in when-sentences, and we may notice that the morphological anomaly of the -ra form within the verb-system of OSp places it in a separate sequential category.

A profile of MSp usage is given in Table 7.5. There is in fact no major structural change from the

OSp situation. The demise of FutSubj has led to a replacement by PresSubj in FUTURE when-sentences, an embryonic trace of which may be argued for in one or two OSp examples; but the association of FUTURE-referring when-clauses with the [+Subj] feature is retained. In the PAST-referring group, CUANDO PAnt/Pret still contrasts with CUANDO Plup/Imp, the [-Punc] sequence still signalling PAST UNIVERSALity. Plup, the descendant of OSp Plup, has ousted -ra (now a [+Subj] form - see the preceding Chapter) in TRANSPOSED PAST examples. Plup, as the [+Past] equivalent of Perf, is well placed to gain the ascendancy over PAnt, which does not have a corresponding [-Past] form, in contexts which require [Past]-AGREEMENT. It is no doubt for this reason too that the -ra form, which equally had no morphologically corresponding [-Perf] form, was weakened; the further lack for the -ra form of a morphologically corresponding [-Perf] form (which PAnt does have) made it doubly weak as a [-Subj] form.

Italian

Much the same kind of remarks can be made for It as have been made for Fr, although we must still count the sequences QUANDO Pret~PAnt/Pret as being available in some spoken dialects.

An area of special interest in the history of It when-sentences is the use of [+Subj] forms in the when-clause. In the OIt texts examined here, the [+Subj] forms appear to be used in the following circumstances: (a) in FUTURE- and PRESENT-referring when-sentences with a CONDITIONAL reading, (b) occasionally in UNIVERSAL- or PAST UNIVERSAL-referring when-sentences, (c) in TRANSPOSED reference examples. It seems likely that the UNIVERSAL usage of the [+Subj] forms may be connected with their use after quando che, "whenever", e.g.:

(52) ... e se io ora sto in peccato mortaio, io starò quando che sia in peccato pestello... (Dec, 175)
"... and if I am living in 'mortar' sin I'll live in 'pestle' sin whenever..."

No difficulty is caused by the use of [+Subj] forms in the when-clause with two different functions since each function is available within different areas of time-reference. However, the use of [+Subj] forms in TRANSPOSED reference when-clauses is rather more difficult to interpret. In the case of TRANSPOSED UNIVERSAL- and TRANSPOSED PAST UNIVERSAL-referring examples, it would be natural to see the use of the [+Subj] forms as corresponding to the usage in UNIVERSAL- and PAST UNIVERSAL-referring sequences, although it is curious that the [+Subj] forms seems to be preferred in the TRANPOSED reference examples, when they are clearly not in the non-TRANSPOSED examples. In the case of other TRANSPOSED examples (like (12) above), however, it is difficult to interpret the usage either as a CONDITIONAL or a UNIVERSAL usage, and such examples may be more plausibly explained by the presence of local conditioning factors of the kind I discussed above in relation to (12). The possibility of using [+Subj] forms in FUTURE-referring when-clauses is still present in MIt, where we have alternatives like:

(53) Quando ci arriverò/arrivi, mi vedrà

The distinction between the two forms probably relies on presuppositions concerning the likelihood of the FUTURE event, rather than on any association with CONDITIONALity (or still less with UNIVERSALity). Battaglia and Pernicone (1968:546), discussing (53), observe:

> Il verbo retto da queste congiunzioni si pone generalmente all' indicativo, perchè indica una circonstanza reale: avvenuta nel passato, oppure in atto nel presente, oppure sicura nel futuro; ma in quest'ultimo caso, poichè l'azione futura può essere considerata come possibile e tuttavia problematica, si può anche adoperare il congiuntivo, specialmente con appena (e non appena), e a volte anche con quando e allorchè...

THE STRUCTURE OF ROMANCE WHEN-SENTENCES

The preceding sections have shown how changes within the verb-system of a language, in that they may affect verb-forms involved in when-sentence sequences, may be responsible for changes within when-sentence structure. The changing function of Perf in MFr and MIt, the disappearance of the -ra form with pluperfect value and FutSubj in OSp - all force changes on when-sentence sequences. Conversely, it may be surmised that the usage of a particular verb-form in a when-sentence sequence (e.g., PAnt in OSp and MSp, the appearance of the Supercompound Perfect in MFr) strengthens the position of that verb-form within the verb-system, and that rejection of a verb-form in a when-sentence (e.g., -ra in OSp) may weaken its position within the verb-system.

It is also instructive to look at how the fortunes of when-sentences in the Romance languages compare with those of other temporal constructions. In MSp, for example, the verb-form after cuando is for the most part identical with the verb-form following other temporal connectives in a similar semantic context. Thus a FUTURE-referring clause always has PresSubj (or PerfSubj) as its verb-form:

(54) Se sentirá débil { cuando / después que / luego que / en cuanto / ⋮ } oiga la noticia

The only exception to this rule concerns an ANT temporal connective. Antes (de) que is always followed by a [+Subj] form, even in cases where other temporal connectives are not:

(55) Se sintió débil { cuando / después que / luego que / en cuanto / ⋮ } oyó la noticia

but

Se sintió débil antes que oyera la noticia

(Other ANT temporal connectives, e.g., hasta que, are in fact more like cuando, etc., since [+Subj] forms are only required when the time-reference of the subordinate temporal clause in FUTURE or TRANSPOSED FUTURE:

(56) Esperaré aquí hasta que llegue el autobús
Dijo que esperaría allí hasta que llegara el autobús
but
Esperó allí hasta que llegó el autobús)

Much the same picture emerges for MIt. Here, FUTURE-referring when-clauses and other temporal subordinate clauses optionally have [+Subj] forms; among the ANT temporal connectives, *prima che* is always followed by a [+Subj] form, whereas *finchè* behaves in the same way as MSp *hasta que*[7]. In MFr, however, the situation is not quite so clearcut, and our parallel fails to a large extent. *Quand* is not normally ever followed by a [+Subj] form; on the other hand, all ANT temporal connectives normally require [+Subj] forms (e.g., *avant que*, *jusqu'à ce que*, *d'ici que*)[8] and even the POST temporal connective *après que*, is often found with a [+Subj] form. This last phenomenon is usually explained through analogy with *avant que*, the antonym of *après que*; it would appear, strangely enough, that MFr has undergone an extension of the use of [+Subj] in temporal clauses when the general tendency of the language has been to reduce the distribution of the [+Subj] forms.

The seeds of these general patterns can be traced to a large extent in the data available to us from CL. POST temporal connectives normally require [-Subj] forms, as do SIM connectives. In the verb-forms of clauses introduced by ANT temporal connectives, a quite marked move towards the use of [+Subj] forms can be discerned during the CL period (see Table 7.2): in post-Ciceronian CL, ImpSubj is increasingly found in the subordinate clause of a PAST ANT temporal sentence with a positive matrix-clause, presumably by analogy with the FUTURE ANT situation, where PresSubj was a possibility in the subordinate clause of a temporal sentence with a positive matrix-clause. Hence we could easily imagine a proto-Romance situation in which [+Subj] forms were the rule with ANT temporal connectives and [-Subj] forms the rule with POST and SIM temporal connectives: this, with the exception of the peculiar (and easily explainable) case of *après que*, is the situation in MFr.

In MSp and MIt a parameter of time-reference seems to have come into play at some stage, since the obligatory [+Subj] form in MSp and the optional [+Subj] in MIt is restricted to FUTURE-referring clauses. Indeed, with the exception of *antes (de) que*/*prima che*, the parameter of FUTURity is more significant in these languages than that of ANTeriority. The evidence from MIt seems to suggest that a modal parameter comes into operation too: the 'hypothetical' reading of a [+Subj] form in a FUTURE-referring *when*-clause may be parallel to the requirement that a [+Subj] form is used in a relative clause with a negative antecedent, so that *quando venga...* may be considered as having the underlying structure

(57) [... Adv_i [(lui) venire Adv_i /FUT/] /FUT/]

The MSp situation differs in that there is no 'modal' overtone to the choice of a [+Subj] form in a FUTURE-referring temporal clause, so that a structural description such as (57) is unmotivated and unnecessary. As far as OSp is concerned, we find that the distribution of FutSubj and PresSubj varies slightly according to temporal connective. FUTURE-referring temporal sentences with connectives other than quando are comparatively rare in the four OSp texts studied, and a composite picture of usage is therefore difficult to obtain[9]. The indications, however, are as follows. ANT connectives (ante(s) que, fasta/hasta que) are consistently followed by PresSubj, e.g.

(58) non deranche ninguno fata que yo lo mande (Cid, 703)

"Let no one break ranks until I give the order."

Of the SIM connectives, mientra que is found with both PresSubj and FutSubj in Cid and Mil, e.g. (from Mil):

(59) mientre que fuere vivo verá plazentería (Mil, 115c)

"While he lives he will see grace."

(60) bien nos verrá emiente mientre vivos seamos... (Mil, 390b)

"It will come sharply to mind while we live..."

Among the POST connectives, de(s)pues que is found with PerfSubj and FutSubj:

(61) despues que vos ayas fecho este sacrifiçio, ofreçer vos los he yo en graçias e en seruiçio... (LBA, 777a-b)

"After you have made the sacrifice I will give them to you in thanks and service..."

(62) ... non sabes quet acaeçra depues que fueres dentro. (PCG, 40.45R)

"You do not know what will befall you after you are inside."

Desque and luego que similarly appear with both PresSubj and FutSubj. If any pattern emerges, then, it is that while ANT connectives obligatorily take PresSubj and quando obligatorily FutSubj, most other temporal connectives are ambivalent between the two forms. In such cases, there does not appear to be any semantic distinction to be drawn.

At this juncture, it is again interesting to compare the situation in MPtg, where FutSubj forms cognate with those of OSp still survive. Here, three kinds of FUTURE-referring temporal connectives can similarly be distinguished: (a) those which require FutSubj (quando, segundo, conforme, (assim) como), (b) those which may take either FutSubj or PresSubj (enquanto (que), assim que, logo que, depois que and sempre que), and (c) those requiring PresSubj (including até que and antes que) (see Willis (1965:§190)). In both MPtg and OSp, therefore, quando belongs to the group which takes exclusively FutSubj, and the ANT connectives to the group which takes exclusively PresSubj.

We may assume, then, that in the first place CL FutPerf, the origin of OSp and MPtg FutSubj, is generalised into the subordinate clauses of both POST and SIM temporal sentences which are FUTURE-referring at the proto-Romance stage from which Sp and Ptg spring. PresSubj in the subordinate clause of ANT temporal sentences (except when-sentences) is a continuation of the CL tendency which Sp and Ptg share with other Romance languages including Fr. The presence of PresSubj in the subordinate clauses of other temporal sentence types in OSp and MPtg may be a result of analogical broadening of the rule requiring PresSubj in ANT temporal sentences (compare the phenomenon of MFr après que), or it may be favoured by the kind of considerations which seem to affect the choice of PresSubj as opposed to Fut in MIt. However that may be, the extension of PresSubj within the temporal sentence system of OSp paves the way for further broadening to FUTURE-referring when-sentences when FutSubj is eventually weakened. It is likely, therefore, that the explanation of diachronic processes in Sp may benefit from a consideration of when-sentences within the whole temporal sentence system.

NOTES

1. Menéndez Pidal clearly regarded the verb-form salie as anomalous when he corrected these two

troublesome lines as follows:

Las palabras son puestas, los omenajes dados son,
que otro dia mañana quando saliesse el sol,
ques tornasse cada uno don salidos son.

The MS edition is essentially the same as the Smith text, except that the caesura is made after manana.

2. Indeed, there are a couple of examples from Erec which appear as when-sentences in the Roques text but as factive complements in the Foerster edition, e.g.:

Molt est grant honte et grant leidure,
quant ceste bataille tant dure... (Roques, 901-2)

Mout est granz honte et granz leidure
Que ceste bataille tant dure. (Foerster, 901-2)

"It is a great shame and a great discredit when/
that this battle lasts so long..."

3. The one example I encountered, in Erec, was rendered differently in the Foerster and Roques editions:

Et Enide aprés lui i cort,
Qui mout estoit joianz et liee.
Quant lor voie iere aparelliee,
As puceles ont congié pris...
(Foerster, 5298-301)

"And Enid followed him, joyful and delighted.
When their way was prepared, they took their
leave of the damsels..."

et Enyde aprés lui recort,
qui molt estoit joianz et liee,
que lor voie ert apareilliee.
As puceles ont congié pris... (Roques, 5250-3)

"And Enid followed him, joyful and delighted
that their way was prepared. They took their
leave of the damsels..."

4. This example could clearly also be read in a way in which the when-clause is not subordinate to the clause to which feroit belongs (i.e., with li rais de le lune feroit ens as a completely separate conjoined sentence.

5. In this example, it may be that the overall context of 'description', in which Imp would be the normal PAST-referring form, determines the verb-form of both constituent clauses. Discourse context may also have an important part to play, since the preceding strophe contains a whole series of Imps which represent 'description' with PAST reference:

Las ondas vinién cerca, las gentes alongadas,
avié con el desarro las piernas embargadas;
las compannas non eran de valerli osadas,
en poquiello de término yazién muchas jornadas.

6. Cornu (1953:149) points out that in written Fr the passé surcomposé is associated particularly with the verbs terminer, achever and finir, and with verbs which imply the cessation of a previous state (e.g., partir, quitter, prendre, etc.).

7. Note, however, that It finchè also has the value of "as long as", in which case its verb is a [-Subj] form (finchè vivrò, aspetterò qui).

8. However, Grevisse (1964:§1018 Rem.) quotes examples with [-Subj] forms when these clauses are PAST-referring for both MFr and older texts. Jusqu'au moment où, a popular alternative to jusqu'à ce que, is followed by a [-Subj] form too.

9. The precise figures are:

Cid: quando, 10; antes que, 6; fata que, 2; mientra que, 1.
Mil: quando, 6; antes que, 1; dessent que, 1; hasta que, 1; luego que, 1; mientre, 6
PCG: quando, 15; fasta que, 1; despues que, 1; luego que, 1; mientre que, 1
LBA: quando, 12; antes que, 7; cadaque, 5; despues que, 1; desque, 6; fasta que, 8; luego que, 1

Table 7.1: CL verb-form sequences with cum

	POST	SIM	ANT	NON-TEMP
PAST	Descriptive: CUM Plup/Perf CUM PlupSubj/Perf Determinative: CUM Plup/Perf	Descriptive: CUM Imp/Perf~Imp CUM ImpSubj/Perf~Imp Determinative: CUM Imp/Perf~Imp	CUM Perf/Plup	CUM ImpSubj~PlupSubj/...
PRES	(CUM Perf/Pres)	(CUM Pres/Pres)	(CUM Pres/Perf)	CUM PresSubj~PerfSubj/...
FUT	CUM FutPerf/Fut	CUM Fut/Fut	CUM Fut/Fut/Perf	CUM FutSubj/...
UNIV	CUM Perf/Pres	CUM Pres/Pres	CUM Pres/Perf	CUM PresSubj/...
PAST UNIV	CUM Plup/Imp CUM PlupSubj/Imp	CUM Imp/Imp CUM ImpSubj/Imp	CUM Imp/Plup (CUM ImpSubj/Plup)	CUM ImpSubj~PlupSubj/...

Table 7.2: CL verb-form sequences with other temporal connectives

	POST (postquam, ubi, ut, etc.)	SIM (dum, dummodo, etc)	ANT (antequam, priusquam)
PAST	POSTQUAM Plup~Perf~Pres/...	DUM Imp~Pres/...	Matrix S positive: ANTEQUAM Perf/... ANTEQUAM ImpSubj/... Matrix S negative: ANTEQUAM Perf~Pres/...
PRES	POSTQUAM Perf/...	DUM Pres/...	ANTEQUAM Perf(~Pres)/...
FUT	POSTQUAM FutPerf/...	DUM Fut/...	Matrix S positive: ANTEQUAM Pres~PresSubj/... Matrix S negative: ANTEQUAM FutPerf/...
UNIV	POSTQUAM Perf/Pres	DUM Pres/Pres	ANTEQUAM Perf(~Pres)/Pres
PAST UNIV	POSTQUAM Plup~PlupSubj/Imp	DUM Imp/Imp	ANTEQUAM Imp/Imp

Table 7.3: MFr when-sentences

	POST	SIM	ANT
FUT	QUAND Fut~FutPerf/...	QUAND Fut/...	QUAND Fut/FutPerf
PRES	(QUAND Perf/Pres)	(QUAND Pres/Pres)	(QUAND Pres/Perf)
PAST	QUAND Plup~Perf/Perf (spoken) QUAND PAnt~Pret/Pret (written)	QUAND Imp~Perf/Imp~Perf (spoken) QUAND Imp~Pret/Imp~Pret (written)	QUAND Perf/Plup (spoken) QUAND Pret/Plup (written)
UNIV	QUAND Perf~Pres/Pres	QUAND Pres/Pres	QUAND Pres/Perf
PAST UNIV	QUAND Plup~Imp/Imp	QUAND Imp/Imp	QUAND Imp/Plup

Table 7.4: MFr verb-form sequences with other temporal connectives

	POST	SIM	ANT
FUT	APRES QUE Fut~FutPerf (Pres Subj~PerfSubj)/...	PENDANT QUE Fut/...	AVANT QUE PresSubj~PerfSubj/ Fut~FutPerf
PRES	APRES QUE Pres~Perf (PresSubj~ PerfSubj/Pres	PENDANT QUE Pres/Pres	AVANT QUE PresSubj~PerfSubj/ Pres~Perf
PAST	APRES QUE Perf~Plup (PerfSubj)/ Perf, Pret~PAnt/Pret	PENDANT QUE Imp/Perf~Imp, Pret	AVANT QUE PerfSubj/Perf~Plup, ImpSubj~PlupSubj/Pret~Plup
UNIV	APRES QUE Pres~Perf (PresSubj~ PerfSubj)/Pres	PENDANT QUE Pres/Pres	AVANT QUE PresSubj~PerfSubj/ Pres~Perf
PAST UNIV	APRES QUE Imp~Plup (PerfSubj)/ Imp	PENDANT QUE Imp/Imp	AVANT QUE PerfSubj/Imp~Plup ImpSubj~PlupSubj/Imp~Plup,

Table 7.5: MSp when-sentences

	POST	SIM	ANT
FUT	CUANDO PresSubj~PerfSubj/...	CUANDO PresSubj/...	CUANDO PresSubj/FutPerf
PRES	(CUANDO Perf/Pres)	(CUANDO Pres/Pres)	(CUANDO Pres/Perf)
PAST	CUANDO PAnt~Pret/Pret	CUANDO Imp~Pret/Imp~Pret	CUANDO Pret/Plup
UNIV	CUANDO Perf~Pres/Pres	CUANDO Pres/Pres	CUANDO Pres/Perf
PAST UNIV	CUANDO Plup~Imp/Imp	CUANDO Imp/Imp	CUANDO Imp/Plup

Table 7.6: MSp verb-form sequences with other temporal connectives

	POST	SIM	ANT
FUT	DESPUES (DE) QUE PresSubj~Perf Subj/...	MIENTRAS PresSubj/...	ANTES (DE) QUE PresSubj~Perf Subj/Fut~FutPerf
PRES	DESPUES (DE) QUE Pres~Perf/ Pres	MIENTRAS Pres/Pres	ANTES (DE) QUE PresSubj~Perf Subj/Pres~Perf
PAST	DESPUES (DE) QUE Pret~PAnt/ Pret	MIENTRAS Imp/Pret~Imp	ANTES (DE) QUE ImpSubj~Plup Subj/Pret~Plup
UNIV	DESPUES (DE) QUE Pres~Perf/ Pres	MIENTRAS Pres/Pres	ANTES (DE) QUE PresSubj~Perf Subj/Pres~Perf
PAST UNIV	DESPUES (DE) QUE Imp~Plup/Imp	MIENTRAS Imp/Imp	ANTES (DE) QUE ImpSubj~PlupSubj /Imp~Plup

Table 7.7: MIt when-sentences

	POST	SIM	ANT
FUT	QUANDO Fut~FutPerf~PresSubj~PerfSubj/...	QUANDO Fut~PresSubj/...	QUANDO Fut~PresSubj/FutPerf
PRES	(QUANDO Perf/Pres)	(QUANDO Pres/Pres)	(QUANDO Pres/Perf)
PAST	QUANDO Plup~Perf/Perf, PAnt~Pret/Pret	QUANDO Imp~Perf/Imp~Perf, Imp~Pret/Imp~Pret	QUANDO Perf~Pret/Plup
UNIV	QUANDO Perf~Pres/Pres	QUANDO Pres/Pres	QUANDO Pres/Perf
PAST UNIV	QUANDO Plup~Imp/Imp	QUANDO Imp/Imp	QUANDO Imp/Plup

Table 7.8: MIt verb-form sequences with other temporal connectives

	POST	SIM	ANT
FUT	DOPO CHE Fut~FutPerf/...	MENTRE Fut/...	PRIMA CHE PresSubj~Perf Subj/ Fut~FutPerf
PRES	DOPO CHE Pres~Perf/Pres	MENTRE Pres/Pres	PRIMA CHE PresSubj~PerfSubj/ Pres~Perf
PAST	DOPO CHE Plup~Perf/Perf, PAnt~Pret/Pret	MENTRE Imp/Imp~Pret~Perf	PRIMA CHE ImpSubj~PlupSubj/ Pret~Plup
UNIV	DOPO CHE Pres~Perf/Pres	MENTRE Pres/Pres	PRIMA CHE PresSubj~PerfSubj/ Pres~Perf
PAST UNIV	DOPO CHE Imp~Plup/Imp	MENTRE Imp/Imp	PRIMA CHE ImpSubj~PlupSubj/ Imp~Plup

Chapter Eight

CONCLUSIONS

GENERATIVE GRAMMAR AND STRUCTURAL MORPHOLOGY

In Chapters 2 and 3 of this study, I hope to have shown that a full description of verb-form usage can only be achieved when the verb is seen from a syntagmatic, as well as from a paradigmatic, point of view. A generative model of language is particularly suitable for the expression of the syntagmatic determining of verb-forms. It can provide for the participation of verb-forms in syntactic rules: I discussed in Chapter 2, for example, the choice of surface verb-forms in the complements of verbs of reporting, command and supposition, and the relevance of this data to an account of simple sentence verb-form usage. Elliptical surface structures (i.e., those involving deletion transformations) are also easily handled by a generative model, and I have suggested that some verb-form usages are most appropriately explained by their participation in such structures (complement structures with a deleted matrix clause, and conditional sentences with a deleted protasis, for example). I have also shown how a generative grammar can provide for the introduction of categories like temporal adverbial classes, which are essentially semantic in nature, as abstract underlying structures. A generative grammar therefore describes without difficulty surface verb-forms which are either (a) the product of syntactic processes (and hence 'derived' from distinct or more abstract underlying forms), or (b) introduced in accordance with relations of congruence contracted with other basic categories.

As regards paradigmatic relations among verb-forms, we have seen that the notion of a 'verb-system' may be construed in two ways. First of all, it is a concept of purely morphological importance -

though I have shown how the careful description of such a morphological set (as in the featural matrices proposed in Chapter 2) is advantageous in the statement of the syntactic and other rules in which verb-forms participate. Secondly, there is the question of how and whether the terms of a 'verb-system' can be awarded distinctive characterising properties. In Chapter 3 I argued that there is no rigorous way in which this can be done, although it is convenient and intuitively satisfactory to make use of the notion of the 'residual value' of some verb-forms, i.e., the value or values which a verb-form may be said to have when shorn of all surface context except the obligatorily cooccurring verb-stem. More generally, however, in Chapter 3 I showed the importance of the notion of paradigmatic opposition in the description of Pret and Perf in English and Sp, and insisted on their being handled within a generative model by essentially parallel processes (congruence with abstract adverbials), rather than primacy being given to their different syntagmatic forms.

When structuralist approaches to verb-form usage attempt to transcend the purely morphological level they are likely to be incomplete and rest on rather ill-defined descriptive bases. My reading of the work of many structuralists (discussed in Chapter 2) suggests that the most perceptive of them indeed felt these deficiencies and struggled to reach beyond the limits inherently placed upon them.

DEFICIENCIES OF THE GENERATIVIST POSITION

Yet while the techniques of generative grammar undoubtedly allow us to progress with greater ease in a description of verb-form usage, they too tend to impose undesirable limits. A syntactically-orientated model of description can only be a partial model of verb-form usage, and it is necessary to take into account factors of general semantics, pragmatics and discourse if anything like a full description of verb-form usage is to be obtained. Of particular interest and complexity was the pattern of semantic readings associated with combinations of verb-stem, verb-inflection and adverbial, which was described in terms of aspectual properties. I am of the opinion that even though many problems of verb-form usage which have been previously thought of as 'semantic' in nature can be dealt with more revealingly in 'syntactic' terms, the 'extra-syntactic' dimensions of semantics and pragmatics ought not to be ignored.

My examination of the syntax of conditional and when-sentences in Chapters 4 and 5 tends towards the same overall view. First, the surface forms of each of these sentence-types represent several different kinds of general semantic relation between the constituent clauses which do not always have reflexes characterisable in purely syntactic terms. Secondly, the selection of verb-form sequences in both genuine conditionals and temporal when-sentences appears often to be related to purely semantic factors (in the case of conditional sentences, on the presuppositions associated with the truth-value of protases and apodoses, and in when-sentences, on the precedence-relation between the events or states of matrix clause and when-clause. Conditional sentence verb-form sequences may also be dependent on pragmatic factors of attenuation ('polite formulae') and other 'marked' situations (doubt, fear, threat, etc.) - these were discussed chiefly in Chapter 6. The analysis I presented of the syntactic structure of conditional sentences in Chapter 4 suggests that a discourse- rather than a sentence-based grammar may be the only adequate way of dealing with such sentences.

A disposition to bring semantics and pragmatics firmly within the descriptive model and to extend interest beyond the single-sentence boundary would bestow on generative grammar the ability to deal with the phenomena of verb-form usage I have adduced for consideration in this study.

STRUCTURALIST SYNTAX

In Chapter 1 I mentioned the possibility of describing discontinuous units of syntax in a structuralist way - a possibility that might well be left out in the cold both by the lack of an underlying level of analysis in structuralist description and by the neglect of paradigmatic relations on the part of generativist grammar. My analysis of conditional sentences in Chapter 4, in which I propose that protasis-apodosis verb-form sequences be viewed as single units or 'modules' makes just such a possibility viable. The close-knit patterning of such verb-form sequences suggests it is valid to regard them as constituting a 'system' of paradigmatic oppositions, definable according to two clearcut semantic parameters of time-reference and truth-value presupposition. Verb-form sequences in when-sentences

(Chapter 5) do not pattern so neatly; yet here again there is clearly a dependency between matrix-clause verb-form and when-clause verb-form, and there are advantages in relating a general semantic property to a verb-form sequence rather than attempting to describe atomistically the value of each verb-form.

The kind of syntactic structuralist approach I am proposing is in fact not inconsistent with the extended concept of generative grammar which I have envisaged above. I am suggesting that in this study I have identified linguistic units which have a regular semantic value but which are discontinuous to the extent that they transcend sentence-boundaries; and that even where such units cannot be so conveniently established with definite semantic values, it may be necessary to incorporate into the grammar the notion of structured semantic relations which hold between sentences and regularly determine the choice of verb-form sequences.

STRUCTURALISM AND THE DIACHRONIC PERSPECTIVE

The advantages of viewing conditional sentence verb-form sequences in a structuralist way and the extraordinary suggestiveness of the structuralist approach to language change in an interpretation of the history of Romance conditional sentences were fully stated in Chapter 6. In this area, the need to examine paradigmatic relations between units emerges forcefully. I also presented many opportunities of observing conditional systems in a state of flux, where several alternant sequences coexist; and it does seem that in such cases the seeds of change can be observed in a synchronic state. The many different reflexes of the conditional system in the languages of Romania illustrate well the varying results that the same structural tendencies of analogy and symmetry may produce. I believe that in the development of the Romance conditional sentence we are entitled to claim yet another supporting example for the dynamic structuralist theory of language change.

However, syntagmatic structure is also of considerable significance in understanding diachronic processes. The development of Cond in Fr, Sp and It, for instance, is no doubt parallel to that of Fut because of the participation of the latter in a number of syntactic structures in which a [+Past] equivalent was required. I pointed out more generally in Chapter 7 how the choice of verb-form in a when-sentence must be understood through comparison with the choice of verb-form in other kinds of temporal clause.

The reinstatement of the study of paradigmatic relations within synchronic linguistics and an interest in syntagmatic relations within diachronic linguistics represents a considerable broadening in scope. It is a necessary broadening if we are not to find ourselves in the anomalous position of holding a view of language change which is based on 'dynamic structuralism' alongside a synchronic view which is rooted in a branch of transformational-generative grammar. Now the overall view of language which I have presented in this study does not provoke such inconsistency. On the synchronic plane, while I have adopted an 'extended' generative model of language, I have pointed out the intuitive appeal of a structuralist view of verb-forms which derives from surface structure and is not inconsistent with a generative model: it is not surprising, therefore, if structural considerations affect the history of individual verb-forms (I think particularly of the disappearance of a structurally anomalous form like OSp FutSubj, which syntactically was fairly strong). I have argued the importance of treating conditional verb-form 'modules' in a paradigmatic structuralist way on the synchronic plane: similarly, I have suggested the crucial significance of the structuralist principle in explaining their diachronic trajectory. I have shown too that a consideration of syntagmatic context is indispensable for a proper study of verb-form usage in the synchronic perspective: so it is on the diachronic plane, where syntagmatic context and synchronic structure are undeniably essential in the full history of verb-forms and the structures in which they participate.

TOWARDS THE FUTURE

I reach the end of this study with, above all, a sense of inadequacy in which the shortcomings of my own work figure not least. Yet I must regret too that despite the apparent wealth of published material on the Romance verb, Romance linguists must in some respects simply sit down and start again. Few of our accounts of the standard languages, our monographs on individual dialects, or our linguistic atlases provide the kind of subtle syntactic, semantic and pragmatic information that I believe we need before we can really begin to break open the fascinating comparative pattern of Romance verb-forms. Our rich treasure-house of textual monuments must yet again be searched for the same kind of information that will have to back up any historical syntax of the Romance verb. As yet, we have not the data before us: the deficiency is a substantive one. I hope that my limited work on medieval texts in this book may serve as a preliminary model for the kind of programme that surely needs to be undertaken.

My concern for the general theory of language description is less acute. It has been constantly in the melting-pot and is likely to remain there. There are signs that one by one the limitations against which I have argued are being broken down: in particular, the 'empirical' sociolinguistic approach to historical linguistics signalled by the work of Weinreich, Labov and Herzog (1968) must surely herald the reinstatement of diachronic studies and throw down a challenge to the synchronic/diachronic dichotomy that has been with us for too long. There are as yet few signs of *rapprochement* between traditional structuralists and generativists, however. Generativists concerned primarily with model-building continue to regard eclecticism as a cardinal sin; structuralists are nervous of models which seem to be of little help in describing the data with which they have traditionally been preoccupied. I hope to have suggested, however, that it is only through a meeting of these two approaches that further study of the Romance verb will prosper.

REFERENCES

Alarcos Llorach, E. (1959) 'La forme CANTARÍA en espagnol (mode, temps et aspect)', Boletim de Filologia, 18, 203-12

Anderson, J.M. (1973) 'On existence and the perfect', Foundations of Language, 10, 333-7

Anglade, J. (1965) Grammaire élémentaire de l'ancien français, Paris

Austin, J.L. (1962) How to do things with words, Oxford

Austin, J.L. (1963) 'Performatif-constatif', in C.E. Caton (ed.), Philosophy and Ordinary Language, Urbana, Ill., pp. 22-3

Badia Margarit, A.M. (1972) 'Por una revisión del concepto del 'cultismo' en fonética histórica', in Studia Hispanica in honorem R. Lapesa, Madrid, Vol. 1, pp. 137-52

Bally, C. (1933) 'Les notions grammaticales d'absolu et de relatif', Journal de Psychologie, 30, 341-54

Banfield, A. (1973) 'Narrative style and the grammar of direct and indirect speech', Foundations of Language, 10, 1-40

Battaglia, S. and Pernicone, V. (1968) La grammatica italiana, 2nd ed., Turin

Bédier, J. (1922) La Chanson de Roland publiée d'après le manuscrit d'Oxford et traduite par J. Bédier, Paris

Bertinetto, P.M. 'Il carattere del processo ("Aktionsart") in italiano. Proposte, sintatticamente motivate, per una tipologia del lessico verbale' in Tempo verbale - strutture quantificate in forma logica, Accademia della Crusca, Florence, pp. 11-90

Bever, T.G. and Langendoen, D.T. (1971) 'A dynamic model of the evolution of language', Linguistic Inquiry, 2, 433-63

Bolinger, D.L. (1956) 'Subjunctive -ra and -se: free variation?', Hispania, 39, 345-9

Bolinger, D.L. (1974) 'One subjunctive or two?', Hispania, 57, 462-71

Bosque, I. (1976) 'Sobre la interpretación causativa de los verbos adjetivales', in Sánchez de Zavala (ed.), Estudios de gramática generativa, Barcelona, pp. 101-17

Bourciez, E. (1946) Eléments de linguistique romane, 4th ed., Paris

Brunot, F. (1913) Histoire de la langue française des origines à 1900, Vol. 1, Paris

Brunot, F. and Bruneau, C. (1949) Précis de grammaire historique de la langue française, 3rd ed., Paris

Bull, W.E. (1968) Time, tense and the verb: a study in theoretical and applied linguistics, with particular attention to Spanish, Berkeley and Los Angeles

Campbell, R. and Wales, R. (1970) 'The study of language acquisition' in Lyons, J. (ed.), New Horizons in Linguistics, Harmondsworth, pp. 242-60

Chomsky, N. (1957) Syntactic Structures, The Hague

Chomsky, N. (1966) Cartesian Linguistics, New York

Chomsky, N. (1968) Language and Mind, 1st ed., New York

Clédat, L. (1910) 'Futur dans le passé et conditionnel', Revue de Philologie Française, 24, 141-9

Clédat, L. (1927) 'Futur dans le passé, ses valeurs modales', Revue de Philologie Française, 39, 17-41

Closs Traugott, E. (1969) 'Toward a theory of syntactic change', Lingua, 23, 1-27

Closs Traugott, E. (1972) The History of English Syntax, New York

Cohen, M. (1964) Le subjonctif en français contemporain, Paris

Comrie, B. (1976) Aspect, Cambridge

Cornu, M. (1953) Les formes surcomposées en français, Berne

Cressey, W.W. (1969) 'Relative adverbials in Spanish: a transformational analysis', Language, 44, 487-500

Crystal, D. (1966) 'Specification and English tenses', Journal of Linguistics, 2, 1-34

Damourette, J. and Pichon, E. (1936) Essai de grammaire de la langue française, Vol. 5, Paris

Elcock, W.D. (1960) The Romance Languages, 1st ed., London

Forsyth, J. (1970) A Grammar of Aspect. Usage and Meaning in the Russian Verb., Cambridge

Foulet, L. (1919) Petite syntaxe de l'ancien français, Paris

Fourquet, J. (1966) 'Deux notes sur le système verbal français', Langages, 3, 8-18

Frei, H. (1929) La grammaire des fautes. Introduction à la linguistique fonctionnelle., Geneva-Paris-Leipzig

Gallagher, M. (1970) 'Adverbs of time and tense', Chicago Linguistic Society: Papers from the 6th Regional Meeting, pp. 220-5

Gamillscheg, E. (1913) 'Studien zur Vorgeschichte einer romanischen Tempuslehre', Sitzungsberichte der Kaiserlichen Akademie der Wissenschaften in Wien, 172.6
Gamillscheg, E. (1957) Historische Syntax der französischen Sprache, Tübingen
Garey, H.B. (1955) 'The historical development of tenses from Late Latin to Old French', Supplement to Language, 31
Geis, M.L. (1970) 'Time prepositions as underlying verbs', Chicago Linguistic Society: Papers from the 6th Regional Meeting, pp. 235-49
Gessner, E. (1890) 'Die hypotetische Periode im Spanischen im ihrer Entwickelung', Zeitschrift für Romanische Philologie, 14, 21-65
Gildersleeve, B.L. and Lodge, G. (1895) Gildersleeve's Latin Grammar, 3rd ed., London
Gili Gaya, S. (1948) Curso superior de sintaxis española, 2nd ed., Barcelona
Gili Gaya, S. (1972) 'El pretérito de negación implícita', in Studia Hispanica in honorem R. Lapesa, Vol. 1, Madrid, pp. 251-6
Gobert, D.L. (1966) 'Tense variations in complex hypothetical utterances in contemporary French', The Philological Quarterly, 45, 464-8
Grandgent, C.H. (1907) An Introduction to Vulgar Latin, Boston, Mass.
Grevisse, M. (1964) Le bon usage, 8th ed., Gembloux-Paris
Guillaume, G. (1937) 'Thèmes de présent et système des temps français. Genèse corrélative du présent et des temps.', Journal de Psychologie, and in Langage et science du langage, Paris and Québec (1964), pp. 59-72
Hall, R.A. (1950) 'The reconstruction of proto-Romance', Language, 26, 6-27
Halle, M. (1964) 'Phonology in a generative grammar', in Fodor, J.A. and Katz, J.J. (eds.) The Structure of Language: Readings in the Philosophy of Language, Englewood Cliffs, N.J., pp. 334-52
Hanckel, W. (1929) Die Aktionsarten im Französischen, Berlin
Harmer, L.C. and Norton, F.J. (1935) A Manual of Modern Spanish, London
Harris, J.W. (1975) 'Diphthongization, monophthongization and metaphony revisited', in Saltarelli, M. and Wanner, D. (eds.), Diachronic Studies in Romance Linguistics, The Hague
Harris, M. (1971a) 'The history of the conditional complex from Latin to Spanish: some structural considerations', Archivum Linguisticum, 2, 25-33

Harris, M. (1971b) 'The verbal systems of Latin and French', Transactions of the Philological Society, 1970, 62-90

Harris, M. (1972a) 'Problems of deep and surface structure, as reflected in a diachronic analysis of the French verbal system', Journal of Linguistics, 8, 267-81

Harris, M. (1972b) 'Systems or rules: a false dichotomy?', Archivum Linguisticum, 3, 87-93

Harris, M. (1982) 'The "Past Simple" and the "Present Perfect" in Romance', in Vincent, N. and Harris, M. (eds.), Studies in the Romance Verb, London, pp. 42-70

Herczeg, G. (1976a) '"Se"/"Quando" + "Presente/ Passato del congiuntivo', Archivio Glottologico Italiano, 61, 146-55

Herczeg, G. (1976b) 'Sintassi delle proposizioni ipotetiche nell'italiano contemporaneo', Acta Linguistica Hafniensia, 26, 397-455

Herman, E. (1933) 'Aspekt und Aktionsart', Nachrichten der Gesellschaft der Wissenschaften zu Göttingen Phil.-Hist. Klasse, pp. 470-80

Hoenigswald, H.M. (1963) 'Are there universals of linguistic change?', in Greenberg, J.H. (ed.), Universals of Language, Cambridge, Mass.

Holt, J. (1943) 'Etudes d'aspect', Acta Jutlandica, 15, 1-94

Hornstein, N. 'Towards a theory of tense', Linguistic Inquiry, 8, 521-57

Imbs, P. (1955) Le subjonctif en français moderne, Strasbourg

Imbs, P. (1960) L'emploi des temps verbaux en français moderne: essai de grammaire descriptive, Paris

Iordan, I. and Orr, J. (1970) An Introduction to Romance Linguistics, its schools and scholars (revised, with a suppement 'Thirty Years On', by R. Posner), Oxford

Jensen, J.S. (1970) Subjonctif et hypotaxe en italien, Odense

Jespersen, O. (1933) Essentials of English Grammar, New York

Joos, M. (1968) The English Verb, 2nd ed., Wisconsin

Jungemann, F.H. (1956) Teoría del sustrato y los dialectos hispano-romances y gascones, Madrid

Kahn, F. (1954) Le système des temps de l'indicatif chez un Parisien et chez une Bâloise, Geneva

Kany, C.E. (1951) Spanish American Syntax, 2nd ed., Chicago

Kayne, R.S. (1975) French Syntax, Cambridge, Mass.

Kempson, R.M. (1975) Presupposition and the delimitation of semantics, Cambridge

Keniston, H. (1937a) The Syntax of Castilian Prose, New York
Keniston, H. (1937b) Spanish Syntax List, New York
Kiparsky, P. (1968a) 'Linguistic universals and linguistic change', in Bach, E. and Harms, R. (eds.), Universals in linguistic theory, New York
Kiparsky, P. (1968b) 'Tense and mood in Indo-European syntax', Foundations of Language, 4, 30-57
Kiparsky, C. and Kiparsky, P. (1971) 'Fact", in Steinberg, D.D. and Jakobovits, L.A. (eds.), Semantics: an interdisciplinary reader in philosophy, linguistics and psychology, Cambridge
Klum, A. (1959) 'Qu'est-ce que détermine quoi? Réflexions sur les rapports entre les verbes et les adverbes exprimant une date.', Studia Neophilologica, 31, 19-33
Klum, A. (1961) Verbe et adverbe, Stockholm
Kuhn, T.S. (1962) The Structure of Scientific Revolutions, Chicago
Lakoff, G. (1968) 'Counterparts, or the problem of reference in transformational grammar', Indiana University Linguistics Club
Lakoff, G. (1970) Irregularity in Syntax, New York
Lakoff, R.T. (1969a) Abstract Syntax and Latin Complementation, Cambridge, Mass.
Lakoff, R.T. (1969b) 'A syntactic argument for negative transportation', Chicago Linguistic Society: Papers from the 5th Regional Meeting
Lakoff, R.T. (1970) 'Tense and its relation to participants', Language, 46, 838-49
Lakoff, R.T. (1971) 'If's, and's and but's about conjunction', in Fillmore, C.J. and Langendoen, D.T. (eds.), Studies in Linguistic Semantics, New York
Lamérand, R. (1970) Syntaxe transformationnelle des propositions hypothétiques du français parlé, Brussels
Langacker, R. (1969) 'Pronominalization and the chain of command', in Reibel, D.A. and Schane, S.A. (eds.) Modern Studies in English: Readings in Transformational Grammar, Englewood Cliffs, N.J.
Langer, S.K. (1927) 'A logical study of verbs', Journal de Psychologie, 24, 120-9
Lapesa, R. (1951) 'La apócope de la vocal en castellano antiguo: intento de explicación histórica', in Estudios dedicados a Menéndez Pidal, Vol. 2, Madrid
Lapesa, R. (1975) 'De nuevo sobre la apócope vocálica en castellano medieval', Nueva Revista de

Filología Hispánica, 24, 13-23
Le Bidois, G. and R. (1935-8) Syntaxe du français moderne, ses fondements historiques et psychologiques, 2 Vols, Paris
Lehmann, W.P. (1962) Historical Linguistics: an Introduction, New York
Leone, A. (1974) 'SE + condizionale', Lingua Nostra, 35, 113-7
Lepschy, A.L. and Lepschy, G. (1977) The Italian Language Today, London
Lewis, C.T. and Short, C. (1879) A Latin Dictionary, Oxford
Lleó, C. (1979) Some optional rules in Spanish complementation: towards a study of the speaker's intent, Tübingen
Lorian, A. (1964) L'expression de l'hypothèse en français moderne, Paris
Lozano, A.G. (1972) 'Subjunctives, transformations and features in Spanish', Hispania, 55, 76-90
Lozano, A.G. (1975) 'In defense of two subjunctives', Hispania, 58, 277-83
Lucot, R. (1956) 'Remarques sur l'expression de l'aspect', Journal de Psychologie, 53, 447-53
Lyons, J. (1968) Introduction to Theoretical Linguistics, London and New York
Marchand, H. (1955) 'On a question of aspect: a comparison between the progressive form in English and that in Italian and Spanish', Studia Linguistica, 9, 45-52
Martinet, A. (1955) Economie des changements phonétiques, Berne
Martinet, A. (1970) Eléments de linguistique générale, Paris
Matthews, P.H. (1974) Inflectional Morphology, Cambridge
Mendeloff, H. (1960) The Evolution of the Conditional Sentences Contrary to Fact in Old Spanish: a Dissertation, Washington
Menéndez Pidal, R. (1929) Orígenes del español. Estado lingüístico de la Península Ibérica hasta el siglo XI., 2nd ed., Madrid
Moliner, M. (1967) Diccionario de uso del español (H-Z), Madrid
Murphy, A.B. (1963) Aspectual Usage in Russian, Oxford
McCawley, J.D. (1971) 'Tense and time-reference in English', in Fillmore, C.J. and Langendoen, D.T. (eds.) Studies in Linguistic Semantics, New York
Naro, A.J. (1972) 'On "f > h" in Castilian and Western Romance' and 'A reply', Zeitschrift für Romanische Philologie, 88, 435-47; 459-62

Nunn, H.P.V. (1922) An Introduction to Ecclesiastical Latin, Oxford (References are to the 1958 ed.)

Nutting, H.C. (1925) The Latin Conditional Sentence, University of California Publications in Classical Philology, 8, 1, 1-185

Nyrop, K. (1930) Grammaire historique de la langue française, Vol. 6, Paris

Palmer, F.R. (1965) A Linguistic Study of the English Verb, London

Piaget, J. (1968) Le structuralisme, Paris

Pignon, J. (1942) 'Emploi du conditionnel-temps en proposition principale', Le Français Moderne, 10, 28

Pohl, J. (1964) 'Aspect-temps et aspect-durée', Le Français Moderne, 32, 170-8

Popper, K.R. (1959) The Logic of Scientific Discovery, London

Price, G. (1971) The French Language: Present and Past, London

Prior, A.N. (1967) Past, Present and Future, Oxford

Prior, A.N. (1968) Time and Modality, 2nd ed., Oxford

Rallides, C. (1971) The Tense-Aspect System of the Spanish Verb, The Hague

Ramsden, H. (1959) An Essential Course in Modern Spanish, London

Rauta, A. (1947) Gramática rumana, Salamanca

Reichenbach, H. (1947) Elements of Symbolic Logic, New York

Reid, T.B.W. (1970) 'Verbal aspect in French', in Combe, T.G.S. and Rickard, P. (eds.), The French Language: Studies presented to L.C. Harmer, London, pp. 146-71

Rivarola, J.L. (1972) 'Sobre F > h en español' and 'Nota final', Zeitschrift für Romanische Philologie, 88, 448-58

Rivero, M.-L. (1972) 'On conditionals in Spanish', in Casagrande, J. and Saciuk, B. (eds.), Generative Studies in Romance Languages, Rowley, Mass.

Rohlfs, G. (1954) Historische Grammatik der Italienischen Sprache und ihrer Mundarten, Vol. 3, Berne

Ross, J.R. (1969) 'Auxiliaries as main verbs', in Todd, W. (ed.), Philosophical Linguistics, series 1, Great Expectations, Evanston, Ill., pp. 77-102

Ross, J.R. (1970) 'On declarative sentences', in Jacobs, R.A. and Rosenbaum, P.S. (eds.), Readings in English Transformational Grammar, Waltham, Mass., pp. 222-72

Saronne, E.T. (1970) 'La questione dell'aspetto verbale in italiano', Lingua e Stile, 5, 271-81

Saussure, F. de (1916) Cours de linguistique générale, Paris (References are to the 1967 ed.)

Schane, S.A. (1968) French Phonology and Morphology, Cambridge, Mass.

Schane, S.A. (1973) Generative Phonology, Englewood Cliffs, N.J.

Schogt, H.G. (1968) Le système verbal du français contemporain, The Hague

Searle, J.R. (1970) Speech Acts, Cambridge

Seuren, P.A.M., (1969) Operators and Nucleus, Cambridge

Sten, H. (1952) Les temps du verbe fini (indicatif) en français moderne, Copenhagen

Stockwell, R.P., Schachter, P. and Hall Partee, B. (1973) The Major Syntactic Structures of English, New York

Tassie, J. (1963) 'Le conditionnel, tiroir uniquement modal', Revue Canadienne de la Linguistique, 9, 20-31

Togeby, K. (1965) Structure immanente de la langue française, Paris

Väänänen, V. (1963) Introduction au latin vulgaire, Paris

Vendryes, J. (1942-5) Review of Holt (1943), Bulletin de la Société linguistique de Paris, 42, 84-8

Verdín Díaz, G. (1970) Introducción al estilo libre en español, Revista de Filología Española Anejo 91, Madrid

Wagner, R.-L. (1939) Les phrases hypothétiques commençant par 'si' dans la langue française des origines à la fin du XVIè siècle, Paris

Wędkiewicz, S. (1911) Materialen zu einer Syntax der italienischen Bedingungssätze, Beihefte zur Zeitschrift für Romanische Philologie, 31, Halle

Weinreich, U., Labov, W. and Herzog, M.I. (1968) 'Empirical foundations for a theory of language change', in Lehmann, W.P. and Malkiel, Y. (eds.), Directions for Historical Linguistics, Austin, Texas and London

Whorf, B.L., ed. Carroll, J.B. (1956) Language, Thought and Reality: Selected Writings of Benjamin Lee Whorf, Cambridge, Mass.

Willis, R.C. (1965) An Essential Course in Modern Portuguese, London

Wilmet, M. (1968) 'L'imparfait dit hypochoristique', Le Français Moderne, 36, 298-312

Woodcock, E.C. (1959) A New Latin Syntax, London

Wright, L.O. (1932) The -ra Verb Form in Spain, University of California Publications in Modern Philology, Berkeley

Wright, L.O. (1933) 'The earliest shift of the Spanish -ra verb-form from the indicative function to the subjunctive: 1000-1300 A.D.', Language, 9, 265-8

Yvon, H. (1946) 'Notes sur notre vocabulaire grammatical. Le mot "conditionnel".', in Etudes dédiées à M. Roques, Paris, pp. 149-68

Yvon, H. (1952) 'Faut-il distinguer deux conditionnels dans le verbe français?', Le Français Moderne, 2), 249-65

Yvon, H. (1953) 'Indicatif antérieur ou suppositif probable d'aspect composé?', Le Français Moderne, 169-77

Yvon, H. (1958) 'Suppositif, subjonctif et conditionnel', Le Français Moderne, 26, 161-83

TEXTS

OFr

Rol: La Chanson de Roland, ed., F. Whitehead, Oxford, 1968 [early 12th Century].

Erec: Chrétien de Troyes, Erec et Enide, ed. W. Foerster, Halle, 1890. (Reference is also made to the edition of M. Roques, Paris, 1968.) [Mid 12th Century, Champagne].

Marie: Marie de France, Lais, ed. A. Ewert, Oxford, 1969 [mid to late 12th Century].

Auc: Aucassin et Nicolete, ed. F.W. Bourdillon, Manchester, 1919 [early 13th Century, Hainault).

OSp

Cid: Poema de Mio Cid, ed. C.C. Smith, Oxford, 1972 [probably early 13th Century].

PCG: Primera Crónica General de España, ed. R. Menéndez Pidal, Madrid, 1955, pp. 1-50 [second half of the 12th Century]. (This work is referenced by page, line and column.)

Mil: Gonzalo de Berceo, Milagros de Nuestra Señora, ed. B. Dutton, London, 1971 [mid 13th Century].

LBA: Juan Ruiz, Arcipreste de Hita, Libro de Buen Amor, ed. M. Criado de Val and E.W. Naylor, Madrid, 1965 [mid 14th Century]. My transcription follows the conventions used by D.J. Gifford and F.W. Hodcroft (Textos lingüísticos del medioevo espanol, Oxford, 1966) in their rendering of the edition by J. Ducamin (Toulouse, 1901).

OIt

Nov: Le cento novelle antiche, o Libro di novelle e di bel parlare gentile, detto anche Novellino, ed. L. di Francia, Turin, 1948 [late 13th Century].

Inf: Dante, La Divina Commedia, Inferno, ed. C.H. Grandgent and C.S. Singleton, Cambridge, Mass., 1972 [early 14th Century].

Dec: G. Boccaccio, Decameron, ed., C. Segre, Milan, 1966, pp.1-178 [mid 14th Century].

INDEX